YALE ORIENTAL SERIES · RESEARCHES · VOLUME XII

THE ORIGIN OF BIBLICAL TRADITIONS

HEBREW LEGENDS IN BABYLONIA AND ISRAEL

LECTURES ON BIBLICAL ARCHÆOLOGY
DELIVERED AT THE LUTHERAN THEOLOGICAL SEMINARY
MT. AIRY, PHILADELPHIA

BY

ALBERT T. CLAY

I0137560

NEW HAVEN

LONDON · HUMPHREY MILFORD · OXFORD UNIVERSITY PRESS
MDCCCCXXIII

Published by
The Book Tree
Post Office Box 724
Escondido, CA 92033

Call (800) 700-TREE for a FREE BOOK TREE CATALOG
with over 1000 Books, Booklets, Audio, and Video on
Alchemy, Ancient Mysteries, Anti-Gravity, Atlantis, Free
Energy, Gnosticism, Health Issues, Magic, Metaphysics,
Mythology, Occult, Rare Books, Religious Controversy,
Sitchin Studies, Spirituality, Symbolism, Tesla, and much
more. Or visit our website at www.thebooktree.com

PREFACE

Where did our oldest Bible stories really come from? This schloarly work shows that our oldest Bible stories originated in ancient Babylon and Sumeria. The entire proof is laid out in the early part of the book, followed by an Appendix which includes translations of the creation stories from the Sumerians, Babylonians and Phoenicians.

This is an excellent scholarly book, perfect for those researching the beginnings of mankind. In addition to creation stories, Clay covers the stories of the Garden of Eden, the Fall of Man, the Great Flood, and the Tower of Babel. These originals were found on clay tablets, written in cuneiform by the Sumerians. Cuneiform is the very first form of writing ever known on the earth. This is mainly a book on linguistic and archaeological studies by Clay, first published by Yale University Press, so the information is top notch and reliable. It is highly recommended for serious researchers and those curious about the early gods and man's origins.

This book contains irrefutable proof that our oldest Bible stories came from far older sources, and are the oldest stories on the planet. These stories reveal incredible secrets when examined and studied closely, and are, in my estimation, the most important and revealing stories mankind has ever been able to preserve. We are lucky to have found and translated them. This book holds great wealth for those willing to reach in and explore.

Paul Tice

THE ALEXANDER KOHUT MEMORIAL PUBLICATION FUND

The present volume is the fourth work published by the Yale University Press on the Alexander Kohut Memorial Publication Fund. This Foundation was established October 13, 1915, by a gift to Yale University from members of his family for the purpose of enabling scholars to publish texts and monographs in the Semitic field of research.

The Reverend Alexander Kohut, Ph.D. (Leipzig), a distinguished Oriental scholar, in whose memory the fund has been established, was born in Hungary, April 22, 1842, of a noted family of rabbis. When pastor of the Congregation Ahavath Chesed in New York City, he became one of the founders of the Jewish Theological Seminary, and was a professor in that institution until his death. He was a noted pulpit orator, able to discourse with equal mastery in three languages. Among his contributions to Semitic learning is the monumental work *Aruch Completum*, an encyclopædic dictionary of the Talmud, in eight volumes. Semitic and Oriental scholars have honored his memory by inscribing to him a volume of Semitic Studies (Berlin 1897).

Other Kohut Memorial Publication Funds have recently been established in Vienna and Berlin, and at the newly-founded Jewish Institute of Religion in New York. An Alexander Kohut Research Fellowship in Semitics was established at Yale by his family in 1919.

FOREWORD

The first battery against the prevailing view that the Hebrews had borrowed their religious traditions from Babylonia, was opened up in the Reinicker Lectures, for 1908, delivered at the Protestant Episcopal Theological Seminary, Alexandria, Virginia, resulting in a publication entitled *Amurru the Home of the Northern Semites, a Study showing that the Religion and Culture of Israel are not of Babylonian Origin.* After a period of fifteen years, during which time many discoveries bearing upon the subject have been made, the theme was again discussed in lectures delivered at the Lutheran Theological Seminary, Mt. Airy, Philadelphia, as offered here in this monograph.

I had hoped before presenting my recent researches on the subject, as well as a review of those made during the past fifteen years, to be able to devote myself to the study of certain other cuneiform texts, which I feel also represent Babylonized Amorite or early Hebrew literature. Since, however, there are now more than sufficient data available to show the complete baselessness of the contentions of Babylonism, and also because some scholars do not seem to be able to distinguish between efforts made to reconstruct the civilization and history of a lost empire and the riding of a hobby horse, it has seemed advisable to present at this time the material that has been assembled.

When the first assault was made against the prevailing understanding that Israel had borrowed its traditions from Babylonia, as far as I know, all Assyriologists, and Biblical scholars generally, had accepted this point of view. It is this that has been dubbed "Babylonism." The term "Sumerism" refers to the view of some Assyriologists, who believe in the Sumerian origin of the traditions, which have been handed down by the Babylonians and Israel.

Pan-Babylonism, as developed by several German scholars, who have endeavored to show that even parts of the New Testament have evolved from the circle of Babylonian mythology, when even Marduk is transformed into Christ, is only briefly touched upon; for if early Israel did not borrow its religious traditions from Babylonia, it seems unreasonable to suppose that this was done by the Christian Jew.

Although the thesis is quite revolutionary, I feel that I have previously given sufficient evidence to prove that it is correct. Certain scholars, however, who have resisted it, have systematically discussed details, or extraneous suggestions, and have avoided facing the real issue. In presenting here the results of my investigations, as they are to-day, it has seemed necessary to reproduce the views of many friends, with which I totally disagree, and upon which the theories rest. It is my hope that all will fully realize that in doing so I have had but one thought in mind, and that is to present the facts and theories upon which Babylonism and Sumerism are based, as well as reasons why they should be abandoned, in such a way that what is offered the Biblical student will carry conviction. Having taken a stand against the prevailing view that the Hebrew traditions originated in Babylonia, I should regard it a mistake not to make an attempt to bring the issue to a conclusion, since I feel that sufficient material is at hand to effect this.

It was fully expected that the titles of the recent monographs would not meet with the approval of certain scholars any more than did the title of the first contribution. As an illustration of this opposition let me refer here to a criticism that has been offered by a scholar and friend. In his review of *The Empire of the Amorites*, which on the whole was gratifying (see Chapter I), the following lines occur: "Clay argues that there was a 'great empire of the Amorites' in which he gives powers of great magnitude to

'mighty Amorite rulers,' and builds for them an 'imperial city . . .
which was powerful enough to rule the land from the Mediterranean
to Babylonia.' All this and much more is based on fragmentary
evidence piled high and even higher on names of places, names of
deities, or fugitive allusions in Babylonian and Assyrian texts all
of periods far later than the '3rd, 4th, and 5th millenniums' in
which this supposed and subjective empire is presumed to have
held sway. One dislikes intensely to say it, but the book presents
no objective, positive evidence that there was such an 'empire.'
The word 'empire' is quite inexcusable, no kings' names of those
who ruled it being known, and no imperial city of theirs ever having
been excavated."[1]

The statement that my position is "based on fragmentary evidence . . . all of periods far later than the 3rd, 4th, and 5th,
millenniums," is, however, an unintentional misrepresentation of
fact. I admit that the evidence presented in the monograph to
prove the actual existence of an empire, which was all that I had
to offer at the time, was slight; but, nevertheless, it is there. On
pages 89 and 104, there is written: "The earliest Amorite king,
who by his inscriptions informs us that he had conquered Babylonia,
is . . . um-Shamash, (also read Ishar-Shamash), king of Mari, and
Patesi-gal of Enlil, which means that he was suzerain over the land
. . . at least part of Babylonia . . . and refers unquestionably to
one of those early periods when Amurru was the dominant power
in Babylonia."

But while admitting the title was used when the evidence was
slight, I am pleased to be able to say that more recent discoveries
have completely established the view that there was such an empire.
Two years ago a fragment of an early dynastic tablet was discovered
in the collection of the University of Pennsylvania, which enables
us to fill out the break in the list of ruling kingdoms, and restore

---

[1] Rogers, *American Historical Review* 25, 700 f.

the three missing ones that had ruled Babylonia in the fourth millennium B. C.   One of these kingdoms was the Amorite city Mari,[2] which fact is in strict accord with what I have maintained. In other words, the city Mari, which name was synonymous with Amurru,[3] is here found ruling Babylonia.   This puts the question of the use of the word "empire" beyond any further dispute.   We now have, however, also other very important light on the subject.

From an omen tablet in the Pierpont Morgan Library, considered in connection with other known facts, we now obtain the information that Humbaba had humiliated Babylonia[4] a thousand years earlier, in the fifth millennium B. C.   Even a predecessor called Zu, the "storm bird," had apparently also done this.

In view of these facts, I feel quite certain that the reviewer, as well as others who have shared his opinion, will withdraw the assertion that the use of "the word 'empire' is quite inexcusable."[5] The concluding part of the same sentence, however, namely, "no imperial city of theirs ever having been excavated," is unfortunately correct.   If one had been excavated, it is highly probable that investigations along these lines would have been unnecessary.

There are those also who contend that the word "Hebrew" was unjustifiably used in my recent work, entitled *A Hebrew Deluge Story in Cuneiform*.   Of course this assertion is based on a dis-

---

[2] See Legrain, *Museum Journal* 1920, 175 f. and Clay, *Jour. Amer. Orien. Soc.* 41, 243 f.

[3] See *Empire of the Amorites*, p. 68 and *Jour. Amer. Orien. Soc.* 41, 257, note 75.

[4] Clay, *A Hebrew Deluge Story* 42 f; and *Babylonian Records in the Library of J. Pierpont Morgan* IV, 14:65.

[5] It appears to me that the astrological and omen texts, which unquestionably go back to a very early time, and which refer to the king of Amurru as well as the kings of Akkad, Elam, and Subartu, should have been sufficient evidence to make such opposition seem precarious.   In the omen literature there are many references to the king of Amurru; to cite a single example, "If there was an eclipse of the sun on the 16th day, the king of Akkad will die, and the king of Amurru will seize the throne." (*ZA* 16, 220).

agreement with my basic position. The criticism is satisfactorily answered in the pages which follow.

For the laymen, let me explain here the use of the terms Amorite and Hebrew. The name of the land west of Babylonia, as far as the sea, was called Amurru by the Babylonians and Assyrians. This is only a geographical term, embracing the entire land, having had its origin, doubtless, in the name of a city, as the terms Babylonia and Assyria had their origin in the city-names Babylon and Ashur. This country was occupied by the Aramaeans, Hebrews, Phoenicians, Canaanites, and other peoples. The use of the term Hebrew, Amorite or Amoraic, for the early language of Amurru, is intended to designate the early West-Semitic language used in this land, of which we have traces in early cuneiform inscriptions, and which in time developed into what has been preserved for us, which we call Biblical Hebrew, Phoenician, Aramaic, etc. In other words, the term Hebrew for this early language, is to be regarded as used here in the same sense that the Semitic language of the "plain of Shinar" is called Babylonian; although in the early period the upper part of the land was called Akkad, and still earlier Uri, or Uru. We have an exact parallel in calling Anglo-Saxon early English.

The great antiquity of the Amorite civilization, as well as the Amorite origin of the Semitic Babylonians, has quite recently been unreservedly accepted by Professor Ungnad of Breslau (see Chapter I). When this becomes general—in the light of the data we now have, it cannot be otherwise—and when these contentions as regards the traditions which Israel and Babylonia had in common, are accepted—nor can this also be otherwise in the light of the facts here presented—a readjustment of a far-reaching character will have to be made in every work on the early history of the Near East. Besides the restoration to history of a great civilization, that of the Amorite Empire, it means that the political and religious history of Babylonia, as well as of the Sumerians, must be greatly modified; it means that Egyptologists will doubtless feel inclined to take cognizance of even greater influence than heretofore from Syria; it means that the Classical scholar will appreciate that the civilization, reputed to have furnished Greece with many myths, was very ancient and very real; it means that Israel need not be regarded as semi-barbarous Arabs from the desert, who borrowed their religion, their institutions, and even their ancestry from Babylonia; but that their civilization, including their traditions, was deeply rooted in their own past history; and it means the abandonment of many pet theories such as the Arabian cradle-land-wave-theory-of-migration to account for the Semites in Syria and Babylonia. In a word, it is impossible to realize at present how far-reaching in extent are the modifications of prevailing views that acceptance will require.

In the same review above quoted, in referring to my withdrawal of one of the many identifications which had been previously made, there is written the following: "It is a pity that other scholars are not so transparently honest." It seems to me that it is not unreasonable to express the hope in this connection that others will manifest the same spirit. If, in the light of recent research, scholars are convinced that the views which they have published on this subject need modification, especially as regards the traditions of the Old Testament, which are being taught generally in our colleges and schools, as well as in the pulpit, it is to be earnestly hoped they will let this fact become known.

Although I have entered the arena with a thesis of a far-reaching and revolutionary character, and have tried to show that the views of all my fellow Assyriologists are wrong, I am gratified with the manner and spirit of those who have opposed it, for among all the many reviews and articles written by American and foreign scholars,

I know of but a single source—which happens, I regret to say, to be that of a former pupil—which could be said to be aggressive.

During the past years certain scholars, other than Assyriologists, have not only sympathetically followed in these investigations, but have wholly or in part accepted their results. I deeply appreciate the encouragement they have given; for after all the specialist in Hebrew, Arabic, and Aramaic, who also is able to weigh the vagaries of the Assyriologists, is in the best position to judge the merits of the issue; although it is possible even for the student of general history to do this intelligently, especially in the greater part of the discussion which follows. I should like very much to have before the reader of these lectures all that these scholars have written. However, I shall confine myself here to the views advanced in the interests of Babylonism or Sumerism, which are responsible for the deeply rooted conviction that Israel borrowed its religious literature from Babylonia.

I desire, in conclusion, to thank also my colleagues, Professors C. C. Torrey, E. W. Hopkins, A. M. Harmon, and Ellsworth Huntington, as well as my former colleague, James A. Montgomery, for suggestions and references which are indicated in connection with their names; and also Doctors E. M. Grice and Samuel Feigin, who have read the proof, and the Reverend George A. Kohut of New York, who has not only read the manuscript, but also, as on previous occasions, made possible the early publication of the work on the Alexander Kohut Memorial Publication Fund.

ALBERT T. CLAY.

May 19, 1923.

CONTENTS

I

INTRODUCTORY REMARKS

When the writer first proposed the thesis which is here restated under very different conditions, the prevailing understanding as regards the antiquity of the history, culture, and religion of Syria, including Palestine and Mesopotamia, which lands the ancients called Amurru, was as follows:

Arabia was the home of the Semites. The Arabs first entered Babylonia about 2800 B. C. and gave that land its first Semitic inhabitants, who under the leadership of Sargon created a great empire. About 2500 B. C., a wave of Arabs entered Canaan, and furnished it with Semites. A little later another wave poured out of Arabia and overflowed Syria. These were called Amorites; and they established the Hammurabi dynasty. About 1400 B. C., Arabia again "spat out," and a wave of Arabs called the Aramaean, under Joshua, furnished Palestine with its Hebrews. It was not thought possible that a civilization and culture existed in Aram in what had been known as the patriarchal period, for the people in that land, at this early time, were still in the state of barbarism. Abraham, Isaac, and Jacob, therefore, were considered by some to be Babylonian gods; and by others as the personification of Arab tribes, clans, or ethnological groups that came into Canaan under Joshua; Israel's sojourn in Egypt was generally regarded as a myth.

With such conclusions concerning the early history and civilization of this part of Western Asia, it naturally became comparatively easy for the Biblical student to accept the idea that Israel had borrowed its culture from the Babylonians, the people who had repeatedly invaded Syria and Palestine. It really only required a small additional step to accept the idea that Israel's religion had

(19)

been extensively influenced by the Babylonian, and that they had borrowed their traditions and their institutions from that land; even that they had Hebraized Babylonian mythological kings or gods into patriarchs, in order to create an ancestry for their people.

Naturally this background, painted by Assyriologists for the Israelite religion and culture, was unfavorable to the idea that their traditions and religions were rooted in their own past history. Besides, the intelligence of the people who lived in Syria and Palestine, it was held, was not much above that of the "brute beast." Beyond the confines of Egypt and Babylonia were barbarism; the Hebrews were really semi-civilized Arabs from the deserts, who had adopted as their deity Yahweh, the god of the Kenites.   The beginning of their history was when these Arab hordes were brought into Palestine under the leadership of Joshua.

When such leading Assyriologists as the late Professors Delitzsch and Winckler of Berlin, Professor Zimmern of Leipzig, Professor Jensen of Marburg, and others, had reached such results; and when such Old Testament scholars as Professor Gunkel of Berlin, wrote that "as long as the Israelite religion was in its vigor, it assimilated actively this foreign material [referring to Babylonian myths]; in later times when the religion had become relaxed in strength, it swallowed foreign elements, feathers and all," Biblical scholars everywhere, it seems, were influenced to accept these conclusions. In England, where the original seeds of this movement had been sown, scholars and students readily followed the lead.   In America, the position was conceded as correct by almost every scholar, and the theories were made palatable for the student, who was taught that the Hebrew priests, knowing this Babylonian mythological material, deliberately or unconsciously appropriated it for their religious literature.

This has been the prevailing understanding for years; and these views are thoroughly rooted everywhere; in nearly every production written by scholars, it has been assumed that they are well established; Bible teachers have been made to feel that these conclusions are final.

It was therefore not without some intrepidity that in 1907, after setting forth the generally accepted view as regards the origin of the creation story in a book entitled "Light on the Old Testament from Babel," I expressed myself in these words: "and yet it is also quite within the range of possibility and reasonableness to conceive the idea that both stories have a common origin among the Semites who entered Babylonia, prior to their amalgamation with the Sumerians, and who may have also carried their traditions into Palestine." And again: "Taking these things into consideration it is not impossible that the idea of a conflict with this primaeval power of darkness, which perhaps is echoed in the New Testament doctrine of evil angels, was brought into Shinar or Babylonia as well as into Palestine by the Semites themselves; in which case it would have found its way into Canaan, millenniums prior to the time this story assumed the form in which it is preserved in the Old Testament."[1]

At the time, there seemed to be little known that could be used to make such a view appear plausible. To prove that these stories were indigenous in Syria, as I believed they were, it was necessary to show first that civilization actually existed in that land in the centuries prior to Abraham. In the absence of excavations, the only light that could be thrown upon the subject had to come from the Egyptian and Babylonian inscriptions. Fortunately the first ray was at hand.

One day in working on the business documents of the "Murashû Sons of Nippur," I discovered that the name of a god written ideographically KUR-GAL in cuneiform, was scratched in Aramaic characters, reading 'wr. That is, for this ideogram, which meant

[1] *Light on the Old Testament* p. 75.

"great mountain," the equivalent in Aramaic was 'wr (the characters that compose the name Ur of the Chaldees), which I proposed to read 'Ur, and held that it was the same as Amur(ru),
for in many cases the Babylonians used m, where the Aramaeans
used w.[2] This was the opening wedge for the thesis.

In texts published shortly afterwards by Professor Peiser of
Königsberg, the correctness of my reading was fully established;
for in them he found that the name Amurru was written with the
ideograms KUR-GAL and Mar-Tu.[3] In other words, the Aramaic
writing showed that Amurru was also read Urru or Uru. This at
the time seemed to me to be a discovery of far-reaching importance;
and subsequent developments have proved that this supposition
was not incorrect.

On the same documents I discovered also that the name of the
god written ideographically Nin-IB was scratched on the clay
tablet in Aramaic characters 'nwšt; and this name I read En-
Mashtu = En-Martu, and regarded it as Amorite.[4] But what I
proposed, Assyriologists did not accept. About a dozen different
explanations, by as many scholars, were promptly offered;[5] none
of which agreed with my own; and about a dozen more have since
been published in explanation of this Aramaic name.[6] Some
even tried to read the characters differently. However, Professor
Montgomery, a year or two later, in working on an Aramaic ostracon
from Nippur, fortunately found the same name written no less than
five times, showing that my reading of the characters was correct.

A few years later, it was my good fortune to discover the reading
of the second element of the ideogram of this name, Nin-IB, on the

---

[2] Babylonian Expedition of the University of Pa. X p. 7 f.
[3] Urkunden aus der Zeit der dritten babylonischen Dynastie, p. viii.
[4] Babylonian Expedition X 8 f., and xviii f.
[5] See Clay, Amurru p. 196, note.
[6] See Clay, Empire of the Amorites p. 73. Others have since been published.

Yale Syllabary, namely *Urta*,[7] which proved that my understanding
that the name referred to *Martu* was correct; for *Martu* or *Wartu*
became *'Urtu*. ⸱ The prefixed element *Nin*, "lady," had come to
be read *En* or *In*, "Lord"; for the deity, who had been originally
feminine in its native land, was regarded as both masculine and
feminine in Babylonia.[8] In short, the new reading proved conclusively that the god, whose name is written ideographically
Nin-IB, and which was read *En-Urta*, was originally the consort
of the Amorite Uru, who in time, just as I had proposed, became
masculinized. This occurred, as is well known, with other deities.
But let us return to the story.

Following the discovery of these two names written in Aramaic,
I endeavored to show that the Nîsin dynasty (2357–2154 B. C.)
was Amorite. I said that "the name of the kings of the Nîsin
dynasty seem to show West Semitic influence, and that the capital
was doubtless a stronghold of this people."[9] This conjecture was
based on the fact that the name of the founder of the dynasty was
compounded with Uru, namely Ishbi-Urra, and that other Amorite
names occurred in the list: Urra-imitti, Idin-Dagan, UR-En-
Urta, etc. Further I proposed, on the basis of a study of the nomenclature, that the Akkad dynasty (2847–2665? B. C.) was also
West Semitic; and, in short, conjectured that for two millenniums
prior to the time of Hammurabi, Western Semites at times were
able to conquer Babylonia. This being true, I maintained it ought
to follow that a civilization existed in Amurru, which could have
produced myths and legends.

In 1909, I published a monograph entitled *Amurru, the Home of
the Northern Semites*, in which I boldly attacked the prevailing
view concerning the origin of the creation story, the sabbath, the

[7] *Miscellaneous Inscriptions* 53:288.
[8] See Clay, *Jour. Am. Or. Soc.* 28, 139 f.
[9] Clay, *Ibidem*.

antediluvian patriarchs, the deluge story, as well as concerning the historicity of Abram, Isaac, and Jacob. The reception that the thesis received was gratifying, especially on the part of Semitic scholars who had not published their views on the subject; but naturally, the Assyriologists who had developed Babylonism, and those scholars who had popularized its theories by their publications, were not disposed to hurriedly acknowledge that their position was no longer tenable; nor were the hosts of Biblical instructors, who, having accepted the verdict of the world's great Assyriologists, and for years having taught their conclusions, disposed to change their views, because a lone voice had proposed a reversal of them.

I had not long to wait for confirmation of an important part of the thesis. A few years later Professor Barton published an inscription which substantiated my view that the Nîsin dynasty was Amorite, for it showed that Ishbi-Urra, the founder of the dynasty, had come from Mari, which city is in Amurru.[10] Professor Poebel a little later discovered dynastic legends and lists which showed contact with Amurru in a very early period.[11] Many other facts also came to light, which confirmed my view that the Amorite civilization synchronized with the earliest in Egypt and Babylonia.[12]

Since the appearance of the monograph *Amurru*, I have systematically fortified the thesis it contained by presenting one fact after another in articles, and in other publications. In 1919, *The Empire of the Amorites* appeared, and in it I attempted to reconstruct two or more millenniums of history for the land, prior to 2000 B. C., and more recently, in *A Hebrew Deluge Story in Cuneiform and other Epic Fragments in the Pierpont Morgan Library*, I have presented data of a crucial character in support of the entire thesis.

---

[10] *Babylonian Inscriptions* 9:4, 22.
[11] *Historical Texts* (*UMBS* IV 1) 13 ff.
[12] Clay, *Jour. Amer. Orien. Soc.* 41, 241 ff.

The question now is, what is the situation to-day? What do we
know about the two or more millenniums of history of Syria prior
to Hammurabi, which was almost a perfect blank when these
investigations were begun?

We have pierced the wall of silence and darkness at certain points,
and the views we get by peering through these small and large aper-
tures are most illuminating. In order to review fully what is seen,
with all its bearings upon contemporary history, it would be necessary to reproduce here *The Empire of the Amorites* and *A Hebrew
Deluge Story in Cuneiform.* However, a bare outline of the vistas
that we get will suffice for our purpose.

We have already referred to the discovery that the Amorites
founded the Nîsin dynasty (2357–2154 B. C.). Quite recently
letters of Ibi-Sin, the last king of the previous dynasty have been
published, in which he complains that Ishbi-Urra, the Amorite, is
making trouble in the land.[13] As we have already mentioned, this
"man from Mari" succeeded in overthrowing the Ur dynasty,
when two Amorite dynasties, Nîsin and Larsa, were established,
and a little later a third, that of the city of Babylon.

A breach in the wall of darkness gives us a view of Amurru a
thousand years earlier, at about 3300 B. C., when we ascertain that
the capital of Western Asia was then in Amurru at Mari, on the
Euphrates; which city was powerful enough to rule Babylonia
during the reigns of several kings. About a thousand years prior
to this period we were able to make another breach; and this time
the aperture is so large that we get a scene covering the reigns of
three Babylonian kings, when we become acquainted also with
three kings who ruled in the Lebanon region. We find that Zu,
designated the "storm bird," who lived in Syria, had humiliated
Enlil, the chief god of Babylonia, and had robbed him of his prerogatives as "lord of land," when a shepherd named Marad, prob-

[13] Legrain, *Historical Fragments* (*UMBS* XIII) 3, 6 and 9; see pp. 28 ff.

ably the Biblical Nimrod, later called Lugal-Marad, "King Marad," came to the rescue, and with some kind of strategy, ensnared Zu, and pursued him as far as "the distant mountain Sâbu," in the Lebanon range. By his success he was not only able to throw off the yoke of the West, but he conquered Aleppo and Tidnum.

During the reign of Lugal-Marad's successor, named Tammuz, who also had conquered this region, we get, with the aid of later traditions, a remarkable picture of the age, when Ashirta, whom the Babylonians called Ishtar, was queen of the land of Aleppo. She was a Cleopatra of that age, and had many wooers. We learn from the inscriptions that her palace stood amidst the cedars of Lebanon.

Tammuz, who had been born in the cedar forest, and had become a ruler of Babylonia, with his capital at Erech, was one of her lovers. It was while hunting with Ashirta in a wooded gorge of what was later called the Adonis river, tradition tells us, that he had lost his life. Here in this valley his mangled body had been buried, and a great shrine had been erected. The cult, that was apparently inaugurated by this woman in Syria, as is well known, played one of the most important rôles in the life, religion, and history of the ancient world.

Some time after the death of Tammuz, a man named Humbaba usurped a throne in that region, and was able to humiliate Babylonia. It was then that Gilgamesh, the successor to Tammuz, together with his confederate Engidu, fought with Humbaba, and succeeded in restoring the prestige of his land. The data which we can assemble bearing on these three reigns enable us to reconstruct what can be regarded as a chapter in the earliest known history of man.[14]

But let us leave this picture for a moment to discuss a criticism that has been offered as regards these early characters being historical personages, for in previous years they have all been con-

[14] Clay, *A Hebrew Deluge Story* 42 ff.

sidered to be deities, especially because they had been worshipped as such in later periods of Babylonian history. In the light of recent discoveries, however, there is every reason for believing that they were heroic characters who were deified after death. This seemed conclusive following the discovery of the dynastic lists and legends, referred to above, which Poebel recently published.

While it was anticipated that the statement that Ishtar was historical would not be readily accepted, it was somewhat of a surprise to have a young scholar in the British Museum write thus: "In the summary of the early history, few will follow Professor Clay, in considering Gilgamesh and the rest as actual historical figures because their names occur in a king-list, especially when it is remembered that the figures giving the length of his reign are quite impossible."[15] In a criticism received in a friendly communication, another wrote: "You are doing, or attempting to do, precisely the same thing in this twentieth century for Babylonian mythology what Euhemerus attempted to do many centuries ago for Greek mythology."

The fact that Euhemerism, as it was developed, was in time completely disregarded, does not prove that Euhemerus was wrong. As far as I can ascertain, since the excavations at Troy, and in the light of other discoveries, not a few classical scholars hold that many of the so-called Greek and Roman gods were heroic personages. Fortunately Assyriologists are in a better position to judge of the merits of such a question, yes even than Euhemerus himself, who although he had access to the great libraries of his day, doubtless did not have any original manuscripts of the early period. We have hundreds of thousands of *original* inscriptions, written during the several millenniums that preceded the time of Christ.

Thirty years ago Gilgamesh, although called "ruler of Erech" in the epic bearing his name, was regarded as a god. A little later,

---

[15] Sidney Smith, *Luzac's Oriental List* 33, p. 82.

inscriptions were found which informed us that he built the walls of Erech. Later the personal inscriptions of many other so-called gods came to light, and even records of their operations by others, resulting in many of them being transferred from the realm of mythology to the pages of history. What seemed even more conclusive was the finding of many liturgical texts belonging to the cults of certain well-known kings, some of whom were adored as divinely sent redeemers able to intercede for the living. In brief, no one would question to-day that the gods Dungi, Bur-Sin, Gimil-Sin, Ishme-Dagan, etc., were kings. And although some of the very earliest of these deified kings in the recently published dynastic lists were credited as having ruled even longer than some of the Biblical antediluvians, there seemed to be no reasons whatsoever for believing them to have originally been deities.

It is on this experience of the past decades, and because of many other reasons, that the characters referred to above were regarded as deified kings: namely, Lugal-Marad, who had delivered the land from an invader; the profligate Ashirta (Astarte or Ishtar) "the queen of Aleppo," whose cult included the licentious rites which appealed to the sensuality of mankind; her paramour, Tammuz, of whom it is even said in the Adapa Legend that he had been "a king"; and Gilgamesh, "ruler of Erech," who also delivered the land out of the hands of the Amorite Humbaba (previously regarded as an Elamite god). All of them, it seems to me, had been kings and queens. I feel that this view will ere long be accepted by all scholars.

Let us now return to the vistas that discovery and research have given us of the early history of Amurru. At present we cannot peer through any breach of an earlier period; but we hope ere long, by the help of the excavator's pick and spade, to break through at points in the millenniums which preceded, as well as all along the line of the later periods. There can be little doubt but that this land sent its people, centuries earlier than the time we now know of, into the alluvium, called in the Old Testament Shinar, where by their skill they harnessed the rivers, and established permanent homes. Some of the first settlers had gone down to the shore of the gulf, and there on the land's end had founded a shrine which they dedicated to the worship of their god Ea (see *infra*). Others built temples in various parts of the land near the great rivers, and dedicated them to El and other gods of Amurru. Yes, even tradition tells us that the kings who ruled the land before the deluge came from Syria, as is shown by the Amorite names they bear (see Chapter VI).

It ought to be added here that as we peer through these breaches we have not yet been able to see any of those migrations of hungry tribes from Arabia, of which in the past we have so frequently heard. I refer to the theory that Arabia is the home of the Semites, and that "waves" of migration emanated periodically from that land. Amurru does not seem to have had to depend upon the desert for its inhabitants, for Semites found the fertile valleys and plains of Amurru, as well as its forests, its minerals, and other treasuries, at a very early period. In other words, we seem to have every indication that the civilization existing in the now earliest known period in Amurru, was then already ancient. The theory that the Semitic cradle rocked in the deserts of Arabia has received no substantiation as yet from these investigations; it still remains theory, pure and simple.

After assembling these facts for the reconstruction of the millenniums of history prior to Abraham, facts which make it possible to believe that such stories as the creation and deluge might be indigenous in Syria, we ask, has there been any change in the point of view of scholars; have the Babylonists modified their views?

Certain of our foremost scholars who had taken no part in developing Babylonism promptly expressed themselves as being skeptical of its conclusions; but until quite recently I cannot say that Assyriologists who had written on the subject have done more than make certain modifications.

Let me repeat here what I regard as being the first recognition of the thesis on the part of an Assyriologist, and especially as it touches upon the antiquity of the Amorite civilization.   On this, my former distinguished colleague and friend, the late Professor Jastrow, wrote as follows: ". . . but, granting that Professor Clay has pressed his views beyond legitimate bounds, there can no longer be any doubt that in accounting for the later, and for some of the earlier aspects of the Sumero-Akkadian civilization this factor of Amurru must be taken into account; nor is it at all unlikely that long before the days of Sargon, a wave of migration, from the north and the northwest, to the south and southeast, had set in, which brought large bodies of Amorites into the Euphrates valley as well as into Assyria."[16]

While, as stated, several West Semitic scholars had expressed themselves as being favorable to the thesis, this was the first recognition received on the part of an Assyriologist.   There are others who have more recently endorsed the contentions that Syria and Palestine have been occupied by Semites from the earliest times, "i. e., from the late Neolithic period;"[17] as well as those who have admitted "that there is an element of truth at the bottom of them."[18] There has followed, however, confirmation of a more pronounced character.

In a review of The Empire of the Amorites, Professor Rogers writes, "that the book is crowded with the proofs that Amorites lived and influenced the course of human history and that we must find a place for them larger than most of us had dreamed before Clay began these investigations more than a decade ago.   It is his

[16] Jastrow, Religious Belief in Babylonia and Assyria 26 f.

[17] Albright, Jour. Pal. Orien. Soc. II, p. 135.

[18] Sayce, Expository Times, 1922, Nov. p. 76.

due to say that he has opened new windows into the dimly seen and darkly understood lands of Western Asia as the early kingdoms were founded. He has not demonstrated the existence of an empire [on this see the Foreword], but of an influence, and that is quite enough."[19] There has, however, appeared more recently what is even more decided in character.

Professor Ungnad of Breslau, in a brochure which has just appeared, now fully admits corroboration of my basic position. He writes that the Arabian and African origin of the Semites is becoming more and more improbable as investigations advance; that the Semites were already in Syria, 4500 B. C.; that it was a highly cultivated land; that the Semitic Babylonians came from Amurru; that the great Amorite Empire, which the Semites had created, had been destroyed by the Hittites and Egyptians; and that the Amorites very probably had an alphabetic script long before the earliest that is known.[20] It is needless to say that this is in complete accord with what I have been maintaining as regards the early history and civilization of the Amorites.

If these points bearing on the great antiquity of the Amorite civilization are generally acknowledged—and they will be, for the proof has already been presented—I feel that the foundation upon which my entire structure rests is established. This is, therefore, an all-important gain; for without it, or rather the evidence upon which it is based, an early civilization would have to be postulated for Syria, out of which emanated the influences which were exerted upon Babylonia and Egypt. This is now unnecessary. Moreover, with this historical background established, I hope in the present monograph to force many vital conclusions with reference to the origin of religious and cultural elements that found their way into Babylonia; among which are the creation and deluge stories.

---

[19] Rogers, *American Historical Review* 25, 700 ff.
[20] Ungnad, *Die. ältesten Völkerwanderungen Vorderasiens.*

In doing so, I realize that I shall have many hands against me. To inform the teacher that the views which he has taught, and which his student has accepted, should be abandoned, or reversed, is not likely to be hailed with delight. This, nevertheless, must follow; for I believe that I can now present the problem in such a way that all, even those who have not studied Assyriology, can judge for themselves the merits of the position which is now so generally accepted, as well as what is here proposed: namely, its abandonment.

If what the lone Assyriologist here presents is not effective in certain quarters, there will be no disappointment. It is a great deal to expect scholars to nullify what they have written, covering in some instances many decades, as long as there is anything to which they can cling. I am thoroughly convinced, however, that in time even their opposition will take care of itself; for in the pages which follow there is more than sufficient evidence, not only to show that their position is baseless, but to establish the thesis that Amurru is the home of the traditions that we will discuss.

In the course of the discussions under the various topics, I will give the criticisms that scholars have already made of my previous efforts, even some from an aggressive source that do not merit any notice. In presenting hundreds of facts and details, there naturally is plenty of room for slips. A few of these which I have discovered, or to which attention has been called, are cheerfully acknowledged. But let me add here that I know of no criticism of a vital character that has been made, thus far, which has not been, or is not here fully answered.

II

THE FOURFOLD ARGUMENT

In discussing the problem of the origin of traditions handed down by Israel and the Babylonians, the arguments are grouped under four heads, bearing upon migrations, climate, names, and linguistic evidence.

The first argument I desire to use in establishing my thesis is based on a study of invasions or conquests and migrations, and what their respective bearing is in connection with the cultural and religious influences of the one nation upon the other. This study I feel will be found to have a most important bearing in the solution of the whole problem before us, especially in view of the proof that for years has been offered for the Babylonian origin of the stories in Genesis, and of Israel's culture and religion in general, as well as for the claim that before Israel entered Canaan it was a domain of Babylonian civilization. With that in view we will briefly review what is at present known concerning the conquests or invasions and migrations emanating not only from Syria and Babylonia, but also from Egypt; because, like Babylonia, Egypt is a great alluvium which has been closely connected with Syria.

There were other peoples who played a rôle in the politics of the Near East in the early period, as the Elamites, Hittites, etc., but having rather meagre knowledge of their history and religion, as well as for other reasons, we will confine the survey to the three nations mentioned.

From a study of the movements of nations in antiquity, it seems to the writer that the following two principles can reasonably be laid down. First, while the conquering invader leaves such evidence of his presence in the land as victory steles, material objects, social and linguistic influences, his influence upon the religion of the land is either exceedingly meagre, or nil. Secondly, when migrations take place, including also the exiling or enslaving of peoples, the religion and culture of the people migrate with them; and their influence is found in the land to which they go.

Let us now take a survey of the conquests or invasions and migrations as well as other related influences under the following heads: first, Egyptian conquests or invasions of, and migrations to, Amurru; secondly, Amorite conquests or invasions of, and migrations to, Egypt; thirdly, Babylonian conquests or invasions of, and migrations to, Amurru; fourthly, Amorite conquests or invasions of, and migrations to, Babylonia.

EGYPTIAN CONQUESTS OF AMURRU

No references are made in the Egyptian inscriptions to contact with the Amorites in the earliest period. About 3000 B. C., the city of Byblos in Phoenicia is mentioned in the Pyramid texts. The reports concerning the excavations recently conducted at that city by the French offer interesting confirmation of these references; for we are informed that inscriptions have been found there belonging to the early period, including those of Mycerinus, Unas, and Phiops I., and that an Egyptian temple was erected there at a very early time.[1]

The first known Egyptian campaign to Asia was in the reign of Athothis, about 2900 B. C.[2] Snefru, of the Third dynasty, mentions bringing to Egypt forty shiploads of cedar from Lebanon. Sahure of the Fifth dynasty (about 2735 B. C.), sent a fleet against the Phoenician coast. At Abushir, a relief has been discovered showing four ships filled with Amorite prisoners, also from the Phoenician coast. Uni of the Sixth dynasty, invaded the land.

[1] Montet, *Syria* II 333 ff.
[2] See Borchardt, *Mitteilungen der Vorderasiatischen Gesellschaft* 17, 342 ff.

We have a tale of an adventure in Amurru by one named Sinuhe, in the time of Sesostris I. In the reign of Sesostris III (1887–1849 B. C.), a district called Sekmen, perhaps Shechem in Palestine, was pillaged. Ahmose I, Thutmose I, and Thutmose II also invaded Syria. Thutmose III, as is so well known, completely subjugated the land, and brought it under the control of Egypt. His successors lost it to the Hittites and the Habiri in the time of Amenhotep IV. The operations of Seti I, Rameses II, Merneptah, Sheshonk, Necho, and others in Palestine and Syria, are well known.

The social and political influences exerted by Egypt upon Amurru, as determined by excavations, are shown by such archaeological evidences of their presence in the land as victory steles, scarabs, pottery, etc. These have been found in practically every site that has been excavated in Palestine. One needs only to examine the collections of Palestinian antiquities in Jerusalem, Constantinople, and elsewhere, to be fully convinced of this fact. However, it is to such political or cultural matters that Egyptian influence is confined.

Besides these expeditions to Syria and the conquest of that country, and the establishing of a temple at Byblos, we know of the missionary efforts to establish the worship of Amen in that land. Thutmose III dedicated three cities to that deity in the Lebanon district; Seti I set up his own statue in Bashan, representing himself as offering a libation to Amen. Rameses III also dedicated cities in Syria to Amen-Re, and built a shrine for his worship in Canaan. At the time of the Egyptian supremacy in the land, if the local ruler refused to sacrifice to the Egyptian gods, it was a sign of open revolt. Although the expressed devotion to "the sun" in the Amarna letters retained the Amorite name of Shamash, it was nevertheless intended to show obeisance to the Egyptian god. Such facts show us that rulers doubtless officially sacrificed to Amen. Even the people were taxed to support the shrines that had been established. The story of Wenamon (about

1100 B. C.), some years after this supremacy came to an end, would seem to show that the prestige of the god had not entirely ceased at that time. Nevertheless, in spite of these efforts, there does not seem to have been any permanent influence made upon the religions of Canaan by the Egyptian religion. A study of the place names does not show any. Certainly the literature of the Old Testament does not betray any.

This lack of influence of the Egyptian religion can only be explained as being due to the fact that the Egyptians did not colonize in Syria. They had fortresses and outposts in the land, but apparently when the service of the Egyptians came to an end, they preferred to return to the Nile valley. As far as is known, there were no migrations to Amurru from Egypt; excepting, of course, the return of the sons of Israel. There is a perfectly sane reason for this fact. While there are certain plains or valleys, like the Jordan, Esdraelon, and the Shephelah, which attracted peoples from other parts, as well as such districts as Aleppo, Haran, Damascus, etc.; and while the land "yielded figs and vines," and "more plentiful than water was its wine, copious its honey, and plenteous its oil," how do these compare with what was so easily obtained in the Nile valley? Imagine an Egyptian choosing to leave "the flesh pots" of his land, with its opulent fertility, to dwell in Palestine.

It is becoming popular to regard the sojourn of the sons of Jacob in Egypt as a myth. This, of course, is based on a mere conjecture. For me it is rather difficult to believe that such a tradition, with all that it involved, could have taken such a hold upon a people and their literature without there being a historical basis for it; especially when we recall that in their temple service, and in an annual festival, right under the eyes of Egypt, the history of their serfdom and bondage was recited, and their deliverance commemorated.

True, the Hebrews did not bring back to Palestine such customs and evidences of their sojourn as did Judah, for example, when it returned from Babylonia. In Egypt and in Israel, sacrifices were offered, libations poured, and vestments were worn by the priests; and it seems they also had in common such things as the ark with its adornments, the breast-plate, and doubtless other ceremonial paraphernalia. Although the use of many of these things was universal at the time, it is nevertheless reasonable to suppose that Egyptian patterns which were familiar to Aaron, the high priest, would have influenced those of the Hebrews, even though the signification attached to these things was altogether different in Israel.

It would be impossible to understand how, when Moses codified the precepts of Israel, he was not influenced by Egyptian law, perhaps even by the legal language; and it is difficult to understand how Israel could live in a land fairly surcharged, as one has said, with eschatological ideas where the people were so busy attending to the needs of the dead, and yet not develop such an idea as the Egyptian had of the resuscitation of the departed. It seems, however, that even the Hebrew doctrine of the resurrection belongs to a later period. It should also be noted that while Egyptian scarabs, the symbol of immortality, are found in the ruins of the land, we have as yet no indication that any of them are to be associated with the Hebrew religion.

The fact that Israel had lived in the delta more or less removed from the chief centres, must at least in part explain this; but it would seem that the tenacity for their own belief, which has been so characteristic of the Hebrews in all ages, is doubtless the chief reason why they were not influenced by the religion, and even very little by the culture of the Egyptians.

I have dwelt at some length on this subject because of the claim that the Hebrews have so readily assimilated the beliefs of the Babylonians. This, as we shall see, is not only without any verification, but, it seems to me, shows a lack of appreciation of the loyalty which Jews have always displayed for their faith.   And, moreover, it is amazing to find certain Jewish scholars themselves not only accepting such conjectures of the Babylonists, but popularizing them.

In summing up the religious influences of the near neighbor Egypt upon Amurru, we can only come to the conclusion that they are practically nil; and that this must be attributed to the fact that Egyptians did not migrate to that land.

Amorite Conquests of and Migrations to Egypt

Let us now inquire what knowledge we have concerning Amorite conquests or invasions of, and migrations to, Egypt.   While from what is here presented an extensive influence of Amurru can be inferred, we have unfortunately no historical records from that land to give us data concerning their conquests or migrations.   The absence of any historical inscriptions from this region, of course, is well understood as being due to the lack of excavations having been conducted there until quite recently, excepting in Palestine; and also to the fact that a perishable writing material was very generally used.   We are, however, in hopes that the French will find such inscriptions at Byblos; or when excavations are conducted at such sites as Aleppo, Antioch, Kedesh, Haran, Mari, that cuneiform tablets will be found similar to such archives as have been discovered in Hittite regions.   But while records from early Syria are wanting, we can, however, definitely show that Amurru not only invaded Egypt, but migrated to that land.

Egyptian scholars agree that extensive Semitic influences had already been exerted upon the language of Egypt at the very beginning of the historical period.[3]   Craniological research has shown the same thing.   The influence of Byblos as early as 3000 B. C., and the veneration of the goddess of that city in Egypt, imply migra-

[3] Mueller, *Orientalistische Literaturzeitung* XI 403 f.

tions from Amurru. In the dark period from about 2350 B. C., at the very time the Amorites occupied the thrones of Babylonia, it is conceded that many Semitic loan words were introduced in the Egyptian language.[4] The same thing occurred in Babylonia. This lexicographical and grammatical influence upon the Egyptian language, in the absence of historical data, speaks loudly as regards migrations. Since Amurru was then politically in the ascendency, there can be little doubt as to the origin of this Semitic influence. This is confirmed by Professor Flinders Petrie who informs us of the discovery of "a remarkable cylinder of jasper with the name of Khandy . . . a Syrian king ruling Egypt." This, he further tells us, "seems to show the political influence of the VIIIth dynasty, and is closely in accord with Professor Clay's view of an early Amorite kingdom."[5]

It is now generally conceded that the Hyksos, who invaded and held Egypt in the early part of the second millennium B. C., were Semites from Syria. It was also about this time that the sons of Jacob went down to Egypt. We even have a remarkable mural painting, belonging to the time of Sesostris III (1887–1849 B. C.), depicting thirty-seven men, women, and children, from Syria, headed by their chief, Abesha, bringing presents. Abesha is the same name as the Hebrew Abshai of the Old Testament. The scene presents a picture of a civilized people.

The late Professor W. M. Mueller of Philadelphia, in his work on Egyptian Mythology, has informed us that a considerable part of Egyptian religious thought was influenced by Amurru. Even Amorite myths were adopted. An illustration of this is to be found in the conflict between the god of light and the primaeval monster of the abyss, known as "the Creation myth," in other words the

---

[4] Bondi, *Dem Hebräisch-phönizischen Sprachzweige angehörige Lehnwörter;* also Burchardt, *Alt-kanaanäischen Fremdworte und Eigennamen im Aegyptischen.*

[5] See *The Expository Times,* Dec. 1921, p. 121.

story which the Babylonians also borrowed. This, he tells us, reached Egypt some time after 2500 B. C., and gave rise to the story of the gigantic serpent, 'Apop, the enemy of the sun-god.

It would seem to me this Amorite myth had migrated with the people to Egypt in the dark period, above referred to, beginning about 2350 B. C. This is a strikingly significant point in this whole discussion, because at this time, as mentioned above, the Amorites also invaded Babylonia.

Mueller also informed us that only faint traces of the creation of the world from the carcass of the abysmal dragon are found, but other ideas bearing on the conflict with the monster recur in many variant forms. Isis and Osiris are identified with the Tammuz and Ishtar legends of Syria.[6] Following the Hyksos occupation, he further tells us, the worship of Asiatic deities became fashionable in Egypt, being propagated by many immigrants, mercenaries, merchants, etc., from Syria. Among the gods of Amurru worshipped in Egypt are Ba'al, Resheph, Shalman, Astarte, Qedesh, Nikkal, and Anat.[7]

In summing up the influences exerted by Amurru upon Egypt, and *vice versa*, we can only conclude that Egypt has left no impress upon the religion, and even little upon the culture, of Syria and

[6] I cannot follow Langdon (*Journal of Egyptian Arch.* VII 133 ff), who has tried to show that the Egyptian religion is related to the Sumerian because of certain similarities found in rituals of the Tammuz and Ishtar cults and those of Osiris and Isis, especially because they bore the same relation to each other: namely, as brother and husband. The Tammuz and Ishtar cult, I maintain, is West Semitic. Further, I see in other evidence offered to prove such a relationship between the Egyptians and Sumerians nothing beyond the fact that Egypt and Sumer had certain ideas in common; other ancient nations had them as well. I refer to the theory of emanation from the union of a god and goddess; figurines of the mother goddess and child; etc. Moreover, I think Langdon could prove much more effectively that the linear writing of the American Indian is a "survival of the Old Sumerian writing" than are the Egyptian "pottery marks," for a large collection of Indian glyphs can be assembled, which are strikingly similar to the Sumerian.

[7] Mueller, *Egyptian Mythology* 104 ff.

Palestine; and that this was due to the lack of migrations to that
land. On the other hand, we must conclude that the influence of
Amurru upon Egypt was exceedingly great; and that this was due
to the fact that migrations to that land took place.

BABYLONIAN CONQUESTS OF AMURRU

Let us now turn to Babylonia, and inquire what light we
have concerning that land's conquests of, and migrations to,
Amurru.

One of the earliest Babylonian kings known, Etana, who tells us
he subdued all lands, very probably invaded Syria. Lugal-Marad
and Tammuz, prior to 4000 B. C., we know conquered the West.
The consort of the latter, called Ishtar in Babylonia, the writer
feels he has shown, as already mentioned, was Ashirta, a queen
who ruled at Aleppo. Gilgamesh, who followed Tammuz, overthrew
Humbaba of the Lebanon district. All this occurred before 4000
B. C.[8]

Lugal-zaggisi, king of Erech, conquered the Westland as far as
the Mediterranean, as did also his successor Sargon (c. 2850 B. C.),
and a little later, Narâm-Sin. Gudea, the patesi of Lagash, we
know, secured building materials in Amurru. The kings of the
Fourth Ur dynasty likewise had considerable to do with this land;
for they held it in subjection until the Amorites, about 2350 B. C.,
overthrew their rule. Chedorlaomer, king of Elam, and his allied
kings, as we learn from the fourteenth chapter of Genesis, invaded
Palestine after the land rebelled against his suzerainty. That
Elam held the suzerainty of Amurru at this time, is fully confirmed
by the inscriptions.

For about a dozen centuries, following the Hammurabi period,
the land was unmolested by the Babylonians. The Assyrians, however, under Shamshi-Adad I, about 2000 B. C., conquered the

[8] *A Hebrew Deluge Story* 45 f.

Lebanon district; and in the first millennium B. C., completely subjugated the land. We need not rehearse here the Assyrian suzerainty of Syria and Palestine, for this is familiar to all.

I desire, in reviewing these conquests and invasions, to point out that while the Babylonians often humiliated Syria and Palestine, and held it in subjection for long periods, we have no knowledge of any migrations to that land, excepting of course when the Jews returned to their Zion, from the Babylonian captivity.

No one will question that Babylonian customs and personal names migrated with Judah when it returned from the captivity. Moreover, it would be remarkable if such had not been the case. But when we are asked to believe that during the exile, Israel's religion absorbed much from the Babylonian, when the creation and deluge myths, etc., were adopted, this is a totally different matter; and, I maintain, it is untenable.

We should also mention here the fact that Sargon II replaced the Hebrews which he carried away from Samaria with men from Babel, Cutha, etc. Their influence, moreover, does not seem to have been felt upon the religion of the Samaritans. Doubtless not many moons passed before a large portion of them had trekked back to their fertile land.

The trade routes passed through the district of Samaria, and there was constant intercourse with the heathen, resulting in many apostatizing; for the claim is that their prophets "prophesied by Ba'al," and caused the people to err; nevertheless, in the years following the capture of Samaria, the Jews did not charge the people with idolatry. In short, there is no evidence of any foreign influence upon the religion and culture of the Samaritans at this time.

There is one other movement which has been very much overworked in efforts to make Babylonism appear reasonable. Abraham, the son of Terah, we learn from Genesis, went from Ur of the Chaldees to Haran, whence he migrated to Palestine. This is looked upon by some scholars as the migration from Babylonia of the Terahites.

The identity of Mugheir in Southern Babylonia with Ur of the Chaldees, although possible, is by no means certain, and especially since the Jews who lived in Babylonia did not know the site, thinking that Warka (ancient Erech) was Ur, and also because St. Stephen refers to Ur as being in Mesopotamia (Acts 7 : 2).

I have given reasons elsewhere for believing that 'Ur ('wr) is to be identified with Mari on the Euphrates in Mesopotamia, which city apparently was the great seat of worship of the god 'Ur ('wr); and which city, although very important in the time of the patriarchs, was practically lost sight of in later centuries.[9] However, this is a mooted question, and need not enter into this discussion, especially since Babylonia was filled with Amorites at this time.

It is reasonable to conjecture that this tradition may be an echo of a fair-sized migration, headed by Terah; but this could only be interpreted as being a return of Amorites to their ancestral home; for Abram was an Aramaean. It may even represent the descendants of some who had been forced to dwell in Ur.

While, therefore, it is possible to conjecture that Ur was in Southern Babylonia; that the Amorite Terahites while they lived there "drank deeply" of the mythological fountains of the land,

---

[9] Since Mar^{ki} and $Mar-Tu^{ki}$ (= $Amurru$ = Uru) are used interchangeably, and since the name 'wr is also written Ur, I have had no hesitation in identifying Mar or War with Ur. (See *Empire of the Amorites* 100 ff.). It would be interesting to have Albright give the proof for his assertion that this is not tenable for philological reasons (*Jour. Palestine Or. Soc.* I, p. 77). Following are Albright's philological reasons for identifying Ur of the Chaldees with Arbail. He arrives at this as follows: *Arpakshad* is identified with $Arrapha$ = $Arrapka$ = $Arpak$. $Arpakshad$= *Arpak shadē*. The similarity between Arphaxad and 'Ur Kasdum is explained thus: The most important city near Arrapka was Arbela (*Urbillu, Urbel, Arbail*). Urbel in Arphaxad, the home of Abram, was corrupted to Arkel, which was emended into *'Ur Kasdim (Jour. Bib. Lit.*, XXXVII 134 f.).

as some have suggested; that they carried Babylonian myths
with them to Haran, and then to Palestine, where they became a
vital part of the religious conceptions of the Phoenicians and
Hebrews—while all this were possible, it must be understood as
being simply conjectural. But, moreover, all this does not explain
how the Egyptians, centuries before the time of Abram, through
contact with Syria had borrowed "the myth of the combat between
the god of heaven and light and the abysmal dragon of the ocean,"[10]
otherwise generally known as the Creation story.

We find, therefore, that while many conquests and invasions by
the Babylonians of the land of the Amorites are known, there is
no trace of any migrations on the part of the Babylonians. In
explanation of this fact, as in the case of Egypt, we need only compare the land of Amurru with the alluvial plain with its prodigious
fertility.

If, therefore, it is correct that the Babylonians did not migrate
to the West, then according to the principle laid down we should
find that while cultural influences may have been felt in Amurru,
we should not expect to find that the Babylonian religion had
influenced that land.

Let us now inquire what excavations and research have revealed
in the form of actual proof that Babylonia has exercised such an
extensive influence socially as well as religiously upon Canaan or
the Hebrews, as has been so confidently asserted; or upon what
tangible archæological evidence the Babylonists have based the
statement that Canaan was a domain of Babylonian civilization.

We need not repeat here the story of the Amarna letters, that
in the middle of the second millennium B. C., the Babylonian language was used all over Western Asia and Egypt as the *lingua
franca* of that era. This was unquestionably a literary age. The
ability to write in the script of the Babylonians was no mean

[10] Mueller, *Egyptian Mythology* 104 ff.

accomplishment. Education must have been widely spread. All classes of society and both sexes seem to be represented in these writings. The political domination of Babylonia, in some earlier era, probably in the time of Hammurabi, doubtless brought about this use of the language and script. Among the peoples we know used it are the Egyptians, the Amorites or Canaanites, Hittites, Mitanneans, and peoples in Cappadocia and Cyprus. Doubtless all civilized peoples of the ancient world studied this *lingua franca* of that era.

The Amarna tablets have furnished the background and the backbone for the Babylonist view that the religion and culture of Israel are Babylonian. I know of no efforts to show that other than Amorite lands were thus influenced; Canaan especially is centred upon in this connection, because, it is claimed, it was occupied by a semi-barbarous people.

It is generally conceded that this use of the Babylonian language resulted in many Babylonian words creeping into the language of the country; doubtless other Babylonian words also found their way into usage through commerce and political occupation. Knowing what the influence of the French language was wherever it was used as the diplomatic or inter-commercial language, we know exactly what should be expected. It is also reasonable to infer that the scribes in Palestine, who had to know the Babylonian language, would have had copies of Babylonian legends and other kinds of model texts in order to study it, for as is well known, two such texts were found in Egypt; which discovery the Babylonists have stressed so hard in their efforts to show the influence of the Babylonian religion. But it would be just as easy for them to prove that when French was studied in England and Germany for a similar purpose, the people of these lands appropriated the Marseillaise, or the legend of Jeanne d'Arc as their own, as it would be to prove that Canaan or Israel appropriated in this age the myths and legends of Babylonia for their own religious literature. In short, I contend that without other evidence of an archæological character to show Babylonian influence upon the religions of Canaan, this argument is futile.

Let us now enquire what has been found in the shape of archæological material in the numerous sites excavated in Palestine, as well as what research in general has produced to substantiate the idea that Canaan, when Israel entered the land, was a domain of Babylonian culture. What light on the subject is obtained from the material objects that have been discovered?

At Gezer one of the *maṣṣĕbôth*, or stone pillars, which Macalister discovered, was polished with the kisses of worshippers; this he regarded as possibly the central object of veneration. This *bætylos* or *beth-el*, "house of God," as Professor Sayce calls it, is declared by him to "take us back to Semitic Babylonia." The belief that the stone was a "shrine of divinity," he tells us, "belonged to an age of reflection and points to a Babylonian source."[11] I cannot follow in this. The *maṣṣĕbāh*, or stone pillar, has not been found in Babylonia; and I know of no worship similar to it in that land.

Concerning seals found in Palestine, Professor Sayce writes: "It is true that a few seal-cylinders have been met with in the excavations on the city sites, but with the exception of one found at Taanach I do not know of any that can be said to be of purely Babylonian manufacture; most of them are of Syrian make, and represent a Syrian modification of the Babylonian type."[12]

It is really surprising, in view of the use of the Babylonian language and script in Canaan, that, like Egyptian scarabs, many Babylonian seals should not have been discovered there. But let us here examine the one that has been credited as Babylonian. The inscription reads: "Atanakh-El, the son of Khabṣim, the ser-

[11] *Archæology of the Cuneiform Inscriptions* 147 f.
[12] *Ibidem* 151 f.

vant of Ne-Uru-Gal."[13] The personal names are Amorite, and the deity, who was worshipped in Babylonia, is also Amorite. Other names of the same deity are Urra-Gal and Urra. There are also three Egyptian hieroglyphs on the seal. The scene, which is rather crudely drawn, can scarcely be said even to be patterned after a Babylonian model. This is the only seal that the above-mentioned writer even considers to be Babylonian. In short, this seal must be grouped with those of Syrian manufacture.

At Ta'anach a bronze sword was found similar in shape to one which belonged to the Assyrian king Adad-nirari. Here again we can only express surprise that more such objects have not been found, since we know that Babylonia and Assyria had dominated Canaan in many periods.

At Ta'anach tablets were found in a jar, in apparently what was the residence of the chief man of the town, named Ashirta-washur. They refer to political as well as to private affairs. They were written in the Amarna period.[14] There is absolutely nothing found in the tablets to show any other influence from Babylonia except that they are written in the language and script of that land, which, as already mentioned, was then used throughout Western Asia and Egypt.

To say, therefore, that these few tablets and "letters are a final proof, if any were needed, of the complete Babylonian nature of Canaanite civilization in the country before the Exodus"[15] is a conclusion that I cannot follow. One could just as easily show the complete French nature of any country's civilization during the last century, in the absence of any other documents but some written in French.

Professor Nowack, in his review of the excavations at Tel-el-

---

[13] Sellin, *Tell Ta'annek* p. 28.
[14] See *Ibidem* 113 ff., and *Empire of the Amorites* p. 54.
[15] Sayce, *Archæology of the Cuneiform Inscriptions* 150 f.

Mutesellim writes: "It is a disturbing but irrefutable fact that until down to the fifth stratum—*i. e.* to the beginning of the eighth century—important Assyrian influences do not assert themselves. It is most significant that at Megiddo not a single idol from the Assyrian-Babylonian pantheon has been found."[16] Even the Assyrian influence that this writer acknowledges, is based on seals; but these, as we have seen above, are recognized generally to be of Syrian origin.

The results of the excavations by Mr. Macalister were the same; concerning which Professor Sayce has written as follows: "What makes it the stronger is that Mr. Macalister has opened a long series of graves beginning with the neolithic race and coming down to Græco-Roman times, and that while the influence of Egypt is sufficiently visible in them, that of Babylonia is almost entirely absent."[17] I think it would be even more accurate to say, that it is entirely absent.

I find that Professor Gunkel says that the system of measures, weights, and money, used in Israel was Babylonian. Even were this a fact, it would prove no more in this connection than it would to say that Greece has adopted from the Sumerians the division of the circle into three hundred and sixty degrees. As far as I can understand, the Babylonians and the Hebrews only had the manah, shekel, and kor, in common; and whether these terms had their origin in Amurru or Babylonia, is a question on which there is no light; and moreover, it is also a question of comparatively little consequence in this connection. The ancient, like the modern, readily adopted the science of his neighbor; but not his religion.

Professor Gunkel also tells us of the influence of Babylonia upon Israel in the use of particular numbers, *e. g.*, 7 and 12; because the "Tablets of Creation" were written on seven tablets, and the Gilga-

[16] *Theol. Literaturzeitung*, 1908, No. 26.
[17] Sayce, *ibidem* p. 151.

mesh epic was written on twelve, etc.[18]   Of course a similar argument could be used in connection with any series of books that
happened to appear in seven or twelve volumes.

. In studying all the antiquities that have been found in Palestine,
we can only conclude that besides the inscription which Shalmaneser
III cut alongside that of Rameses II on the cliff at the mouth of
the Dog River, a short distance north of Beirut, in Syria, and
besides several letters and contracts already referred to, written in
the intercommercial language of the era, we can correctly say with
Professor Sayce that "the more strictly archæological evidence of
Babylonian influence upon Canaan is extraordinarily scanty";[19]
that there are "few material evidences of intercourse with Babylonia."[20]

This must be conceded as remarkable, especially since we know
that Palestine was on the highroad between Babylonia and Egypt,
and because of the Egyptian antiquities which have been found in
the land.   Certainly from these results, it is obvious that the claims
of pan-Babylonism do not appear in a very favorable light.

It is generally held that the Bible had certain precepts in common with those found in the Hammurabi code, e. g., "eye for eye,
and tooth for tooth," as well as certain laws which are comparatively similar, including the behavior of Jacob and Laban, or Hagar
and Sarah, which coincide with certain laws of the code.   In the
light of the recent discoveries, I do not think that even these facts
furnish any definite criteria on the subject; for aside from the
question of interdependence, it is now admitted that Hammurabi
was an Amorite; and that for two hundred and twenty-five years
before the time he codified the laws, the land was governed by
Amorites; and moreover, Hammurabi, in the code states that ' he

[18] Gunkel, *Israel and Babylon* p. 21.
[19] *Ibidem* p. 151.
[20] *Ibidem* p. 154.

put the laws of Aleppo into execution." Exactly what importance is to be attached to this saying, of course, is at present a question. Further, we know that the early laws in the Yale Collection, written in Sumerian, which are a prototype of the Hammurabi Code, are the "laws of Nisaba and Khani," two Amorite deities.[21]

It is not improbable that Hammurabi may have promulgated his laws in Amurru. These, however, exclude all legislation bearing on religious matters, and in consequence had no influence upon the vast body of religious laws in the Mosaic Code.

And now let us face the reasons given for the assertion that Babylonian theology had made its way to Canaan, and extensively influenced the religions of that land. This is based upon the fact that certain deities known from the Babylonian inscriptions were also worshipped in Palestine. It is said that "the deities of Canaan were to a large extent Babylonian, with Babylonian names. The Babylonian gods Ana, Nebo, Rimmon (Ramman), Hadad, and Dagon meet us in the names of places and persons, and Ashtoreth, who shared with Baal the devotion of the inhabitants of Palestine, is the Babylonian Ishtar with the suffix of the feminine attached to her name."[22]

In view of this contention that in Palestine certain gods of Babylonia were worshipped, it becomes necessary to digress here sufficiently to discuss this assertion and ascertain upon what basis it rests.

It is scarcely possible that the writer would say to-day that Hadad or Rimmon had his origin in the Babylonian Adad. Practically all scholars now agree, as far as I know, that at an early date the Amorite Hadad was carried into Babylonia. This fact, however, must be regarded as very significant. Let us repeat. It is now generally conceded that the Amorite Hadad migrated to

[21] See Clay, *Miscellaneous Inscriptions* p. 19.
[22] Sayce, *Archæology of the Cuneiform Inscriptions* (1908) 152 f.

Babylonia in an early era; and there his name was written Adad, Addu, Adadi, Adada, Dadda, Dadi, etc. These variant forms of the name in Babylonian inscriptions would in themselves show that the deity was foreign.

Dagon, whose worship in Palestine is known from the Old Testament, was in previous years, as we have seen, also regarded by Assyriologists as Babylonian. His first appearance known to me in cuneiform is in a personal name in the inscription of Manishtusu (c. 2775 B. C.), which, it might be added, is full of Amorite names. Dungi about 2419 B. C. dedicated a temple to Dagan. Two rulers' names of the Amorite dynasty of Nîsin contain the god's name. The Amorite king, Hammurabi, calls himself "the warrior of Dagan." This deity was not recognized as belonging to the pantheon of Babylonia.

In Canaan, the Philistines worshipped Dagan at Gaza (Judg. 16:23), and at Ashdod (I Sam. 5:1). There was also a temple of Dagan near Joppa (Josh. 10:41), at present called Beit Dejan. There is another, southeast of Nablus. Josephus mentions a fortress, Dagon, above Jericho (*Ant.* XII 8:1).

It is now recognized by scholars, through the discovery of a few tablets in Mesopotamia, that in the kingdom Khana, on the middle Euphrates, there was a great centre of Dagan worship; and most scholars, I think, are now willing to concede that this was probably the main centre of the worship; and also that he was an Amorite god.

In presenting the above facts I have had in mind letting the non-Assyriologist know what a change the discovery of a few tablets in the Amorite land has brought about; and at the same time to call attention to the fact that in Amurru we have these many geographical names connected with Dagan, while in Babylonia there are none; which fact is paralleled in what we know concerning other gods discussed in what follows.

Nebo, or Nabû, was worshipped at Borsippa near Babylon. The first mention of Nabû and his temple, known to me, is in the reign of Hammurabi, when that king informs us he cared for and built a throne for Nabû. In this Amorite period names compounded with Nabû appear, many of which can be proved to be Amorite. Nabû does not appear in the Akkadian Name Syllabary, but he does in the Amorite; which fact is very significant.[23] In subsequent years Nabû was included in the Babylonian pantheon. In the late period, Babylonian nomenclature is again filled with Amorite names compounded with Nabû.

In Palestine and the surrounding territory, there was first of all Mount Nebo, where Moses died (Nu. 33:47). There was a city Nebo in Moab (Nu. 32:3), probably near the mountain, and one in Judah (Ezra 2:29). According to Jerome's *Onomasticon*, there was a Nebo six miles west of Heshbon, probably the present Neba on the Dead Sea.

Whether we will later find another centre of Nebo worship elsewhere in Amurru, as we did that of Dagan, remains to be seen; but knowing of these several geographical names in Palestine mentioned in the early period, and especially Mount Nebo; and also the fact that Nabû was worshipped only at one city in Babylonia, besides many other facts, referred to above,[24] there can be no doubt as to Nabû being Amorite.

Ashirta, who also appears in a number of geographical names in Palestine,[25] I feel I have conclusively shown recently, was Amorite; and that the original seat of her cult, as mentioned above, was at Aleppo, where she ruled at the time of Tammuz and Gilgamesh, kings of Erech. Her name was written in Hebrew, Phoenician, Moabitish, Aramaic, South Arabic and Ethiopic, in every instance

---

[23] Chiera, *Lists of Personal Names* (*UMBS* XI 2), p. 152.
[24] See also *Empire of the Amorites* p. 180 f.
[25] See *ibidem* p. 172.

with an initial '*ayin*. When her name first appears in cuneiform, it is written Ashdar, Eshdar, Ishdar; later usually Ishtar. It has always been difficult to understand how Assyriologists have been able to satisfy themselves as to the way the West Semitic forms of this name, which are always written with an initial '*ayin*, could have arisen from the Babylonian Ashdar or Ishtar, in which, in not a single instance, was there even an attempt to reproduce the laryngeal.

I know of no effort on the part of Babylonists to show that Ana was worshipped in Palestine.[26] The goddess Anoth, or Antu, however, is generally recognized as having been worshipped in that land.

Antu appears in an inscription, found at Seripul, of Anubanini, king of Lulubu, as the consort of Anu. While Anu of Erech was the father of the gods, and was always foremost in the triad, Anu, Enlil and Ea, the goddess Antu does not occur in early Babylonian inscriptions as being worshipped in that city. This includes the Cassite and even subsequent periods. In the late texts, Antu, especially with the meaning "goddess," was introduced at Erech, and coupled with the name of Anu.

In Palestine, Bêth-Anôth, probably the present Beit 'Ainûn, is a city mentioned in Joshua (15:59). Seti I, and Rameses II, refer to Bêth-Anôth. Sheshonk captured a city by that name in Judah. Jeremiah grew up at Anathôth, at present called 'Anâtâ, near Jerusalem.

The worship of the Amorite Anôth was carried comparatively early to Egypt. At Thebes there was a priesthood of the goddess in the time of Thothmes III (1479-1447 B. C.). Rameses II gave his daughter a name which meant "daughter of Anôth."

---

[26] The name is probably found in *Bêth 'Anî'* (Bethany), and in the personal name '*Aner*, written *An-ram* in the Septuagint. The deity is Amorite, see *Empire of the Amorites* p. 169.

It is not impossible that 'Ana on the Euphrates, in Amurru, was the chief centre of this worship, for close by is 'Anatho, which apparently was a twin city of 'Ana.[27]   Since the worship of Anôth was not recognized in Babylonia prior to the late period, certainly the origin of the deity is not to be found in that land.   Here, it seems to me, is another very obvious and vital point for the Babylonist to explain.

Another deity worshipped in Palestine, who has generally been regarded as Babylonian, is the one whose name was written ideographically ^{d}Nin-IB; for Bît ^{d}Nin-IB is mentioned in the Amarna tablets as being near Jerusalem.

There are one or two occurrences of ^{d}Nin-IB in the Babylonian inscriptions known to me in the Akkad period.   But in the nomenclature of the Nîsin dynasty (2357-2154 B. C.), when Amorites flooded the country, many names are found compounded with that of the deity, including a king's name.   Thereafter, at Nippur, this deity became very prominent.

Recent discoveries in Babylonia, as already mentioned, have shown that the ideogram ^{d}Nin-IB is to be read En-Urta, "Lord Urta," and that the deity, who had originally been feminine, had become masculinized in Babylonia.

Elsewhere I have shown that the name of the great Amorite god, Uru, is to be found in the name Jerusalem, which in ancient times was written Uru-salim and Ur-salimmu in cuneiform.   In view of this fact it would seem highly probably that the Amorite city had originally been dedicated to the worship of Uru.   And it also seems reasonable that the shrine Bît ^{d}Nin-IB, or Bêth Urta, "shrine of Urta," which was close by the city, was dedicated to the consort of Uru.   In view of these facts, and many others presented elsewhere,[28] there can be little doubt that this deity is Amorite.

[27] See ibidem 116 f.
[28] See The Empire of the Amorites.

Such a deity as "Moloch," whose name was carried to Babylonia, where it was written Malik, as well as the gods Attar, Adon, Gir, etc., need not be discussed here, since they are now generally regarded as Amorite or West Semitic. This concludes the list of deities who have been identified with the West, as far as I know, that have been, or could be cited as Babylonian. In short, not a single one of these deities is Babylonian.

Before leaving this subject let us inquire of the Babylonists why such leading gods of Babylonia, as Enlil, "the lord of lands" in the early period, and Marduk, the Bêl of Babylon, who usurped Enlil's position, and from the time of Abraham was the chief deity of the land—why, if their contentions have anything in them, are these gods not named as having also been worshipped in Canaan?

It was perfectly clear in the case of Egypt, why the religion of that land made no impression upon Syria. The same is true of Babylonia. People from that rich alluvial deposit did not migrate. In short, while we know that the Philistine, the Hittite, Girgashite, and other peoples, had representatives in Palestine, there is not a word in the Old Testament, or in any other inscription, to show that the "Babylonite" lived there, except those whom Sargon brought to Samaria.

It seems to me that this brief review of the facts bearing on the question before us, leads to the conclusion that Babylonians did not migrate from the alluvial plain to Canaan; from which it follows that the Babylonian religion was not carried to that land.

Although pan-Babylonism, as already stated, is such an extreme position that it has practically exploded itself, there is, however, a phase of it that should at least be briefly mentioned in this connection. The late Professor Winckler of Berlin, who founded what is generally called the "Astral-mythological School," attempted to reconstruct the astrological system of the Babylonians. By his work he has contributed considerably toward a better understanding of the subject; but in connection with his researches he has also attempted to show that the Israelite cult was dependent upon a Babylonian original; and that the astral-mythological element is extensively found in the Old Testament.

In Winckler's efforts to prove his contention he made use of the following kind of facts: Abram must be a moon-god, for he went from Ur to Haran, two places identified with that deity. The 318 men Abraham assembled in going after Lot, are the 318 days of the year when the moon is visible. Kirjath-arba, a city in which Abraham lived, means "city of four"; and this refers to the four phases of the moon. The word Beersheba means "seven wells"; this represents the seven days in each phase of the moon. The four wives of Jacob are also the four phases. His twelve sons are the twelve months; Leah's seven sons are the gods of the week; the 1200 pieces of silver which Benjamin received, are a multiple of the thirty days of the month; and his five changes of raiment are the five intercalary days of the Babylonian year.

Although others have popularized this phase of Winckler's theories, I feel that we need simply have stated some of the arguments upon which they are based. Moreover, his followers seem to be comparatively few. Let it suffice to say that Israel's law required that the man who worshipped the sun, moon, or any of the hosts of heaven, should be put to death (Deut. 12:2–7). That such were worshipped in Palestine is very evident; but it cannot be shown that the worship penetrated the religion of Israel.

We know that Egypt established shrines to Amen in Palestine, and that they disappeared without leaving a trace. It is not impossible that the Babylonians may have attempted to do a similar thing. Even had they succeeded, if that had been done, it would prove nothing as regards the religion of Israel. I doubt, however, whether they ever made attempts to do this. Certainly there is not the slightest evidence that they did.

In reviewing all the material that has been used in the past to show the influence of the Babylonian religion upon that of Canaan (without considering the stories of creation, deluge, etc., which are discussed below), I feel that there is absolutely nothing upon which the theory rests.

These are some of the reasons why I cannot follow those scholars who have promulgated the idea that Canaan was "a domain of Babylonian civilization"; that its religion "had its roots in the Valley of the Euphrates"; that "Babylonian myths were in current circulation in Israel," and that "when Israel entered the land all these ideas were a part of the mental possession of the people."[29]

Amorite Conquests of and Migrations to Babylonia

And now let us inquire whether we have knowledge of any Amorite conquests of Babylonia, or of any migrations to that land. In Genesis we have an echo of the Semitic migration when they went eastward into "the plain of Shinʳr," and built Babel. We find that it can be shown that most of the names of the antediluvian kings of Babylon were Amorite (see Chapter VII). We find also that the first five postdiluvian kings bore Amorite names.[30] It is needless to enlarge upon the significance of these facts. Through a recent discovery, we now know that a usurper named Humbaba, who ruled in the Lebanons, had humiliated Babylonia in the time of Gilgamesh, about 4200 B. C., and that Ishtar, the queen of Aleppo, as mentioned above, was the consort of his predecessor, Tammuz, king of Erech. About a thousand years later, the Amorite city Mari, on the Euphrates, as we have already seen, ruled Babylonia during the reigns of three kings. Many other rulers of Babylonia, in the centuries which follow, bear Amorite names, as Enbi-

---

[29] *History of the Religion of Babylonia and Assyria* p. 136.
[30] See *Empire of the Amorites* 80 f.

Ashdar, Ishu-El, Zi-mutar, Uzi-watar, El-muti, etc.   Later, in the
time of the Akkad dynasty, about 2800 B. C., we find the nomenclature of the city of Akkad well filled with Amorite names.[31]   The
same is true of the Ur dynasty, from 2474 B. C.   About 2350 B. C.
the Amorites overthrew the Babylonian rule and completely dominated the land, establishing three contemporaneous dynasties, the
Nîsin, the Larsa, and the Babylon; Hammurabi, the Amraphel of
the fourteenth chapter of Genesis, being the sixth king of the last
mentioned.   We know from the thousands of legal and business
documents that the nomenclature of this time was especially full
of Amorite names.   It was in this period that the early version of
the Deluge story was transcribed, which the writer feels he has
shown is Amorite.   Again, in the Assyrian period and in the Neo-
Babylonian time, especially after Nebuchadnezzar had carried Judah
into captivity, we find many Amorite names and, in particular,
hundreds of Jewish names.

With the knowledge, therefore, that there was such a constant
influx of Amorites in almost every period down to 2000 B. C., as
well as in the late periods, we would expect to find that the land
was thoroughly permeated with the religions of the Amorites.
There is a mass of evidence to prove that this is a fact.

The most high god, El, of the Amorites, was early brought into
the land.   The city of Babylon was dedicated to his worship for
the name of this metropolis means "Gate (*Bâb*) of El."   The city
of Der was likewise dedicated to him, for that name was written
Dûr-El, i. e., "Fortress (*Dûr*) of El."   Erech very probably also
had El as its patron deity (see also Chapter III).

The god Uru, found in five of the antediluvian names of kings,
seems to have been brought into the land in many different periods,
when migrations took place.[32]   The name of the god Amurru is

---

[31] See Scheil, *Delegation en Perse* II 41 ff.
[32] See Chapter II, and also *Empire of the Amorites* 66 ff.

but another form of this name, for in Aramaic, as we have seen, it was written '*wr* (= Ûru). At Cutha, he was worshipped under the name of Urra, Urra-gal, "the great Uru," and Ne-Uru-Gal or Nergal.

Urta, or En-Urta, who, as we have seen, was originally the consort of Uru, was worshipped especially at Nippur, where, as mentioned above, the goddess was masculinized. A study of the nomenclature of that city indicates that the time when this cult became popular, synchronized with the rule of the Amorites in the Nîsin-Larsa-Babylon period.[33]

Adad, the Hadad of the Old Testament, as we have seen, was early brought into the land by the Amorites, as was also Dagan, familiar to us as the Old Testament Dagon. The gods Ea, Nisaba, Nebo, Ashirta, Adgi, Attar, Gir, Khani, Sharru and many other Amorite deities, the Semitic emigrants, who moved into Babylonia, brought with them. This is a natural conclusion. History records no exception to the rule that migrating people have carried their religion with them. And it is certainly reasonable to infer that they carried with them also their legends. But this is not only a perfectly reasonable supposition; it can also be satisfactorily proved to be a fact.

Before leaving the subject of migrations let me digress to say here that what is true of Syria in its relation to Egypt and Babylonia, is true of Syria in its connections with other lands, such as South Arabia, Greece, and Italy. It is generally admitted for example that extensive religious influences from Amurru were felt in Italy; but it is also admitted, that land gave practically nothing in return to Syria. This movement in the direction of Italy is well attested. Not only did Italy import grain and industrial objects from Syria, but soldiers, workmen, and slaves. The unprec-

---

[33] One occurrence of a name compounded with En-Urta is found in the texts of the previous period. See Barton, *UMBS* IX 1, 58:I:7.

edented wealth and splendor of Rome also became very attractive to the merchant and mercenary, as well as to the excess population; so that there was an extensive movement toward Italy. The migration of Syrians to this land, Professor Cumont informs us, who were faithful to their deities, is responsible for the great religious influence that this part of the Orient exerted upon the Roman religion; but on the other hand, he informs us, Rome has given Syria nothing in return.[34]

This review of invasions, conquests, and migrations, based on the testimony of the monuments, establishes fully the proposed principles laid down in connection with the spread of cultural ideas and of religious influences. This being true, and with the knowledge that the migratory current was from Amurru to Babylonia, and not *vice versa*, it follows that the Amorite religions have influenced those of Babylonia, the land which lies on its border. This, as we have seen, is fully borne out by excavations and research. And this, I maintain, is an exceedingly important argument in showing that the religious literature, including the creation and deluge stories, which Amurru and Babylonia had in common, had its origin in Amurru, whence it was carried with the migrating Semites into Babylonia.

The second argument that I desire to use in connection with my thesis is based on a study of climatic conditions in Babylonia and Amurru, as well as of the forces which are credited with having given rise to the so-called nature-myths, the stories of the creation and the deluge.

The theory of the Babylonian origin of the Hebrew story of creation is largely based upon the idea that it symbolizes the change of seasons from winter to spring; and that this nature-myth had its origin in the heavy winter rains, when the land was

[34] Cumont, *Oriental Religions in Roman Paganism* 8 f.

flooded, which were followed by spring, when life again appeared. Likewise the theory of the Babylonian origin of the deluge story has for its basis the idea of "the yearly phenomenon of the rainy and stormy season, which lasts in Babylonia for several months, during which time whole districts in the Euphrates valley are submerged."

In the chapters which follow I shall show that these theories, which are so vital to the position of the Babylonist, are based on a complete misunderstanding of climatic conditions in Babylonia. Moreover, I think it can be conclusively shown that the force in nature which is said to have given rise to these stories, reflects not the climate of Babylonia, but that of Amurru.

The third argument I propose using in establishing my thesis is based on the study of the names of deities and persons found in the texts involved. This, in my judgment, is perhaps the most important of the four arguments used. Having already assembled in publications perhaps twenty-five thousand names, gathered from the nomenclature of the cuneiform tablets covering several millenniums,[25] it is possible from a study of them to ascertain influences, as well as migrations, that have taken place, in a most remarkable manner. On a basis of the study of the foreign names in the nomenclature of Babylonia, without any other data, it would be possible to reconstruct considerable history of the movements of ancient peoples into that land.

In the earliest dynastic lists now known, we find Amorites and other foreign peoples ruling Babylonia. In the collection of names belonging to the Akkad and Ur dynasties, as we have seen, we find large numbers of Amorite and other foreign names. In the Nisin-

---

[25] See Dhorme, *Bei. zur Assyr.* VI 2, 63 ff.; Huber, *Personennamen;* Ranke, *Early Babylonian Personal Names;* Clay, *Personal Names of the Cassite Period;* Tallqvist, *Assyrian Personal Names;* Tallqvist, *Neobabylonisches Namenbuch;* and the indices to many volumes of texts.

Larsa-Babylon contemporaneous dynasties, there is a great influx of Western Semites. In the Cassite period (1700–1200 B. C.), these are reduced to a minimum, but in place of them we find the nomenclature full of Cassite and Hittite-Mitannian names. In the Neo-Babylonian period we find hundreds of Jewish names; in the Persian period these have greatly multiplied, when large numbers of Persian names are found, including many Egyptian. In the Greek period, many Greek names are found.

We know that the Amorites subjugated Babylonia; that the Hittites invaded it; that the Cassites, Persians, and Greeks in certain periods also ruled the land, and that the Jews were carried into exile to Babylonia. The nomenclature reflects all these movements, and corroborates perfectly the historical data which have already come to light.

In the previous chapter we have seen the importance of such studies, how when, following the discovery that the name Amurru was written 'wr (Úru) in Aramaic, it was conjectured on the basis of this, as well as the study of the names of the Nîsin dynasty, that the dynasty was Amorite; which has since been definitely corroborated.

Another instance that might be cited as regards the importance of these studies is the bearing that a single name often has which occurs in a text. For example, in the well-known Gilgamesh epic the hero fights an enemy in the cedar forests, who was called Humbaba, which name is also written Hubaba. The scenes of this conflict have for years been placed in Elam, not because we know that a single cedar tree ever grew there, but because of the resemblance of the name Humbaba to that of the Elamite god Humba, which is variously written, as Humman, Humba, Humban, Umman, Umba, etc. It will be noticed that in no instance is there a reduplication of the consonant b in the god's name, as in Humbaba. Upon this identification, emphasis also was placed upon the epic being based upon a myth, being in part astral, it was said, and in part a nature-myth.

Scholars years ago called attention to a name which closely resembled it, found in a legend of Lucian, concerning the building of the temple at Hierapolis, which was in the land where cedars grew; but nevertheless scholars continued to identify the character as an Elamite god.

The recent discovery of the name written Huwawa on the early version of the epic found in the Yale Collection; the recent discovery also that Humbaba was a usurper who had humiliated Babylonia, as determined from an omen text in the Pierpont Morgan Collection; and the occurrence of the name in the Amorite Name Syllabary found at Nippur, have now definitely established the fact that Humbaba was an Amorite king whose palace was in the cedar forests of Lebanon.[36]

I have cited this instance to show how important is the correct identification of a single name in a legend; for in many publications Humbaba is regarded as a god of Elam, where cedar forests are supposed to have grown; all of which was based upon this identification, which is now proved incorrect. Naturally if an ancient legend were discovered and it contained but a single name, say for example Agamemnon, unless there was scenery that unquestionably reflected another land, scholars would have little hesitation in giving their view of its origin. In using this argument based on the study of names in connection with the creation and deluge stories, I might add that it will be seen that conclusions rest not upon a single name, but upon many.

The fourth argument that I wish to use in my efforts to prove the Amorite origin of these stories is based on a study of certain

---

[36] See *Empire of the Amorites* 87 f; Jastrow-Clay, *An Early Version of the Gilgamesh Epic* p. 23; and *A Hebrew Deluge Story* 49 f.

literary and linguistic evidence found in them.   I fully appreciate that here there will be a difference of opinion expressed.   This will largely arise from the fact that my point of view is totally different from that of most Assyriologists as regards the relative position of the Babylonian language in the Semitic group.

The prevailing view is that the Babylonian or Akkadian language antedates the Amorite group (*i. e.*, Hebrew, Phoenician, and Aramaic) by many centuries; and that, generally speaking, when these languages have words in common with the Babylonian, especially when they are not found in Arabic, they have had their origin in Babylonia.   This understanding is due to a number of reasons.

Arabia, as already stated, is considered by these scholars to be "the home of the Semites," and its language is the source of all in the Semitic group.   Syria and Palestine received their first Semitic peoples from Arabia about 2500 B. C.   The civilization of Syria and Palestine was therefore of comparatively late development, and was extensively influenced by the Babylonian.

My own understanding of the situation is totally different.   The cradle of the Semites may have rocked in Arabia; this may even have occurred at the North Pole, where some Indo-European scholars think Aryan had its origin.   I only know that it is now proved that the antiquity of the civilization of Amurru synchronizes with the earliest found in Egypt and Babylonia.   I believe that excavations in Syria will reveal the fact that its civilization greatly antedated that of Egypt and Babylonia.   Further, I know that there is no basis for the Arabian wave theory of migrations to account for the Semitic inhabitants of Amurru and Babylonia; and I believe, as already mentioned, that Amorites, who as we definitely know did migrate in all early periods into the Babylonian alluvium, furnished it with its Semitic inhabitants.   Doubtless many Arabs also trekked in from the desert at the same time; but of this we have no evidence.   Further, I believe that what we call Semitic

Babylonian is a dialect of the Amorite language under the influence of the Sumerians, who introduced their script in the land, and who are probably responsible for many of the grammatical peculiarities of the Babylonian language. In other words, I believe that the Babylonian is a broken down Amorite language which in all periods, due to migrations, was influenced by the mother tongue.

To give here all my reasons for this understanding of the language, is impossible, and also unnecessary. I have simple given my view of the origin of the language for the purpose of showing why scholars will differ, at least as regards some of the linguistic evidence which I propose to offer for the Amorite origin of the creation and deluge stories. I shall give some examples, however, which are beyond any cavil; but until the relation of the Hebrew and Babylonian languages is viewed differently than it is at present, it is expected that many will refuse to accept the conclusion that a word is foreign when it has been met with in Babylonian literature, even if it is well known in the Amorite group. It does not matter to them whether it is obsolete, or it is alone found in a list of words where it is explained by a well-known Babylonian word. Nor does it matter whether the root of the word has a wide extended use in Hebrew or Aramaic, and is not found in Babylonian, except in the text of the story under consideration. Fortunately I can produce some linguistic and some literary evidences which lie beyond the possibility of such opposition.

III

THE CREATION STORY

It is generally admitted that certain parallel ideas which are found expressed in the literature of ancient Israel concerning the creation of the world, and in a story of creation as handed down by the Babylonians, have had a common origin. These embrace the ideas that prior to the creation a watery chaos existed; that the deep was personified by a monster, designated as Tehom and Tiamat; that Jehovah or Marduk went forth to battle with this monster, who was slain; after which the firmament, the luminaries, and man were created. These and other points of resemblance, it is generally admitted, leave no doubt as to there being a relationship between the cosmogony of Israel and that handed down by the Babylonians. It naturally followed that either the Biblical conception was borrowed from the Babylonian; or the Babylonian was borrowed from the Biblical; or both were founded on a common primitive source.

Scholars generally have dismissed the second supposition as an impossibility; and the third is excluded on the ground that the stories contain a large percentage of Babylonian ideas. The Biblical conception of creation, therefore, they say, is of Babylonian origin.

George Smith, who found and translated for the first time many of the fragments of the Babylonian story, took the position that it originated in Babylonia. This was also the view of Professor Sayce, another of the pioneers in this field of research, who later wrote concerning the subject: "The elements indeed of the Hebrew cosmology are all Babylonian; even the creative word itself was a Babylonian conception, as the story of Merodach has shown us."[1]

[1] *Religions of Babylonia and Assyria* p. 395.

In the nearly fifty years which have passed since the first translation was made, this has become the prevailing view; and it has been generally accepted everywhere as fully established. "In fact," as the late Canon Driver has written, "no archæologist questions that the Biblical cosmogony, however altered in form and stripped of its original polytheism, is, in its main outlines, derived from Babylonia."[2]

Before considering the arguments for and against this theory, let us briefly review the sources of our knowledge of the Biblical and Babylonian cosmological ideas.

One of the results of the literary analysis of the Old Testament is that scholars generally accept the view that there are two creation stories in Genesis, the second of which begins in the middle of the fourth verse of the second chapter. As is well known, there are other passages in the poetical books of the Old Testament which give us additional light upon Israel's conception of the creation, especially those which refer to a struggle between Yahweh and a being who is regarded as having personified the primaeval ocean. Several different names of this monster are found, as Tehom, Rahab, Leviathan, Dragon (*tannin*) and Serpent (*nakhash*). The first mentioned is the same word which is found in the second verse of Genesis and elsewhere in the Old Testament, where it is translated "deep."

In some of these poetical passages a leading thought can clearly be traced: namely, that Yahweh had a great conflict with this being, after whose defeat the heavens and the earth were created. In this conflict we learn that the hostile creature had helpers, who were also overcome. In some passages, however, the monster represented a nation which was unfriendly to Israel.

The more important of all these passages which have been previously assembled by Gunkel[3] and others, follow:

[2] Driver, *The Book of Genesis*, p. 30.
[3] See Gunkel, *Schöpfung und Chaos* 29 ff.

Psalm 89:9 ff.

    When the waves thereof arise, thou (Yahweh) stillest them.
    Thou hast broken Rahab in pieces as one that is slain;
    Thou hast scattered thine enemies with the arm of thy strength.
    The heavens are thine, the earth is also thine:
    The world and the fulness thereof, thou hast founded them.
    The north and the south, thou hast created them.

Isaiah 51:9 f.

    Put on strength, O arm of Yahweh;
    Arise as in the days of old, the generation of ancient times.
    Art thou not he who cut Rahab in pieces, pierced the Dragon?
    Art thou not he who dried up the sea, the waters of the great Tehom,
    Who made the depths of the sea a way to pass over?

Job 26:12 f.

    He stirreth up the sea with his power,
    And by his understanding he smiteth through Rahab.
    By his spirit the heavens are garnished;
    His hand hath pierced the swift Serpent.

Psalm 74:13 f.

    Thou didst divide the sea by thy strength:
    Thou breakest the heads of the Dragon in the waters,
    Thou breakest the heads of Leviathan in pieces,
    Thou gavest him to be food to the people inhabiting the wilderness,
    Thou didst cleave fountain and flood;
    Thou driest up mighty rivers.
    The day is thine, the night is also thine:
    Thou hast prepared the light and the sun.
    Thou hast set all the boundaries of the earth:
    Thou hast made summer and winter.

Isaiah 27:1

    In that day Yahweh with his hard and great and strong sword will punish Leviathan the swift serpent, and Leviathan the crooked serpent, and he will slay the Dragon that is in the sea.

Isaiah 30:7

    For Egypt helpeth in vain and to no purpose
    Therefore have I called her Rahab that sitteth still.

Psalm 87:4

    Rahab and Babylon I proclaim my votaries.

Besides these passages there are others which refer to Tehom, Rahab, etc.[4]   Primarily, the monster personifies the primaeval waters, but several passages show that it symbolically represents an unfriendly power.   Egypt especially figures in this capacity. This fact reminds us of the Phoenician legend of Sanchuniathon, in which we learn that the god "Kronos (El), visiting the country of the south, gave all Egypt to the god Taautus (Tiamat), that it might be his kingdom."[5]

These, as well as other passages, show that in Israel the belief existed that there had been a great conflict prior to the creation of the heavens and the earth, between Yahweh and a primaeval monster, with whom were associated other beings termed dragons. Some seem to think that this conflict underlies the thought expressed in the second verse of Genesis, because of the use of the word *tehôm*. However, certain of these passages, as already mentioned, also show that this monster symbolically represented an unfriendly nation; the same, as we shall find, was the case also in Babylonian literature.

Throughout the Old Testament the word *tehôm* has the meaning "deep," as well as "the primaeval waters," and their personification.   It is generally held by Babylonists that such a crude conception as the strife between Yahweh and the monster, which idea was borrowed from Babylonia, was not tolerated in the creation story, as it jarred upon the purer theological conceptions and in consequence was suppressed.   The idea, however, of the firmament, to keep back the waters, was retained.

Eusebius has handed down some fragments of the Phoenician cosmogony by Sanchuniathon, which he found in the writings of Philo of Byblos.   In this Phoenician cosmogony, we are told that "as the first principle of the universe he posits murky, windy air,

[4] See Deut. 33:13; Job 9:11 ff; 38:16 f; Psalms 36:6; 41:19; 42:7; 77:16 f; 91:13; 97:7; Prov. 3:20; Isaiah 4:6; Ezekiel 29:3; Amos 7:4; etc.

[5] Cory, *Ancient Fragments* p. 16.

or a breath of murky air, and turbid chaos, dark as Erebus; these were infinite and throughout a long lapse of time limitless" (see Appendix C).

These stories from Amurru, including the Biblical cosmological expressions, it is generally held, make everything emanate from a watery chaos. It is this idea that the Babylonists have asserted was borrowed from Babylonia.

As is so well known, the Babylonians have handed down several creation stories written in Semitic and Sumerian; but only one has any relation to this conception as handed down by the Hebrews; that is, the one which they called *Enuma elish*, "When above", which are the first two words of the story.

One recension of this myth was written on seven tablets, and deposited in the library of Ashurbanipal. These, together with some fragments written in the Neo-Babylonian and Persian periods, have reached the British Museum in a fragmentary condition; and have been studied for years, and translated many times.

During the excavations of the German Oriental Society at the city of Ashur, some few years ago, portions of another recension, written several centuries earlier, were found. These tablets and fragments fortunately fill some important gaps in the narrative previously published. A complete translation of all the parts that have been recovered is given in Appendix A.

The composite character of the creation story, as handed down by the Babylonians, was recognized years ago. During the long process of editing, especially after it had been made a pæan in honor of Marduk, many modifications had taken place. It was also recognized years ago that two different conflicts were embodied in the narrative; and also that in it two or more versions were harmonized.

It is not necessary to discuss here these theories, nor the process that has resulted in the many changes and difficulties that are found in the story. Suffice it to say that there are two conflicts set forth in the epic; the one is found in the first seventy-seven lines, and is immediately followed by the second. The first resulted in the slaying of the primaeval Apsu by Ea; and the second, of his consort, Tiamat, by Marduk. An outline of the first conflict is as follows:

Before the heavens were named and the dry ground was gathered together, the primaeval creators Apsu and Tiamat begat the gods Lakhmu and Lakhamu, who in turn begat Anshar and Kishar; and these brought forth Anu, who begat Ea. The gods annoyed the primaeval Apsu and Tiamat by their deeds. With Mummu, his messenger, Apsu went to Tiamat with a plan to destroy them; but Tiamat was opposed to this.

The all-wise Ea, perceiving the plan of Apsu, cunningly applied an incantation, which resulted in Apsu being overcome by sleep; when Ea bound and slew him. Mummu, who then became violent, was also killed.

Ea then established upon Apsu his dwelling. In his chamber he rested peacefully. He named it *apsû;* and he founded shrines. Around its place he established his dry ground (*giparru*).

The story of the second conflict, beginning with the seventy-eighth line, has been edited to glorify Marduk, the god of Babylon; and also in the interests of the god Ashur. The story of the fight is greatly drawn out by repetitions. An outline of it follows:

Lakhmu and Lakhamu, in the abode of the fates, in the midst of the *apsû*, begat Anshar and Kishar. The primaeval deities sought vengeance because Apsu, their begetter, had been slain. They banded together at the side of the fuming and raging Tiamat, and prepared for battle. We then learn that Tiamat, under the title Ummu-khubur, "mother of the assembly," "who formed all things," bore monster serpents, sharp of tooth, and merciless of attack. She filled their bodies with venom instead of blood. She created vipers, dragons, raging hounds, hurricanes, tempests, etc., to assist her. She took Kingu for her spouse, and exalted him by giving him the tablets of destiny, and the power of deity (*anûtu*).

The all-wise Ea, also perceiving this plot, went and informed Anshar, his father. He said: "Tiamat, who begat us, hates us"; "and all the gods have turned to her." Anshar sent Anu to stand before Tiamat, that her spirit might be appeased, and her heart be merciful; but Anu could not withstand her awful visage and her mutterings. Whereupon, Marduk rejoiced his father by asking to be allowed to accomplish all that was within his heart, when he said: "If I, your avenger, enchain Tiamat, and give you life, proclaim an assembly, and exalt my destiny."

Anshar requested Gaga, his messenger, to repeat everything before the gods, his fathers, and to make ready a banquet for them, that they might decree the fate of Marduk. When Lakhmu and Lakhamu heard what was going on, they cried aloud; and the Igigi wailed bitterly.

The gods assembled; they ate and drank; they prepared for Marduk a lordly chamber; they proclaimed him chief among the great gods. They said: "Thy word is Anu," "we give thee sovereignty over the whole world." They set a garment in their midst; Marduk was told to give the command, and it vanished; then to give another, when it returned. They bestowed sceptre, throne, and ring upon him.

Marduk chose his weapons; he set the lightning in front of him; with a burning flame he filled his body; he stationed the four winds behind him; he created an evil wind, the tempest and hurricanes; he raised the thunderbolts; he mounted his chariot, yoked with four horses, and advanced toward the raging Tiamat; to whom, while she uttered rebellious words, he gave the challenge for the combat. She was like one possessed; she lost her reason, and uttered wild piercing cries; she pronounced her spell.

Marduk spread out his net and caught her; he let loose the evil wind in her face. As she opened her mouth, he drove it in, and it filled her body, which with his spear he burst. When Tiamat was slain, her host of helpers scattered to save their lives; but Marduk took them captive with his net, and broke their weapons.

He took "the tablets of destiny" from Kingu, and slew him. He then stood upon Tiamat's hinder parts, and with his merciless club, smashed her skull. He split her open like a flat fish into two halves; with one half of her he established a covering for heaven. He fixed a bolt; he stationed a watchman; he bade them not to let her waters come forth; and he placed the dwelling of Ea over against the *apsû*. This, in brief, is the story of the fight between Marduk and Tiamat.

In meeting all the arguments that have been presented by Babylonists, as well as all that can be offered in order to substantiate the idea that the cosmology, as found in the Old Testament, and in the *Enuma elish*, originated in Babylonia, and in presenting my own proof that it emanated from Amurru, I will follow the four arguments outlined in Chapter II.

The first of these has been fully presented, namely, that since migrations from Babylonia to Amurru are not known to have taken place, religious influences from Babylonia should not have been felt in that land; and since migrations in all periods from Amurru into the adjoining alluvial plain are known to have taken place, religious influences from Amurru should have been felt in the land; and, moreover, that these postulates have been fully borne out by excavations and research. It follows, therefore, that the religious literature, which Amurru and Babylonia had in common, if it had its origin in either country, was certainly carried by the migrating Semites into Babylonia from Amurru.

As the second step in the consideration of this problem let us now proceed to present the proofs that have been advanced for the

Babylonian origin of the myth. In searching the literature on the subject, I find that there have practically been offered but two arguments, one bearing on climate, and the other on numbers, which are fully considered in what follows.

The second of the two arguments that have been offered, which I think will be found to be rather negligible, is based on the division of the creation days into seven, i. e., six of creation and the sabbath, which is the same as the number of tablets on which the *Enuma elish*, or the Babylonian story, was written, namely seven. This argument has been repeated many times, though not by all Babylonists; and has been quite recently emphasized by Professor Barton, who says: "Each account is arranged in a series of sevens, the Babylonian in seven tablets, the Hebrew in seven days. Each of them places the creation of man in the sixth division of its series. . . . The creation of the firmament he [the J. writer] transposes from the fourth tablet to the second day; the intrigues of the gods of tablet three are replaced by the appearance of the dry land and the growth of grass, and the creation of the heavenly bodies is taken from the fifth tablet and placed on the fourth day."[6]

It should be stated here that the Babylonian story makes no reference to the creation of vegetation, birds, and fishes; nor does it refer to beasts and reptiles, except those created to help Tiamat in her conflict.

There can be little doubt that prior to the time when the Marduk schoolmen used the epic to glorify their deity, when the vain repetitions were doubtless introduced, and the stolen titles of other gods were added to those of Marduk, the epic had been written on fewer tablets; yet we are asked to believe that the division of the Hebrew story of creation into six days and the sabbath, originated in the number of tablets it required to hold this epic, because we find in

[6] See Barton, *Jour. Bib. Lit.* XL (1921) 93 f.

each instance the number "seven," and the fact that the creation of man in both instances is connected with the number "six." I do not think it necessary to multiply words as regards this argument for the Babylonian origin of the Biblical story of creation; let us tabulate, however, the acts of creation for the six days in the Hebrew story, and what the seven tablets contain.

BIBLICAL STORY	THE SEVEN TABLETS
Day 1: Heavens, earth, and light created.	1: Ea-Apsu conflict; *apsû* established. Marduk-Tiamat fight.
Day 2: Firmament created.	2: The fight continued.
Day 3: Gathering of waters: ground and vegetation seen.	3: The fight continued.
Day 4: Sun, moon, and stars created.	4: The fight continued; firmament established.
Day 5: Birds and fishes created.	5: Appointment of the stations of the gods, stars, luminaries, divisions of year.
Day 6: Beasts, reptiles, and man created.	6: Creation of man. Titles of Marduk.
Day 7: The Sabbath.	7: Titles of Marduk.

Now let us face the one all-important argument that has been offered for the Babylonian origin of the Hebrew story. It is regarded as a nature-myth which had its origin in the heavy rains and the annual inundations. The myth, in other words, symbolizes, we are told, "the change of seasons from winter to spring."

Professor Zimmern of Leipzig, in following Professor Jensen, presented the argument thus: the Babylonian "would say to himself, 'The world must first have come into being just as it still comes into being year by year and day by day. Just as in every spring Marduk, god of the spring sun, calls forth the level land that has been flooded by the winter rains, the deep, or Tiamat, so in the first spring, at the first New Year, the world came into being after a combat between Marduk and Tiamat.' "[7]

The late Professor Driver of Oxford, following Professors Jastrow and Zimmern, summed up the argument thus: "During the long winter, the Babylonian plain, flooded by the heavy rains, looked like a sea (Bab. *tiamtu, tiâmat*). Then comes the spring, when the clouds and water vanish, and dry land and vegetation appear. So, thought the Babylonian, must it have been in the first spring, at the first New Year, when, after a fight between Marduk and Tiamat, the organized world came into being."[8]

This is the one important argument on which the Babylonists have based their theory that the Hebrew story of creation was borrowed from Babylonia. You will find it reproduced again and again; it is deeply rooted everywhere. It is, however, entirely fallacious; it is due to a complete misunderstanding of the climatic conditions in Babylonia.

In the first place, the rivers do not flood in the winter—in fact, from October to January inclusive, the water in the river is at its lowest level. Following the melting of the snow in the mountains of Armenia, the rivers flood in March, April, May, and June,[9] in other words, in the spring months after the winter is passed and gone. They are at the highest in April and May. This completely disproves one part of the argument. A similar fate awaits the other part.

Babylonia could well nigh be classed with desert lands. Some farmers, depending upon the rain, do sow in the winter months, and get results, providing the rains materialize; but frequently it happens that they do not. In the winter of 1919–20, the writer found that the rains in Babylonia had not been sufficient to bring

---

[7] Zimmern, *The Babylonian and the Hebrew Genesis* p. 25.

[8] Driver, *The Book of Genesis* p. 28. Cf. also King, *Schweich Lectures* p. 128.

[9] See Willcocks, *The Irrigation of Mesopotamia* p. 5.

out the ordinary verdure, leaving the land even in spring looking like a desert. The crops of the winter season, consisting principally of wheat, barley, beans, and roots, need irrigation from November to May.[10] Without the aid of the rivers and the irrigation ditches, the country would be a complete waste; and it would be no place for man to live. If the rains are scanty on the whole, the native is pleased, because of the damage which heavy rains do to his mud house, or because they beat through the flimsy reed-hut in which he lives. The rivers, in short, furnish the land with its "life blood."

Sir William Willcocks gives us observations on the climate for seven years, taken at Baghdad by the Meteorological Department of India, in which the average rainfall for the year is given as 4.98 inches. In one of the seven years an exceptionally heavy fall of 10.23 is recorded; the lowest being 2.78 inches.[11] The latter amount is about the average given by the German scientists, who have also kept records of the rainfall.

Koldewey, who excavated at Babylon for about sixteen years, informs us that rain is very scanty in Babylonia. He writes: "I believe if all the hours in the whole year in which there were more than a few drops of rain were reckoned up, they would barely amount to seven or eight days. The annual downfall has been registered by Buddensieg at seven centimetres (= 2.80 inches)."[12]

The fall of 2.78 inches of 1909 at Baghdad, which is about the average fall of rain given by the German scientist at Babylon, distributed by months was as follows: October .25 (in two rains); November .25 (four); December .77 (four); January .06 (two); February .70 (five); March .28 (two); April .33 (three); May .14 (two); making in all 2.78 inches.[13] We would compare this fall of

[10] Willcocks, *Ibidem* p. 7.
[11] *Ibidem* 74 ff.
[12] Koldewey, *The Excavations at Babylon* p. 74.
[13] See Willcocks, *Ibidem* 77 ff.

rain with our light summer showers.   Banks, who also excavated in
Babylonia, writes: "The rains are not continuous as in other parts
of the Orient, for they come with no greater frequency than during
a New England summer, and it is then that Babylonia possesses
one of the most delightful of climates."[14]

It is only necessary to contrast this situation with the statements
that scholars have been making for years, in order to ascertain how
baseless they are.   But we need not simply register negative results
in connection with the climate.

Let us now inquire what the meteorological reports of the rainfall in Syria and Palestine inform us.   At Jerusalem, where records
have been kept for over fifty years, the average is 26.16 inches
(13.39 to 41.62); at Haifa the average is 27.75; at Beirut 35.87;
and in the Lebanon mountains, about 50 inches.[15]   Most of the
rain in Syria falls in the three winter months, December, January,
and February.   An average rainfall of 35.87, or 50 inches, naturally
means that in some years there is a much greater fall.   What such
torrential downpours, which occur in the three cold winter months,
mean to the people, and what happens often to the towns situated
in the fertile plains and valleys, it is not difficult to imagine.

We have therefore seen that the flooding of the rivers in Babylonia occurs not in winter; that the average fall of rain is exceedingly small; and that in contrast with this situation, the average
fall of rain for Syria is about ten times as great.   It should necessarily follow, therefore, that if, as scholars say, this is a nature-
myth which symbolizes the change of seasons from winter to spring,
reflecting the climate of the land, and if it had its origin either in
Amurru or Babylonia, it was certainly indigenous in the former.

We have not yet discussed all that this argument of the
Babylonists implies.   This will be covered fully under the

[14] Banks, *Bismaya* p. 352.
[15] See the *International Bible Encyclopaedia* p. 2526.

third head, in the discussion of the names that are contained in the stories.

Under the third division of the discussion as outlined in the second chapter, we now come to an examination of the names of deities with reference to the source whence they came, beginning with the primaeval gods Apsu, Tiamat, and Mummu.

When George Smith first interpreted the creation fragments, he translated Apsu "the abyss," and Mummu-Tiamat "the chaos (or water)," and Tiamat "the sea."[16] For a long time, scholars followed Smith in translating Apsu and Tiamat in this way. The only recent translations, however, that preserve Smith's idea, are those of Dhorme, who translated Apsu "de l'océan" (1907);[17] and Barton, who translated Apsu "Abyss," and Tiamat "Sea" (1922).[18] All other recent translators consider Apsu and Tiamat as proper names, e. g., Jensen (1900),[19] King (1902, 1916),[20] Rogers (1912),[21] Jastrow (1914),[22] Ebeling (1921),[23] Ungnad (1921),[24] Budge (1921),[25] and Luckenbill (1921).[26]

In Babylonian *apsû* means "ocean, deep." Some Assyriologists think, since the ideogram *ZU-AB* is used for this word, that the root of it is the Semitic *zâbu*, "to flow." Others hold that *apsû* is Babylonian; and still others, Sumerian; but all seem to agree, as far as I can see, that it is the origin of the Hebrew *'epes*. In other words, in spite of the fact that there is a clear etymology for the

[16] *Chaldean Account of Genesis* p. 65.
[17] *Choix de Textes Religieux Assyro-Babyloniens* p. 3.
[18] *Archaeology and the Bible* p. 235.
[19] *Keilinschriftliche Bibliothek* p. 2.
[20] *Seven Tablets of Creation* p. 2; and *Schweich Lectures* (1916) p. 122.
[21] *Cuneiform Parallels* p. 3.
[22] *Hebrew and Babylonian Traditions* p. 69.
[23] *Das Babylonische Weltschöpfungslied* p. 14.
[24] *Die Religion der Babylonier und Assyrier* p. 27.
[25] *The Babylonian Legends of Creation* p. 32.
[26] *Amer. Jour. Sem. Lang.* XXXVIII, p. 15.

word in Hebrew, while there is none in Babylonian, it nevertheless is said to have originated in the latter language. While both *apsû* and *tiâmat* are translated "ocean," the former is regarded as referring to "sweet water," and the latter to "salt water." The basis for this remarkable distinction is the connection of Apsu with Ea, "the god of the springs," who really slew him, and Tiamat with the "ocean."

In the Old Testament, the meaning "ocean, deep, abyss" for *'epes* is wholly unknown. It means "the end, nought," etc. It refers to the extreme limit of the earth. It is from the root *'ps* "to come to an end, to cease." Not only the verb is in use in Hebrew, but a derivative, *'ôpes*. The poetical and cosmological idea expressed by *'epes*, occurring in the plural *'ap°sê*, in the phrase "ends of the earth," is found fourteen times in the Old Testament. Let the following passage from Proverbs (30:4) suffice to illustrate its use:

> Who has ascended up into heaven, and descended?
> Who has gathered the wind in his fists?
> Who has bound the waters in his garment?
> Who has raised up all the ends (*'ap°sê*) of the earth?

And let us here inquire as to the meaning of *apsû* in the *Enuma elish*. Besides the personal name, this passage (lines 69 ff) occurs:

> He bound him, namely Apsu, and slew him.
> He established upon *apsû* his dwelling.
> ....
> In his chamber he rested peacefully.
> He named it *apsû*, he founded shrines.
> Around its place (*ashru*) he established his dry ground (*giparru*).

There is here no intimation that *apsû* has anything to do with water. The proper understanding of this passage implies that out of Apsu, Ea made *apsû*, the place upon which he built his dwelling, referring to the temple at Eridu; where he also established shrines;

and around which "place" he created earth. The word *ashru* "place," could scarcely be used in connection with the "ocean." Does this, therefore, sound like "a watery chaos," or the "water beneath the earth"?

This passage appears to me to reflect the movement of the Semites in going to "the end" of land, where Ea's temple was built. The cosmological idea expressed by *apsû* in this story, is identical with that of the Hebrews *'epes*, for to them it was the extreme part of the earth, the land's end, which Apsu personified. That is, to the Semite at Eridu *apsû* was the "dry land" that was created; at the point where, at that time, the land ended and the great waters began.

In this connection, let us look at some other occurrences of *apsû* in the cuneiform literature. The Bilingual Babylonian Story of Creation, or the beginnings of Eridu, which was first translated by Dr. Pinches,[27] in referring to the time before vegetation had been created, and buildings were erected in the alluvial plain (see Appendix B), reads as follows from the sixth line, telling of the time when:

Nippur was not made, Ekur was not built;
Erech was not made; E-anna was not built;
The *apsû* was not made, Eridu was not built;
The holy house, the house of the gods, his habitation was not made.
All lands were sea.
When what was in the sea was pressed out.
At that time Eridu was made, Esagil was built;
The temple...... where in the *apsû*, Lugal-du-azag had dwelt.
Babylon was built; Esagil was finished.

In the last three lines, we can see the work of the priests of Babylon who rewrote the poem to glorify their god Marduk.

Certainly the temple of Eridu and its shrines were not built in the ocean. To translate *apsû* "deep" in the eighth line, as well as

---

[27] *Jour. Royal Asiatic Society* XXIII 393 ff.

in the thirteenth line, as has been done by Assyriologists, I think,
is a mistake. It unquestionably refers to the land on which Eridu
has been built, namely the land's end.

Professor Jastrow in translating *apsû* "deep," as is usually done,
recognized that the line was in contradiction to line ten, "All lands
were sea." He, therefore, proposed that lines nine to eleven belong
to a Nippur version, in contradistinction to the Eridu version.[28]
But by translating *apsû* as *'epes*, this proposal becomes unnecessary.

In a ritual text concerning the restoration of the temple, which
Weissbach published,[29] we find this passage:

> Ea (*Nu-dim-mud*) created *apsû*, his dwelling place.
> Ea pinched off clay from the *apsû*.
> He created Kulla (the brick god) for the restoration [of temples]."

It would seem somewhat difficult to pinch clay for the making of
bricks, off "the ocean," as *apsû* is usually translated in this passage.

In the Gilgamesh story of the flood, Ea advised the hero, as
regards the construction of the ship to cover it with a roof. He
says: "Upon the *apsû* protect it with a *shâshu*" (line 31). The hero
later says: "I laid its hull; I enclosed it with a *shâshu*" (line 60).

I have endeavored to show elsewhere that *shâshu*, the course of
the sun-god in the heavens, is the Babylonian word for "firmament," corresponding to the Hebrew *râqî'a'*, the vault above the
earth; and that it is here used figuratively for the roof or covering
of the ship.[30] With this understanding that *shâshu* is the covering
which rested upon its sides, *i. e.*, the *apsû* or "ends of the ship,"
we have an illustration of the firmament resting upon the *'ap̂sê*
or "ends of the earth." In the *Enuma elish* the *shâshu* is represented by the halved Tiamat, the ends of which also rested on the

---

[28] *Jour. Amer. Or. Soc.* XXXVI p. 283.
[29] *Babylonische Miscellen* XII:25–27.
[30] See *A Hebrew Deluge Story* 73 f.

apsû. This also is the Hebrew conception, as shown by the passage: "The pillars of heaven tremble," Job 26:11.[31]

I have never seen this conception of the earth's construction presented; namely, that the firmament rested upon the "ends of the earth"; nor, as far as I can ascertain, has it been appreciated that the first act of creation in the *Enuma elish* was the founding of the *apsû*.

If *apsû* in Babylonian, as I maintain, originally meant the ends of the earth, and is an Amorite word, how can we explain that in Babylonian it came to have the meaning "ocean, deep"?

When the Amorites descended from the higher lands into the alluvium they went to the land's "end," and there established a city, which we know as Eridu. This to them was a veritable *'epes.* Here, on land only a few feet above the sea, like the present Basra, they established their permanent home. Situated in the extreme delta, through which at that time doubtless many streams in flood season flowed, whereby the water could easily escape, probably on what appeared as a shoal in flood season, they could live with much less labor than farther north where the rivers had to be harnessed. This very probably explains why Eridu was "the first city" built in the plain. It seems to me that this is reflected in the Bilingual Babylonian Creation Story, where we read that "the lord Marduk filled in an embankment at the edge of the sea" (Appendix B:30).

It is not difficult to understand how their deity, Ea, who in their native land had been "god of the earth" (*i. e.*, En-Ki), and also of its springs and fountains which had made the rivers, became at Eridu, where "fountains of the deep" were unknown, the god of the rivers and the ocean. My colleague Professor Hopkins calls my attention to the fact that in Aryan mythology there are several examples of agricultural deities or gods of springs becoming gods of the ocean. Poseidon, though in Homer a god of the sea, has

[31] My colleague, Professor Torrey, has called my attention to this passage.

clear traces of an earlier more general character of a god of nourishing water.   In the Peloponnesus, he was specially honored as god of fertility, not only of crops but also of flocks; the rearing of horses was his peculiar care.[32]

Parallel to this is the growth of Neptune, who about 400 B. C. became identified with Poseidon, when he also became wholly an ocean-god.   In other words, Neptune, like Poseidon, was first a god of springs and fertilizing waters before becoming a sea-god.[33]

Professor Hopkins also calls my attention to the fact that in India, Varuna is god of rain and of sky-water first, before he becomes the ocean-god; later when the people reached the sea, they called their general water-god the god of the ocean; that is, he was always god of water of all kinds; and "ocean" was simply included in his province.   Furthermore, he became "god of the West" on account of the location of the sea (Arabian ocean), as well as "god of the ocean."[34]

There is a passage in the Bilingual Babylonian Story of Creation, quoted above (see also Appendix B), which has never been understood, and which, it seems to me, throws important light on the subject.   After referring to the time before vegetation has appeared, and temples and cities had been built, the phrase "all lands were sea," is followed by the passage in question:

I-nu sha ki-rib tam-tim ra-ṭu-um-ma.

This is immediately followed by the words: "At that time Eridu was built."   The passage, therefore, should refer to what happened between the time when all was sea, and the building of Eridu, and is therefore the crucial one of this story of creation.

Following are some of the translations of the passage.   The words that are italicized represent the word *raṭûma.*

[32] See Fairbanks, *Greek Religion* p. 154.
[33] See Georg Wissowa, *Religion und Kultus der Römer* p. 250.
[34] See Hopkins, *Religions of India* p. 67.

When within the sea there was a *stream*. (Pinches.)[35]
When within the sea the *current* was. (Sayce.)
Da die Mitte des Meers ein *Wasserbecken* war. (Jensen.)
At that time there was a *movement* in the sea. (King.)
Das Feste der Insel war *Wasserfluss*. (Jeremias.)
When the middle of the sea was a *water-basin*. (Rogers.)
At a time when there was a *ditch*(?) in the midst of the sea. (Jastrow.)
At the time that the mid-most sea was [shaped like] a *trough*. (Budge.)
Als die Mitte des Meeres ein *Rinnsal* war. (Ungnad.)

There is a foreign word *râṭu*, found in a text of the late Sargon, and in some explanatory lists,[36] which seems to have been properly identified with the Hebrew *rahaṭ* "trough, basin"; and this is the basis for the translations given above. But it must be quite apparent that a trough, or a current, a basin, a ditch, or a stream, in the midst of the sea, scarcely makes sense, and does not account for the dry ground upon which Eridu was built. There is, however, a Hebrew word which I think may throw light upon the difficulty. In Job (16:11), there are parallel phrases reading thus:

God delivered me to the ungodly
And cast me out (*yirṭēnî*) upon the hands of the wicked.

Practically all commentators have uggested that *yirṭēnî* has been incorrectly handed down, and that it should be *yîr°ṭēnî*, from a root *yaraṭ*, found in a single passage in Numbers (22:32),[37] which also does not seem to be understood. But there does not seem to be any need for this emendation. The root *raṭah*, in late Hebrew meaning "to wring out, press out," seems to be that of the word in the above passage, which is usually translated, "cast out"; and this is also the root of *raṭûma* in the Babylonian story, and not *rahaṭ*. The passage can then be translated: "Then what was in

[35] The publications, in which the translations are found, are given in a foot-note to Appendix B.
[36] See Muss-Arnolt, *Ass. Dic.* p. 961.
[37] See Gesenius-Buhl p. 319; and the recent commentaries on *The Book of Job*, by Driver and Gray, Ball, etc.

the midst of the sea was pressed out (wrung out, cast out)," namely
the "dry land," which was the *'epes*. With this meaning the passage describes the appearance of ground at Eridu, for we know
that the Persian Gulf recedes each year. This is also the Hebrew
conception of the formation of "the dry land," as we learn from
Genesis, and also from the cosmological passage referred to (in
Job 30:4), where the *'epes* was "raised up" from the sea. While
the word *hēqîm* can be translated "established," as is usually done
in the passage, every Hebrew scholar knows that it literally means
"raised up"; and this expresses the cosmological idea that is found
in the Babylonian story.

If my interpretation of *raṭû* is correct, it would seem to be a
word used by the Amorites who lived at Eridu. Moreover, it will
be interesting to have the Sumerist, who holds that this bilingual
story was originally Sumerian, explain why the Sumerian scribe
used the word *rad* (there being no *ṭ* in Sumerian) for *raṭû*; and it
will also be interesting to have him explain why the Sumerians used
the sign *RAD* for the Semitic *rāṭu* "basin," when his own word
for "basin" was *shita*. Perhaps later he will agree that the original
story was Semitic, and not Sumerian.

With this understanding of the passage in question, it becomes
clear how the word *'epes*, meaning "end," became identified with
the sea, which from year to year sent forth more *'epes;* and what is
here more important, how the sea, which contained the *'epes*, came
to be called *apsû*.[38]

---

[38] In understanding that these two words are related, we should attempt to
account for the final long vowel. There seem to be three possible explanations.
One is, that probably *apsû* means "belonging to the *'epes*," referring to the water
which surrounds it, and with which it was so closely identified. The second is,
that it is dual; certainly this is implied here as well as elsewhere. And the third is,
that it is plural, like the word in the common poetic phrase of the Old Testament,
meaning "ends of the earth." Exactly the reverse was advanced by Hommel,
as quoted by Zimmern *KAT*[3] p. 492 note 1.

We have seen above that *apsû* in the *Enuma elish* does not mean "the deep," nor is it connected with that idea. It, therefore, cannot be used to show that in the Babylonian story "the watery chaos" was the first creator. Moreover, taking everything into consideration, it must be apparent that *apsû* in this poem originally personified the end of the earth, around which the "dry ground" was formed; while Tiamat personified the "water."

We now come to Tiamat, the consort of Apsu, who was slain by the god Marduk, and out of whose corpse the firmament was created.

In Babylonian the word *tiâmat* means "sea, deep, abyss." It is found written in the following forms: *ti-a-am-tu, ti-am-tu, ti-amat, tam-tu, tam-du, ta-ma-tu, ti-à(wa)-am-tu,* and *ti-à(wa)-mâ(wa)-ti.*

In an examination of all the dictionaries and glossaries at hand, from the earliest period to the latest, as well as syllabaries and many texts, I could not find a single example of this very common word meaning "sea" that represents the *h* (as is usually done by what is called the "breathing") which all scholars admit it originally contained.[39]

The many variant forms of the word clearly indicate that it is foreign. This is especially shown by the last two examples given above in which *wa* is used instead of *à* and *mâ.*[40] Certainly this comparatively rare usage of the sign by the two scribes indicates that they appreciated that the word contained a weak consonant; but they did not know which. The scribe of the last example even represented the *h* in the word which followed. Yet the word *tiâmat,* for which there is no root in Babylonian, scholars have declared is the origin of the Hebrew *tehôm.*

---

[39] I have no doubt that such an example will turn up if scholars are right as regards the root of *tehôm.*

[40] The former occurs in a building inscription of Nabopolassar *OBI* 84, II:50; and the latter is found in the Creation Story II:81 (*CT* 13, 6:13).

In the Old Testament the very common word *t͏ᵉhôm*, which means the same as *tiâmat*, was also used for the "subterranean waters" and the primaeval waters before the creation. Tehom, who personified the deep, was a swift serpent and a monster of the waters. We not only have the root of the word in general usage in Hebrew, but we have several allied roots, as well as derivatives. We have *hûm, hamam* and *hamah*. These roots being so closely related, scholars are not agreed from which one Tehom is derived. This word is generally regarded as having been borrowed from the Babylonian *tiâmat*; or, as a follower of the Babylonists, in writing on the second verse of Genesis, puts it: "Unquestionably, too, the word [*t͏ᵉhôm*] is derived from the Babylonian *Tiâmat*. And its early use in Hebrew attests early Israelite acquaintance with the Babylonian *Enuma elish* epic, or at least with the Babylonian creation myth in some form or other."[41]

Without taking into consideration the discussion which follows, it has appeared for years almost incredible that Assyriologists could make themselves believe that this corrupted word, which from the earliest times had lost the consonant *h*, and for which there is no etymology in Babylonian, could be the origin of the Hebrew *t͏ᵉhôm* and the Arabic *tihāmat*. Let us now inquire what other light Babylonian literature and art throw on the subject before us.

There is an inscription called the Cuthean Legend in which an early Babylonian king recounts how he was delivered from hordes of "people who had the bodies of birds of the hollow, men who had the faces of ravens," whom Tiamat had suckled, and who "in the midst of the mountain became strong," etc. The king mustered great forces and eventually, after three years' fighting, triumphed over this foreign power which had humiliated his land. The tablet commemorating the deliverance was deposited as a memorial in

[41] Morgenstern, *Amer. Jour. Sem. Lang.* XXXVI p. 197.

the temple at Cutha. Tiamat, it would seem, was here, as in *Enuma elish*, the mother-goddess of that people. They lived in a mountain. It should be added that there is nothing in the legend that connects her or anything else with the sea.[42]

Besides this legend there are several references to Tiamat in fragments of tablets which are either not understood or throw little or no light upon the subject. In one, which is probably astrological, "*tiâmat* the upper," and "*tiâmat* the lower," refer to the upper and lower sea. In another, the "breadth of *ti[âmat]*," which, if correctly restored, has a significance that is not understood.

While references to Tiamat in the literature are exceedingly limited, there are two other legends known which refer to male monsters, who symbolize foreign powers. In the Library of Ashurbanipal, an inscription was preserved which records a fight between Tishpak, a god, and a huge serpent (*ṣîru*) of the river, who was called Labbu, which means "lion," probably "sea lion." This also did not occur prior to the creation, but after "the cities had sighed" because of some oppression. Unquestionably Labbu, who happens to be a male, not a female monster, symbolically represents some unfriendly sea-bordering nation.

A portion of another dragon myth was recently found at Ashur, and published by Ebeling.[43] Unfortunately the text is very fragmentary, but there is enough preserved of it to show that the huge monster had legs, and devoured fish, birds, and beasts, as well as "the black headed people." This is also a male monster of the deep, and is called *ṣîru* "serpent." He unquestionably also represents the national ensign of some foreign nation.

Let us here inquire how Tiamat is described in the *Enuma elish*. In her equipment for the fight, in addition to making weapons invincible, she bore monster serpents, vipers, dragons, hurricanes,

---

[42] See King, *Seven Tablets of Creation I* pp. 140 ff.
[43] *Orientalistische Literaturzeitung* (1916) 106 f.

hounds, fish-men, scorpion-men, tempests, etc. In the entire list
of eleven aids, only "fish-men" are referred to, if that is the correct
translation of the word, to show that she had anything to do with
water. Moreover, there is nothing in the entire poem to connect
Tiamat with the sea, except her name, which, as we have seen, is
the same as *tiâmat* "ocean"; or to show that she personified the
"watery chaos."[44] The comparison of this fact with the statements
of Babylonists is quite illuminating and interesting.

In Babylonian art, we have the following to consider in this
connection. The serpent was introduced in the art in an early
period. It was the symbol of an invader who ruled the country,
whose name has come down to us in a Sumerian form, Nin-Gish-
Zidda. Ushum-Gal "the great serpent" is frequently mentioned in
connection with Tammuz, his son; and was used symbolically thereafter in Babylonia. Since these were foreign rulers, it becomes clear
as to how this symbol was introduced in the land. It is not improbable that the country whence they came, was in the Lebanon
region, for Tammuz is said to have been born among the cedars.[45]
At present there is no way of connecting Tiamat with these emblems.
Of course, it is well known that the worship of the serpent or dragon
prevailed also in Elam, Egypt, Phoenicia, Hatti, Persia, India,
China, Greece, and other lands.

On a large slab found in the palace of Ashurnaṣirpal at Nimroud,
the fight between the storm-god and a winged monster is depicted.
This, however, is also a male monster. Sennacherib, in a building
inscription, tells of his having a great bronze door made on which

---

[44] Deimel has recently propounded a brand-new theory as follows: Tiamat
typifies Rim-Sin, king of Larsa, who reigned as far as the sea (*tiâmat*). Kingu is
Ki-en-gi, the name of Sumer, which in the epic is personified in derision. The
victory of Marduk over Tiamat and Kingu typifies the conquest of Hammurabi
over Larsa and Sumer. (See *Orientalia* 4, 44 f.)

[45] See *A Hebrew Deluge Story* p. 46. The fact that his name is written with two
Sumerian ideograms Dumu-zi is no proof that Tammuz was a Sumerian.

he had portrayed scenes depicting the fight with Tiamat, not by Marduk, but by his own deity, Ashur. There are also a number of seals with scenes of a fight between a deity and a dragon, as well as seals depicting fights with lions and other beasts. In many instances such objects reflect the religious ideas of the people, in distinction from the recognized theological ideas of organized society.

Let us here inquire whether any references in the cuneiform literature, besides the *Enuma elish*, can be cited to show that the Babylonians had such a doctrine as the emanation of all things from "a watery chaos," or "moisture," which it is claimed was borrowed from Babylonia.

In the Bilingual Babylonian Story of Creation, bearing especially on the building of the temple in Eridu, already mentioned, in which after referring to the time before reeds sprouted, trees grew, bricks had been made, or Nippur, Uruk, and *apsû* had been made, the writer says:

> All lands were sea.
> Then, what was in the midst of the sea was pressed out.
>
> Marduk bound reeds upon the face of the water;
> He created ground, and poured (it) with the reeds.

In this cosmological conception, as Professor Jastrow has correctly pointed out, "there is no assumption of a chaotic condition at the beginning of time with the watery element in control."[46] The myth assumes the earth to be in existence, but covered with water. There was, however, no life in it. Professor King also called attention to the fact that in this myth "it is important to note that the primaeval water is not personified."[47]

The conception that this naïve writer gives us of the creation is that the gods made the "dry land" appear in much the same way

---

[46] *Amer. Jour. Sem. Lang.* XXXVI 244 ff.
[47] *Schweich Lectures* 1916 p. 124.

as many of the early cultivators of the land did in order to create fields. This, as already stated above, is a local nature-myth which had its origin in Eridu, and reflects the time when Amorites moved into the uninhabited alluvium. This is the nearest approach to the Amorite cosmology that I know of in the Babylonian literature. In other stories of creation handed down in Sumerian, there is not a semblance of the idea that things emanated from water or a watery chaos. In view, therefore, of all the assertions made by Babylonists on the subject, and also Sumerists, this conclusion must be conceded as most surprising.

In the Old Testament, as we have seen, there are many references to the conflict between Yahweh and Rahab or Leviathan the dragon, who personified the deep, Tehom. There are so many references to this conflict and the primaeval state, and so many poetical allusions to the dragon, symbolizing the deep, chaos, destruction, and death, that one is led to feel that the conception belonged to the very bone and marrow of the religious and philosophic thought of the people. Even in the New Testament we learn that "the earth was compacted out of water by the word of God" (II Peter, 3:5).

We have also seen how in the Phoenician cosmogony all the seeds of creation sprang from the watery chaos; which thought is also paralleled in Homer, who tells us that Okeanos was the source of all things, including the gods. This thought, moreover, was also very widely diffused. The watery origin of created things was known to the Vedic Aryans;[48] even the North American Indians had this doctrine.

With all the light, therefore, that is now available from the cuneiform literature we learn on the one hand that, with the exception of the *Enuma elish*, but one legend mentions Tiamat, who in it is not a goddess of the deep, but the mother-goddess of a moun-

48 See Hopkins, *Religions of India* p. 48.

tainous land which had humiliated Babylonia; and on the other hand, the thought that all things emanated from water is wholly wanting in the literature of the Babylonians.

Where then, we ask, are the data to show that "the elements indeed of the Biblical cosmology are all Babylonian"? Where then is the proof that "attests early Israelite acquaintance with the Babylonian *Enuma elish*," even if we assume that this epic is Babylonian? Where is the basis for the assertion that the doctrine of the emanation of all things from water is based on it, or, in fact, on anything Babylonian? If a more ancient recension of this poem is found, it may contain this idea; for I believe the Amorites brought it into the country; but even then it would have to be admitted that the elimination of the idea in later times proves that the thought was not Babylonian. How will the advocates of the theory explain the omission of the very idea in the literature of the Babylonians that they say the Hebrews borrowed, and with which their own literature was so thoroughly permeated?

It seems to me there can be no other conclusion but that at some early time this idea migrated with the myth to Babylonia with Amorites, where it took on a local coloring at Eridu, and was modified at Babylon, and later at Ashur, during which process the Amorite idea, that all things emanated from water, was lost sight of.

We now come to the name and word Mummu. In the fourth line of the poem, the word is used as a prefix to Tiamat, but in the lines which follow, Mummu is the name of the minister of Apsu. Damascius, who obtained his data from the writings of Berossus, tells us that Mummu was an offspring of Apsu and Tiamat.

The explanation of this word has given rise to an extensive literature. Smith originally translated it "the chaos of water."[49] Zimmern translates it "Urgrund"; Delitzsch, "Noise, the tumult of the Urwasser"; Prince and Haupt, "unfathomable depths,"

[49] *Chaldean Account of Genesis* p. 65.

(from a reduplication of *mu*); Jensen, "Urform"; Dhorme, "tumultueuse"; Barton, "roaring";[50] Deimel, "gebärerin" (from a reduplication of *mu(d)*).[51]   Professor Jastrow held that Mummu, is the offspring of Apsu, the watery expanse, and Tiamat, through the commingling of their waters, and is a term signifying water.[52]

The word cannot be explained etymologically as coming from any root in use in Babylonian.   The meaning "noise, roaring," which unquestionably is correct, is based upon the well-known Hebrew root *hûm*.   Although there are a few occurrences of the Hebrew word in cuneiform, the root is not in use in Babylonian.

It is to be noted that in the story the word or name, aside from its occurrence as a prefix to Tiamat, is not used in any way as connected with water; in fact little light is thrown upon Mummu except that he concurred in the plot of Apsu; and then, because he became violent, after his master had been slain, Ea killed him.

In the Old Testament, *m'hûmah*, with which Smith correctly connected the word, means "tumult, confusion, disquietude," from the root *hûm* "to murmur, roar, discomfit."   This understanding of the word throws light upon its use as a title or prefix to the name Tiamat in the fourth line of the poem.   In view of the fact that Tiamat originally personified "the deep," the meaning "turbulent" would be most appropriate; although, as stated above, the thought implying this, as characteristic of the deity, had been practically eliminated from the myth as the Babylonians have handed it down.

In this connection let us briefly discuss another title of Tiamat, namely *Ummu khubur*, the one "who formed all things."   In line 4, as we have seen, another epithet of the goddess reads, "the bearer of all of them."

[50] See Muss-Arnolt, *Assyrian Dictionary* pp. 552 f.
[51] Deimel makes Mummu the original mother-goddess (see *Orientalia* 4, p. 44).
[52] *Hebrew and Babylonian Traditions* p. 73.

Professor Zimmern translated *khubur* "deep," and Père Dhorme, "totalité," the former being based on the idea that Tiamat was a goddess of the deep, and the latter on the idea that she was "the bearer of all of them"; but there is no root for either idea in Babylonian. All other scholars had left the word untranslated.

The word *khubur* also occurs in the so-called Ea and Atra-khasis Epic, where with the exception of the meaning "totalité," offered by one scholar, it has been left untranslated by all others. In a recent study of the legend, I found that the word was glossed by *pukhru* "assembly." In view of the fact that the context required such a meaning; that in Hebrew and Aramaic the root *khabar* means "to join, associate"; and because there are derivatives like *kheber* "company," *khābēr* "associate," etc., it followed that *khubur* was unquestionably an Amorite word, having the same meaning as the Babylonian *pukhru* "assembly." As in Greek mythology, the council or assembly of the gods is here referred to; the idea figures very prominently in these myths. This being the proper explanation of the word, and since Tiamat was the "bearer of all of them," and the one "who formed all things," I have proposed that the title *Ummu khubur* means "mother of the assembly," and that it was unquestionably Amorite.[53]

It is somewhat fortunate that the word had been left untranslated by all except in the instances referred to, for if it had been construed as belonging to the root mentioned, it doubtless would have been listed as a Babylonian word which the Aramaeans and Hebrews had borrowed from the Babylonians. If my explanation of this word is accepted, it naturally follows that it has an importance of a far-reaching character.

It is therefore not at all surprising to find that three attempts have already been made in reviews which have appeared to explain *khubur* otherwise, and thus avoid admitting that it is Amorite. In

[53] *A Hebrew Deluge Story in Cuneiform* p. 18.

opposition to my explanation Doctor Thompson of Oxford, translates the word "crowd, noise(?)," but offers no etymology.[54] For the meaning "noise(?)" there is none; and if "crowd" is correct, it can only be from the same Amorite root which I have proposed. I see, therefore, no reason whatever for accepting this guess. The second is that of Luckenbill, who, without a semblance of etymological support, translates *khuburi* "numbers." This need not detain us.[55]

Professor Sayce sees in the word *khubur* the name of "the river of death," which the dead had to cross, and which was located in the north.[56] "Mother of the river of death" hardly seems appropriate; but upon what is this meaning based?

Khubur, as is well known, is the name of an important tributary or "companion" river of the Euphrates in Mesopotamia. In two texts, Khuburru is the name of a country in north Mesopotamia, called also Subartu.[57] In a religious text, the words *urukh me-[te]* occurs in one line, and in the following is mentioned the river Khubur.[58] If the restoration is correct, the two words mean "road of death." These passages are brought together and the idea formulated that *khubur* is the name of the river of death which the dead had to cross, and which is located in the north.[59]

If the thought of a "river of death" figures in the Babylonian religion, it depends, as far as I know, upon the above obscure and reconstructed passage. I only desire to add that I can see no

---

[54] *The London Times Literary Supplement*, Oct. 12, 1922, p. 646.

[55] See *AJSL*, 39, 154. Line 4 of the ancient famine story he translates: "the god became disturbed by their (the people's) numbers (size)." Line 8: "because of their numbers, I(?) will proclaim a dispersion(?)." These translations sound as if Luckenbill confused the Biblical stories of the creation, deluge, and the tower of Babel.

[56] *Expository Times*, 1922, Nov. p. 76.

[57] See *Rawlinson WAI*, II, 50:51, and V, 16:19.

[58] Craig, *Religious Texts* I, p. 44.

[59] See Jensen, *Mythen und Epen* 307 ff.

reason for accepting this idea in connection with *khubur* in the texts under consideration, where a meaning like "assembly" fits the context perfectly; nor in the title "mother *khubur*" the epithet of the goddess in the myth, who is credited with being a parent of all the gods. In other words, I see no reason for setting aside my own explanation of the word, and for giving up my firm conviction that it is Amorite.

Before we proceed to consider the names of other deities found in this poem, let me ask for a decision on the question as to whether the words Apsu, Tiamat, Mummu, and *khubur* are Babylonian or Amorite. For these four words used as names and titles, as we have seen, on the one hand, there are no roots in Babylonian, nor are there derivatives from the roots, *i. e.*, it is not possible to explain them etymologically on the basis of known roots in that language. On the other hand, in Hebrew we have not only the corresponding words in use, but in every instance verbal forms from the roots to which they belong, as well as other derivatives. Under these circumstances, let me ask, how can anyone make himself believe that they are of Babylonian origin? It seems to me that it would be about as easy to believe that the word "Ocean" was originally English, from which language it was borrowed by the Greeks, when it became Okeanos.

Lakhmu and Lakhamu in the poem are the parents of the indescribable Anshar, whom they had endowed with an equality of deity, and also the ancestors of Anu and Ea. When Tiamat had planned revenge for the death of Apsu, Anshar sent his messenger to inform his parents and to invite them and all the gods to an assembly and feast. It is impossible to conclude otherwise than that these parents occupied a unique position in the poem, as it was originally handed down. What rôle did they play in the Babylonian pantheon?

In Babylonian literature, Lakhmu and Lakhamu are never mentioned as the ancestors of Anu or Ea; in fact they are unknown in the Babylonian pantheon. In the five large collections of names, we do not find a single instance in which these deities appear. This absence in the nomenclature of the country, where the poem is supposed to be indigenous, is most significant.

In Assyria, the pair is mentioned in several different versions of a list of gods. Naturally the appropriation of the poem to magnify Anshar, the deity of the land, would account for this; but these deities also played no rôle in the Assyrian pantheon; and they are not found in the nomenclature of the land. Moreover, the attempt to replace Lakhmu, the father of Anshar, with the name of Ea, in lines 78 and 89 of Tablet I, confirms the idea that the deity is foreign.

Among the monsters in the poem, created by Tiamat to assist her in her fight, is the goddess Lakhamu (I:134). In a building inscription of an early king of Babylonia, Agum-kakrime, who ruled in the seventeenth century B. C., in describing his adorning the shrines at Babylon, tells us that he had his workmen carve figures of the monsters, over whom Marduk triumphed; among which, as in the myth, he included Lakhamu. Will the Baby-lonists, who hold that this poem originated in Babylonia, explain these facts, including, of course, the fact that this pair are the ancestors of Anu and Ea? Unquestionably, Lakhmu and Lakhamu were foreign deities.

The names of these deities, it would seem, were a part of the narrative as it reached Babylonia, but they doubtless belonged to the West. The identification of Lakhmu with Bêth-Lekhem (Beth-lehem), the name of two cities or shrines in Palestine, has frequently been suggested. It is at least the only plausible identification that has thus far been made.

It has been suggested that the names of the pair which Lakhmu and Lakhamu created, namely Anshar and Kishar, arose through an effort made by Assyrian scholars to include their god Ashur among those of the poem. Kishar is generally thought to be a pure abstraction of the late time. Moreover, both deities seem superfluous. Anshar, it seems to me, has usurped the place of El or Ilu.

In the edict of the gods, when Marduk was made preëminent, they said, "thy word is Anu (originally El)." When Ea exalted him, "he endowed him with an equality of El." These and other passages make it reasonable to suppose that the Marduk schoolmen, who rewrote the epic, belittled El, as they also did Ea, in their efforts to magnify their own deity. The Ashur priests apparently did the same thing by introducing Anshar, and using for him the description of El or Anu.

In reading the magniloquent description of Anshar "who was clothed with the majesty of ten gods" (see Appendix A, I, 83–102), one cannot help feeling that this originally belonged to the all-important god Ilu or El, whose name was later syncretized with, or written Anu. Confirmation of the conjecture is to be found in connection with the number of eyes he is said to have had (see 95 ff); for we learn in the cosmogony of Sanchuniathon, the god Taautus "contrived also for Kronus (or El) the ensign of his royal power, having four eyes, in the parts before and in the parts behind, two of them closing as in sleep." In the sixth tablet Anu, or El, appears as the all-supreme deity. It would seem that the Ashur priests had not completed their task of editing the text in the interests of their deity.

We now come to the fourth group of gods in the creation story, Anu (or El), Ea, and Marduk. It is said in the epic that Anu begat Ea. Although the text is incomplete at this point, we know from other sources that Ea begat Marduk. The chief deities of the early deluge story included Ilu, Ea and Adad; and it seems to me that the same was true of this story prior to its revision by the priests of Marduk. This is also the triad of the Name Syllabary, published by Chiera, which was written at Nippur in the third millennium B. C., but which obviously is of even greater antiquity.

El, we know from the nomenclature, was an Amorite deity of the earliest period. El and Hadad (Adad) were two of the important deities in Syria as late as the first millennium B. C. According to the Phoenician mythology of Sanchuniathon, El or Kronos, was the son of Ouranos "heaven," and Ge "earth," who were the children of Elioun "the most high." El, this mythology tells us, founded Byblos, the first city in Phoenicia, which he gave to the goddess Baaltis; Egypt, he gave to Taautus (Tiamat).

El or An was the foremost deity in early Babylonia. It is not impossible that the Sumerians originally had a deity An, meaning "heaven" or "high," but I doubt it. Like the Greeks who adopted and worshipped Semitic gods under a disguise that was very transparent, I believe that the Sumerians, after they had come into the country, also adopted the gods of the Semites. There are many reasons for this view.[60] The Sumerian An, meaning "high" or "heaven," En-Lil "lord of the storm," En-Ki "lord of the earth," Nin-Kharsag "lady of the mountain," Nin-Edinu "lady of the plain," Nin-Erinu "lady of the cedar," Nin-Mar[ki], "lady of the city Mari," etc.—these are not names; they are epithets. Names of deities, such as El, Ea, and Adad; Osiris, Isis, and Horus; Zeus, Apollo and Hera; or even Yahweh, as everyone knows, are not so easily explained.

I feel that I have satisfactorily shown elsewhere that the worship of Anu was brought by the Amorites into the land, very probably from 'Ana on the Euphrates.[61] It is possible that the Western Semites originally worshipped two gods, named El and 'Ana (or Khana), who in time became syncretized. But probably 'Ana was originally an epithet of El. The Babylonian form of the

---

[60] See also Meyer, *Sumerier und Semiten in Babylonien.*
[61] *The Empire of the Amorites* 116 ff; 168; and 178.

name, Anu, arose from the use of the Sumerian sign *AN* to represent the name of the deity. Certainly a more appropriate sign to represent the name of *'El 'elyōn* the "most high god" of the Semites, namely *AN*, meaning "high" and also "heaven," could not have been selected. That *AN* could have become Semitized into *Anu*, is perfectly clear when we know that the epithet of the storm-god, En-Lil "Lord of the storm," became Ellil. Moreover, An, or Anu, was regarded as the same as Ilu, or El.

At Erech, the name of the temple of this god, as in the case of all names of temples in Babylonia, was written in Sumerian, E-Anna. This name, I believe, originally meant not "house of heaven," but "house of El," *i. e.*, Bêth-El. At Babylon, El is found in the city's name, *Bâb-El*, "Gate of El." While in time, Marduk supplanted El, the original patron deity of the city, we find Hammurabi not only crediting "Ilu, king of the Anunnaki," with having committed the rule of mankind to Marduk, but together with Ellil, as having raised the towers of Babylon.[62] El is also found, as already mentioned, in the name of Der, which was written *Dûr-El*, "Fortress of El." It is obvious that El was also the foremost deity of this city; and yet it was known as "the city of Anu."[63] Certainly this fact seems to confirm the idea that Anu arose through the use of the ideogran *AN* for the name of El. It might be added that the name of the only known king of this city of the early period, is Anu-mutabil.

I believe if a version of the *Enuma elish* is found belonging to the early period, that, like the deluge story, the name of the chief deity will be written Ilu or El, instead of Anu. When the priests of Babylon rewrote the epic, throughout it they ascribed the prerogatives of El to their god Marduk. For example in exalting him, the gods are made to say, "thy word is Anu" (IV:4); but

[62] See *A Hebrew Deluge Story* p. 29.
[63] See *Keilinschriftliche Bibliothek* III 1, 165:4.

in a passage found in the sixth tablet (98), the original name is found, where the gods are made to say: "for us, whatever name we mention, he is our El."

I have already given my conception of the god Ea; how, when this "lord of the land" migrated to Eridu, on the sea, he became the god of the deep, where for millenniums his cult developed independently.

One of the ideograms which represented the name Ea was *En-Ki*, which means "lord of the earth." He was also "lord of springs," and designated as "the potter," "the great artificer," showing his identity with a mountainous land, where metals were found.

Another common ideogram, written *E-A*, meaning "house of water," was used to represent the name of the god Ea. The latter may be a graphic expedient, on the part of the Sumerian scribes, which probably approximately represented the pronunciation of the god's name (which is certainly very close to Jah), and at the same time described one of his characteristics, as god of the water, which he especially became at Eridu. Let me repeat here some of the reasons which I have given elsewhere for the statement that Ea is Amorite.

In the Name-Syllabary found at Nippur, copied in the third millennium B. C., but doubtless of much greater antiquity, Ea is found in a group which occurs a number of times, as follows: Ilu, Ea, and Adad(IM). This, as I believe, was the earliest Semitic triad in Babylonia before Enlil displaced Ea as second in order, and before Ilu was Babylonized, by the use of the sign *AN*, into Anu. It shows also that the explanatory list of gods, which begins with Ilu instead of Anu, and is followed by Ea, not Enlil, very probably also goes back to this early period.

In the same archive at Nippur, an Amorite Name-Syllabary was discovered, also belonging to the early period; and in it the following groups are found, consisting of: El, Ea, and Nebo; El,

Ea, and Ashirta; Dagan, Ea, and Ashirta; also [?], Ea, and Dagan. This Name-Syllabary, which contains only Amorite deities, is a most significant proof that Ea is Amorite.

A study of the nomenclature of the Manishtusu obelisk (about 2775 B. C.), reveals many Amorite names compounded with that of this deity. Especially interesting are such groups as Aku-ilum and Aku-Ea; Ikrub-Ilu and Ikrub-Ea; Iti-Ilu, Iti-Ea and Iti-Dagan, etc.[64]

The lack of excavations in Amurru is again felt, yet with the help of the Amarna letters we are not without some light on the subject from that quarter. In letters from Mitanni, we find Ea is syncretized with Sharru, as Ea-Sharru, in two lists of deities.[65] During the same period this deity was also worshipped in Babylonia, as shown by the personal names.[66] At Calah, Ashur-nâṣir-apal erected a statue to Ea-sharri. Still another reason for regarding Ea as an Amorite deity is to be found in the fact that the god appears in the same position in the triad of the early version of the deluge story, as in the Name-Syllabary, i. e., Ilu, Ea, and Adad.

It is held that Marduk usurped the position of Enlil. I do not think the original story mentioned Enlil. A glance at the closing line of the Fourth Tablet makes it very apparent that his name has been forcibly introduced into the poem at that point. In VI: 43 we have the triad Marduk, Enlil, and Ea.

A careful study of the story will not fail to reveal the fact that Marduk supplanted El. When the gods desired to honor him, as mentioned above, they commanded: "his word is Anu (originally El)." While in the Old Testament, Yahweh slew the dragon, there is little difficulty in understanding that El was the name used at an earlier time. A Greek myth seems to add force to this conclusion.

[64] See Scheil, *Délégation en Perse* II, 41 ff.
[65] See Knudtzon, *El-Amarna-Tafeln* 24:76, 101.
[66] Clay, *Personal Names of the Cassite Period* p. 148.

The story of the contest between Kronos (whose other name was El), and Ophioneus (which name means "dragon"), was handed down by Pherecydes, who, it was understood, did not derive it from Greece or Egypt, but, according to Philo, obtained it from the Phoenicians. Kronos was the leader of one host, and Ophioneus of the other. It reads: "He relates of challenges and combats between them, and that they make a treaty that whichever (side) of them shall fall into Ogenes (for Okeanos "ocean"), shall be conquered, and those, who shall thrust them off and conquer them, shall have heaven."[67] This is obviously another version of the conflict.

The name of the messenger Gaga, is also Amorite. We find that Sennacherib, in giving a list of twenty deities which he invoked at the close of a building inscription, mentions such Amorite gods as Khani, Gaga, Sherua, Nikkal, etc., doubtless in the interests of those who had taken part in the work. Gaga was never included in the pantheon of the Babylonians or Assyrians. The name appears in the Amorite Name-Syllabary; and it is probably found in the name Idin-Kakka, king of Khani (in Amurru). Moreover, I do not believe that scholars will question the Amorite origin of this deity.

In presenting the above facts and theories concerning El, Ea, and Marduk, while I am convinced of their validity, I realize that for some time they will doubtless be regarded as mooted, because the conclusions involved are so different from those commonly accepted. In view of this fact, and in order to avoid having the issue befogged by criticisms of such points, which are not necessarily pertinent, and especially since there is more than abundance of proof without them, I am quite willing that the facts and theories above presented as regards El, Ea, and Marduk, as well as concern-

[67] From Origen, *Contra Celsum* vi 42 (Diels, *Fragmente der Versokratiker* ii, p. 203).

ing Anshar and Kishar, be left out of consideration in this connection. This, however, does not apply to the primaevals, Apsu, Tiamat, and Mummu, nor to Lakmu, and Lakhamu, as well as to Gaga.

The importance of such onomastic studies has already been referred to. There can be little doubt but that we have here a crucial test of the whole thesis. The occurrence of these foreign deities as the chief actors in this poem, unquestionably shows that the poem is of foreign origin.

In discussing under the fourth division of arguments or reasons for the Amorite origin of this story what I regard as literary evidence, I fully appreciate, as already stated, that I am treading, at least in part, on ground that fresh discoveries may modify, but also against which some followers of Babylonism can present a display of philological knowledge, so that the non-Assyriologist may be impressed with its importance. In connection with the deluge story, evidence that is beyond cavil can be presented. In this instance, unfortunately, having only recensions of the poem that belonged to a comparatively late period, after it had been edited several times, we doubtless have little remaining of the original story. Nevertheless, a few words have been preserved for us, and in the very place we should naturally expect to find them, namely in the few lines at the beginning of the poem, bearing on the primaeval period.

The first Amorite word to be noted is *ammatum* in the second line, which, according to the context, should mean "earth, ground, the earth's surface," in contrast to "the heavens." All translators, following Smith, have recognized this meaning. The word is otherwise unknown in Babylonian literature. The variant form *ab-ba-tu*,[68] found in the Ashur version, clearly shows that it is a

[68] See *Keilschrifttexte aus Assur, Religiösen Inhalts* 162 : 2.

foreign word. Probably some day it will be found in a Babylonian explanatory list of foreign or obsolete words. Jensen has correctly compared it with *ammōth* "the ground" of the threshold, Isa. 6:4.[69] It is unquestionably the same word.

The question can here be raised, since in the Hebrew story *adamah* "ground" as the earth's surface, takes the place of this word, whether it is not possible to regard *admatu* as the origin of *ammatu*. But let it be clearly understood that this is a mere suggestion for consideration.

The words Apsu, Mummu, and Tiamat have already been discussed. The fourth word is *gipara*, in line seven. This has been translated "Gefilde" by Delitzsch; "Bäume" by Jensen; "field" by King and Barton; "soil" by Jastrow; "Strauchwerk" by Ebeling; "reeds" by Luckenbill; "Festland" by Ungnad, etc. The context suggests the meaning "dry ground, earth, land." It seems as if it is an Amorite word, like *ipru* or the Hebrew *'āpār*, "dry ground, dirt, earth." As is well known, strong *'ayin* is reproduced by *g* in Babylonian, e. g., *rigmu;* as well as by *g* in Greek, e. g., Gaza. If it should prove correct that *gipar* is the equivalent of the Hebrew *'apar*, we would have an example of weak *'ayin* being represented by *g*. Probably the word in early Hebrew was pronounced also as if it had a strong *'ayin*, for in the Amarna letters, *'āpār* is written *khaparu;* and, moreover, as Professor Torrey has suggested, it may be connected with the Arabic *ghabar* which has the same meanings, "dust, earth, etc."

The Hebrew *'āpār* is used in the same sense in the Old Testament. Note the passage in which "the fruits of the earth of the world" are mentioned (Prov. 8:26). It is also found in passages having a cosmological significance: "who hath measured the waters in the hollow of his hand and meted out the heavens with a span and comprehended the dirt (*'āpār*) of the earth as a measure (Is. 40:12).

[69] Jensen, *Mythen und Epen* p. 302.

The sixth word is *suṣâ* in the same line, which has been translated "Rohrdickicht" by Jensen; and "marsh" or "marshland" by all others except Jastrow, who has surmised its meaning, and translated it "the shoot."

In Hebrew, we have the word *ṣ°'ṣ°'â'* meaning "issue of man" and "issue of the earth." It seems evident that this is the same word that is in the creation story. Note the parallel thought expressed in the following passage: "he that created the heavens and stretched them forth; he that spread forth the earth and the things which come out of it (*ṣ°'ṣ°'â'*)," Is. 42:5.

These six words, including those of the gods mentioned, are in the first six lines. In the lines which follow, besides the title *Ummu-khubur* and the names Lakhmu, Lakhamu, Gaga, etc., discussed above, there seem to be comparatively few distinct indications of the original source. Moreover, the literary marks indicating the origin of the poem, have, as already stated, nearly all been removed or Babylonized by the different redactors.

I feel in this discussion of the Babylonian origin of the Biblical stories of creation, that there is little left to which those who will continue to hold the theory can cling. If they seem to think there is, let us have their evidence; it will be welcome. Beyond the statement that the proof offered in the four groups of evidence is more than sufficient to prove the utter baselessness of the theory, it seems unnecessary to summarize what has been presented in this chapter, as well as what bears on the subject in the one which precedes.

ADAM, THE GARDEN OF EDEN, AND THE FALL

In the past fifty years a number of attempts have been made not only to find Babylonian parallels for the stories of Adam, Eden, and the Fall of Man, but to prove that these stories originated in Babylonian mythology.

In 1875, George Smith announced in an English newspaper that he had found what he had regarded for "the general public the most interesting and the most remarkable cuneiform tablet yet discovered." He said it contained "the story of man's original innocence, of his temptation, and fall."[1] Naturally this announcement was echoed far and wide. However, in a very short time scholars showed that Smith was mistaken in his translation; and his view was abandoned.

Not many years later Delitzsch endeavored to locate Eden in Babylonia, where besides the Tigris and Euphrates he identified the Pison as the Pallicopas canal, and the Gihon as the Gukhande (also called Arakhtu).[2] This view also has been abandoned.

Another effort was also made to locate Eden at Eridu in Southern Babylonia. The Babylonian story of the nature and position of Eden, it was said, is to be found in an incantation text, where: "(in) Eridu a dark vine grew; it was made in a glorious place; its appearance (as) lapis-lazuli planted beside the abyss," etc.[3] The first man, Adam, we are told, was a Sumerian, who had been created in Eridu (the good city); and here, therefore, the Babylonian Semite placed the home of the first ancestor of his race. This

---

[1] *Daily Telegraph* (London) March 4, 1875.

[2] Delitzsch, *Wo Lag das Paradies* 1881.

[3] Sayce, *Hibbert Lectures on the Religion of the Ancient Babylonians* p. 238.

belief, we are further told, the Semite "borrowed along with the other elements of Babylonian culture" . . . "Like the story of the deluge it was part of the Sumerian heritage into which the Semite had entered."[4]

One of the traditions handed down by the Babylonians, referring to Eridu, is known as the Legend of Adapa, which, although it has very slight resemblance to the story of Adam and his fall, it is claimed, was transformed and recast into that story. Others regard this legend as a direct prototype which had certain influences upon the development of the Genesis story.

Fragments of this legend which belonged to the Library of Nineveh, are now found in the British Museum and in the Pierpont Morgan Library; the principal portion of it, however, was discovered among the Amarna archives in Egypt, where it was used as a text-book to study the Babylonian language; this is now in the Berlin Museum.

For many years Professor Sayce has held that Adapa was identical with Adam, and that the name Adapa could be read Adam. More recently it was found that the sign *pa* had the rare value *mu*, which he felt supported his view that *Adapa* is to be read *Adawa*, and that this is identical with Adam.[5] Others, however, have since called attention to the fact that this name is frequently written *A-da-pa*(*d*), which makes the reading *Adamu* impossible.[6] Following is an outline of the Adapa legend.

The god Ea had given great wisdom to a certain sage, named Adapa, who was a priest of Eridu, in order that he might reveal the fate of the land; "but eternal life he had not given him." He was a zealous priest of the sanctuary; he baked bread, and provided food by fishing in the sea. One day while exercising the

---

[4] Sayce, *Archaeology of the Cuneiform Inscriptions* p. 91.

[5] *Archaeology of the Cuneiform Inscriptions* p. 91, note 1.

[6] Langdon, *Sumerian Epic of Paradise* p. 64, note 1.

latter function of his office, the south-wind capsized his boat, when in revenge he broke its wings so that for seven days it blew not upon the land; whereupon he was summoned to appear in heaven, before Anu.

In preparation for his visit to Anu, his god Ea instructed him how to excite the sympathy of the demi-gods he would meet at the portal of heaven. He told him to appear in a mourning garment, and when asked for the reason, to reply that it was because two gods had disappeared from the land. And on being asked who these gods were, to say that they were Tammuz and Gish-Zidda. These, being the same with whom he would be speaking, would look in amazement at one another; and then they would intercede before Anu in his behalf. Ea further instructed Adapa:

> When thou comest into the presence of Anu, they will offer thee
> food of death; do not eat it.
> They will offer thee water of death; do not drink it.
> They will offer thee a dress; put it on.
> They will offer thee oil, anoint thyself with it.
> The advice that I give thee, do not neglect;
> The word that I tell thee, observe.

Adapa made his appearance in heaven as instructed. Everything happened as foretold. Anu's anger was appeased, and he ordered that they

> Bring him food of life that he may eat.
> Food of life they brought him; he did not eat;
> Water of life they brought him; he did not drink.
> A dress they brought him; he put it on. Oil
> They brought him; he anointed himself.
> When Anu saw this he was amazed (and said):
> Now Adapa, why didst thou not eat? Why didst thou not drink?
> Now wilt thou not remain alive. (He replied) Ea my lord
> Said: Thou shalt not eat, thou shalt not drink.
> (Anu said) Take him and bring him back to earth.

The balance of the legend is poorly preserved, and not very well understood. Some lines are suggestive of its having been used, like so many of the legends, for incantation purposes:

> And what evil he imposed upon the people,
> [And] the disease which in the body of men he imposed,
> That will the goddess Ninkarrak allay.
> Let illness depart; let sickness turn aside.
> [Upon] that [man] let his terror fall;
> . . . . . he shall not rest in good sleep.

The significance of these lines is not understood. The balance of the text is missing.

Certain scholars have made extensive comparisons between Genesis and this legend.[7] It seems to me that there is but one clear thought that this legend has in common with the Old Testament, and that is that the gift of immortality was connected with the eating of the food of life; although even this thought is not parallel, for Adam through disobedience ate of the food in order to become like God, and Adapa through obedience to his deity's counsel, refused it. Perhaps the lone thought that Genesis and the Adapa legend have in common is that man forfeited immortality by his own act.

As is well known, many ancient legends have already been recovered concerning men seeking immortality.[8] Naturally it is reasonable to believe that this thought was uppermost in the mind of man in ancient times, as it is at present.

It is interesting, however, to note that Sir James G. Frazer was not sufficiently impressed by this contention even to mention the Legend of Adapa as a parallel to the story of the fall, in his *Folklore in the Old Testament*. He records some stories where men missed the gift of immortality because of disobedience or accidents,

---

[7] See for example, Barton, *Archaeology and the Bible* 260 ff.
[8] Frazer, *Belief in Immortality* I, 59 ff.

and that serpents and other animals had obtained it, for whose subtlety they were hated; but the Adapa Legend is not even referred to.   Among others he includes the Gilgamesh story of how the existence of the magic plant of immortality was revealed; and how the serpent had stolen it while he was bathing.   Another immortality story is to be seen in the Etana Legend.[9]   Doubtless many others will be found as investigations proceed.

Adapa was a priest of Eridu, and "a sage among men."   The reference in the legend to the two kings who had disappeared and had become demi-gods, would show that he lived at a time subsequent to them.   According to the recently discovered dynastic lists they ruled about 4200 B. C.   There is no indication in the poem that it belongs to the beginning of man's history—in fact, everything in it points to an advanced state of civilization.   In this connection I cannot agree, therefore, with those who, believing that Adapa was the ancestor of the human race, do not think "it wise to test mythological and poetic statements by the strictures of logic."[10]   Moreover, if in the light of facts contained in this discussion, especially concerning the migration of religious ideas, there are those who can still satisfy themselves that this legend has furnished the idea for the writer of the Old Testament story of Adam and the fall, nothing that I can add will cause them to change their views.

A few years ago Professor Langdon of Oxford published a Sumerian tablet which was announced as containing the origin of the Hebrew story of Paradise, and as showing that the geographical description of the Genesis story was "obviously derived from Sumero-babylonian cosmology."   In the same tablet he also found the origin of the story of the Fall of Man, which he said "is a masterly combination of the Eridu doctrine known to us in

---

[9] See *A Hebrew Deluge Story* 34 f.
[10] Langdon, *Sumerian Epic of Paradise* p. 40, note 3.

the Semitic legend of Adapa, and the doctrine of our Nippur tablet."
It was held that the tablet also contained the story of the flood.[11]

A verdict was promptly given on these conclusions by a number
of scholars, which was that the proper interpretation of the text
excluded the suggested Biblical parallels.[12] It is now generally
thought that the tablet is a mythical account of the origin of a city,
and the beginnings of agriculture.

Still more recently another announcement has been made of
what is claimed to be the discovery of "the clearest and most
complete account of the Sumerian story of the Fall of Man, as
known to the priestly writers of Nippur."[13] Like the statements
of George Smith and others, this has been echoed and re-echoed
everywhere in the daily press. I regret to say that I cannot follow
the writer; I do not believe that the text has any bearing whatsoever
upon the story of the Garden of Eden or the Fall of Man.

The contentions of Professor Chiera rest largely on the meanings
of several words, which he holds show the mythological character
of the tablet, and which make his Biblical parallel possible. Chief
among these are *kin-gub*, which he translates "garden" or "land,"
and two new words which he regards as representing "two legendary
trees of the garden," namely, *gish-gi-tug-gi*, which he translates
"tree which establishes (the use) of clothing," seeing in the word
that which "brings into more prominent light the story of the fig
tree out of the leaves of which the first wearing apparel was made";

[11] Langdon, *Sumerian Epic of Paradise, the Flood, and the Fall of Man.* See also
Proc. Soc. Bib. Arch. 36, 188 ff and 253 ff., *Jour. Amer. Or. Soc.* 36, 140 ff., and
Amer. Jour. Sem. Lang. 33, 245 ff.

[12] See Sayce, *Expository Times* 1915 88 ff., Jastrow, *Amer. Jour. Sem. Lang.* 33,
91 ff., *Jour. Amer. Or. Soc.* 36, 122 ff., and 274 ff., Barton, *Amer. Jour. Theol.* 1917,
571 ff., and *Archaeology and the Bible* 282 ff., Prince, *Jour. Amer. Or. Soc.* 36, 90 ff.,
Witzel, *Keilinschriftliche Studien* I 51 ff., Albright, *Amer. Jour. Sem. Lang.* 35, 161 ff.,
Mercer, *Jour. Soc. Bibl. Res.* 1818, 51 ff., King, *Schweich Lectures* 1918, p. 126.

[13] Chiera, *Amer. Jour. Sem. Lang.* 39, 40 ff.

and *gi-ŭsh-dù*, which he translates, "the reed which frees from death," which he holds is "a very good name for the tree of life."

The last two mentioned Sumerian words, in the absence of an explanatory list or a context which throws light on their meaning, can be translated in many different ways, since they are both composed of three separate signs or words which have many different meanings.[14] It is possible to select from the more than one hundred values of these signs, without these helps, such combinations having meanings that would fit into almost any explanation, even to making the one group mean "tree of life." Some day an explanatory list will probably be found, when the exact meaning of these words will become known.

The Sumerian word *kin-gub*, as proposed, probably means "garden"; but the context shows it was a vegetable garden, and not as Chiera proposes, "the garden harboring the tree of life." The legend, even on the basis of his own translation, it seems to me, refers to "sons of menials" being sent away from the estate, probably for stealing; who shall not return to lead the ox, to irrigate and till the field, and to cultivate the garden. Others shall do this; and their parents shall eat of the food. Then follows what appears to be the citing of a penalty of "ten measures of barley," apparently referring to the overt act of the "sons of the menials."

This is what has been declared to be "the clearest and most complete account of the Sumerian story of the Fall of Man." It

---

[14] Let us look at the second, namely, the word *gi-ŭsh-du*, which Chiera translates "the reed which frees from death," which he says is a "very good name for the tree of life." It is composed of three signs or words. The first can be read *gi* "reed, land," etc., *gin* "establish, oppress." etc. The second sign can be read *ŭsh* "blood, death," etc., *til* "live, complete," etc., *bad* "remove, open," as well as many other values. The third sign of this group can be read *dù* "break, cook, open," etc., *gab* "cut through," *tukh* "open," etc. All three signs or words have many values and meanings, leaving it absolutely impossible to know what the group does mean until it is found in an explanatory list, or in an inscription where the reading becomes clear from the context.

is from this "myth" and the Biblical account, we are told, that "we gather the idea that the god never intended man to be immortal."

It is not impossible that parallels of the Biblical story of Eden and the Fall of Man will be found, for if the Amorites brought other legends to Babylonia, it is reasonable to suppose that they may have also brought these. It seems to me, however, that the search will have to be continued among the Babylonian and Sumerian legends, not only for the origin of these stories, but even for parallels.

In the light of the excavations conducted in Babylonia, and our present knowledge of its physical geography, it is absolutely clear that civilization could not have had its origin in the lower Tigro-Euphrates valley or delta. We know that it required engineering works on a very large scale before it was possible to make the country habitable;[15] and this involved extensive coöperation and a willingness on the part of many people to be amenable to regulations. Great embankments had to be constructed, to keep the rivers within reasonable channels in flood season; and great basins had to be provided, to retain water so that when the floods receded, it could be used for irrigation purposes. Prior to his entrance into the alluvium, man lived further up the rivers, where apparently his engineering science had developed. Eridu by the sea, it seems, was the first permanent habitation, because it was possible for man to live there with the least amount of effort owing to the fact that the inundating waters could readily escape into the gulf.

Above Hit, where the alluvium begins, there are natural agricultural districts close to the rivers, extending over a wide area. Sir William Willcocks was so very much impressed with the agricultural possibilities of this part of Western Asia, that he has proposed to locate the Garden of Eden in this region. Five or six thousand years ago, he tells us, before "the degradation of the

---

[15] See Sayce, *Archaeology of the Cuneiform Inscriptions* p. 76; Willcocks, *The Near East*, September 29, 1916, p. 521; Clay, *Jour. Amer. Or. Soc.* 41, 261 ff. etc.

cataracts," there was a free flow of water in this district for irrigation purposes.[16]

It appears to me that the theory of Willcocks, who is so well acquainted with this part of the Near East, having studied it topographically and otherwise as an engineer, is very important in this connection, in showing, at least, that this country was probably occupied earlier than the alluvial plain. It was in this part of Amurru that the very ancient kingdom Mari existed, which had not only ruled Babylonia in the fourth millennium B. C., but furnished that land with its gods. Here was found the kingdom 'Ana, also written Khana, which furnished Babylonia with its god Ana, and Palestine and Egypt with his consort Anat. It was from this land that the Semite moved into the alluvium when it was ready to receive man.

We are informed by Egyptian archaeologists that the alluvium of the Nile valley was formed only about six to eight thousand B. C., and that prior to this time, prehistoric man lived in the terraces along the river. From the light thrown upon the subject by excavations, this probably is about the time the alluvial plain of Babylonia was first occupied. It would be difficult to understand, therefore, how any intelligent resident of Western Asia could accept the idea that man first lived in this alluvium. With the evidence everywhere in sight of his colossal doings, in his efforts to harness the two rivers, it is inconceivable that the ancient could satisfy himself that this had been Paradise, and that primaeval man lived there. It is difficult to conceive how even an intelligent Babylonian could have come to such a belief. Moreover, the description of Eden in Genesis precludes the possibility of its being in the alluvial plain; as does also the description by the prophets Ezekiel and Amos.[17] Certainly the Amorites or Hebrews never thought of placing the Garden of Eden in "the plain of Shinar."

---

[16] *From the Garden of Eden to the Crossing of the Jordan* 3 ff.

[17] See Ezekiel 27:23; 28:13; and Amos 1:5.

V

THE HEBREW SABBATH

For years it was held that the Hebrew Sabbath was borrowed from Babylonia: that it had its roots in the Babylonian *shapattu*, or *shabattu*,[1] to which we have been told we owe the blessings of that day; for "the Sabbath-rest was essentially of Babylonian origin."[2] It is even held that "the word Sabbath is Babylonian indeed."[3]

This view has been accepted by many scholars. It is only necessary to examine the Biblical dictionaries, commentaries, and other helps, to ascertain how deeply rooted this idea is at the present time. Let us here inquire upon what basis does the assertion rest that the Hebrew Sabbath is of Babylonian origin.

In the first place there was found in a Babylonian dictionary, or explanatory list of rare words, this formula: *ûm nûkh libbi* = *sha-pat-tum* (or *sha-bat-tum*).[4] This was translated "*shabattu* was the day of rest of the heart," literally "a day of rest." The word *shabatu* was also found in an explanatory list of rare words, but the meaning given for it, namely, *gamâru* "to be full, complete"[5] did not seem at the time to be suitable for the assertions that had been made.

The word *shabattu*, for which there is no etymology in Semitic Babylonian, was said to have been derived by the native lexicographers from the Sumerian *sa* "heart," and *bat* "to cease" or "rest";[6] it was literally translated "heart rest."

[1] Delitzsch, *Babel and Bible* p. 101.
[2] Sayce, *Religion of Egypt and Babylonia* p. 476.
[3] Rogers, *Religion of Babylonia and Assyria* p. 226.
[4] *Cuneiform Texts* 12, 6:24.
[5] See *Zeitschrift für Assyriologie* 4, 272.
[6] Sayce, *Religion of the Babylonians* p. 272.

The second discovery upon which the theory is based, is an inscription giving a calendar of the festivals of the intercalary month Second Elul, in which the duties of the shepherd, or king, are prescribed for the 7th, 14th, 21st, and 28th, as well as the 19th days of the month. It reads: "The seventh day is the feast of Marduk and Zarpanit. It is an evil day. The shepherd of great peoples shall not eat flesh cooked over coals of an oven; he shall not change the garments of his body; he shall not put on clean clothes; a sacrifice he shall not offer; the king shall not ride in his chariot; he shall not speak as a king; the diviner shall not give a decision in the secret place; the physician shall not touch a sick man; it is not suitable to pronounce a curse; at night the king shall bring his offerings before Marduk and Ishtar; he shall offer a sacrifice; the lifting up of his hands is pleasing to the god."[7]

Whether these requirements were to be observed only during the Second Elul, the extra month inserted in the calendar every two or three years, cannot be determined. Although the tablet was found in the Nineveh Library, it doubtless refers to observance by the king at Babylon, as shown by the names of the deities. These days have been regarded as the origin of the Hebrew Sabbath.

Although the words *shapattu*, and *shabatu*, are not used in connection with these days, it was assumed that they were thus called; and although in the hemerology they were designated as "evil days," nevertheless scholars decided arbitrarily that the words *ûm nûkh libbi*, found in the syllabary, referred to them. For years Babylonists based their assertions that the Sabbath was a Babylonian institution on these two points.

Somewhat later it was shown that the expression *nûkh libbi*, which occurs frequently in the lamentation hymns, did not mean "rest of the heart," but referred to the pacification of the gods;

[7] *Cuneiform Inscriptions of Western Asia* IV, 32:28 ff.

and the expression was then translated "day of the appeasement of the heart."

In 1904, Doctor Pinches discovered in a tablet giving the designation of the days of the month, that the 15th day was called shapatti[8] when it became clear that the word shabatu, explained by gamâru, meaning "to be complete, full," apparently referred to the full moon in the middle of the month.[9]

This new light upon the subject required a readjustment of the proof that has been advanced for the Babylonian origin of the Sabbath. However, this was promptly accomplished, and the same conclusion reached, even "that the word Sabbath is Babylonian indeed."

In this contention I cannot acquiesce. There is no root in Babylonian, as already intimated, equivalent to the common Hebrew shabat "to cut off, desist, put an end to." With the knowledge of its extended usage throughout the Old Testament, and knowing how thoroughly the institutions and the life of Israel were bound up with this day, to me it has been inconceivable how Assyriologists could make themselves believe, on the basis of the data given above, that this institution and this word were borrowed from Babylonia.

As the calendar for the intercalary month Elul contained certain requirements of the king on the 7th, etc., days of the month, but not of the common people, an investigation was made by the late Professor Johns to ascertain what the dating of the many contracts would show as regards the observance of these days.

It was found that on the days in question, business was carried on as usual, although the 19th day showed a considerable falling

[8] *Proc. Soc. Bibl. Arch.* 26, 51 ff. Most of the days are simply numbered. Besides the 15th day, the 21st is called *ibbu* "anger"; the 25th *arkhu TIL*, perhaps meaning "end of month"; see Jastrow *Rel. Bab. und Assyr.* II, 510 f.

[9] See also Zimmern, *ZDMG* 58, 199 ff and 458 ff.

off, and in the time of the First Dynasty of Babylon and in the seventh century of the Assyrian period, there was also observed a decrease in the number of business transactions dated on these days, which, however, perhaps can now be explained (see below). This falling off of business did not show itself in the tablets of the Cassite period. The temple documents of that era showed the same average of business transacted on these days, as well as on the 19th of the month.[10]

An examination of the business archives of the Murashû Sons of Nippur, dated in the reigns of Artaxerxes I and Darius II, that is in the time of Ezra, also do not show any abstention from business on these days; they do, however, show that on them the Jews, who figured so prominently in these documents, are conspicuous for their absence as contracting parties. Probably a reinvestigation of the documents of the First Dynasty, and of the Assyrian period, will reveal a similar West Semitic influence on these days, especially as in both these periods Babylonia and Assyria were well filled with Amorites. Another fact has recently come to light which has an interesting bearing in this connection.

The nearest approach to anything resembling the actual observance of a day like the Hebrew Sabbath in Babylonia, is to be found in a series of twenty-three tablets in the Yale Babylonian Collection, which belonged to the temple archives discovered at Warka, the ancient city of Erech. They are monthly records of sheep delivered for sacrificial and other purposes. These tablets are dated between the fifth year of Cyrus (534 B. C.), and the sixth of Cambyses (523 B. C.). The number of sheep that were delivered is specified for each day of the month; for example, five or more sheep were set apart for the "stable," and four or more for the "shepherd of sacrifice," probably referring to the stable of the

[10] Johns, *Expository Times* XVII 567.

royal or official household, and the shepherd in charge of the temple sacrificial animals.[11]

These entries are made for each day of the month; but following the entry for the 7th, 14th, 21st, and 28th days, there is written in some of the records an additional item, namely, "one *khitpi*," which word apparently means "offering";[12] and in the others the words "one kid for an offering." There is, however, a variation in the days. Nine of the records have the same succession of seven days, but on the rest of the tablets the previous day is occasionally mentioned, as the 6th, 13th, 20th, and 27th; and in one instance the 26th day. This would simply show that the kid for the offering was in some instances delivered on the day previous to the one appointed.

These tablets show the first actual observance of anything in Babylonia that suggests the existence of a parallel to the Sabbath. Moreover, it very probably is more than a parallel; we may have here proof of the observance of the Hebrew Sabbath in Babylonia; but by whom?

We know that Nebuchadnezzar carried Judah into captivity. We find that the nomenclature in Babylonia, following this event, contains many Hebrew names. The Murashû archives, a century later, are full of them.[13] And we know also with what considera- tion Cyrus treated the foreign peoples of the land from the very beginning of his reign. In these tablets we find that from the fifth year of Cyrus, the keeper of the city's live stock at Erech, in addition to the five and occasionally more sheep, which he daily delivered to the official stable, and four and occasionally

---

[11] Clay, *Miscellaneous Inscriptions* 75 ff.

[12] The only occurrence of this word known to the writer is on an Aramaic inscrip- tion found in the Serapaeum at Memphis; for which the translation "offerings" has been offered; cf. *ibidem* p. 77.

[13] Clay, *Business Documents of the Murashû Sons of Nippur.*

more to the shepherd of the sacrificial animals, gave a kid for an "offering," on the 7th, 14th, 21st, and 28th days.

While it is not specified who received these four kids each month, knowing that thousands of Hebrews were in the land, it seems reasonable to conjecture that they were given to Hebrew menials who were in the employ of the court or temple, so that they could keep their feast in accordance with their religion.

There have already been published hundreds of hymns from Babylonia, and hundreds of ritual texts. The mass of this kind of literature is ten times greater than that found in the Old Testament. We have also a large body of laws from the early and late periods. In these, as well as in the mass of other texts, besides what is referred to above, there is not a semblance of an idea corresponding to the Hebrew Sabbath, nor any reference to the word (i. e., shabbat, not shapattu or shabattu).

Whether in view of the fact that the "new moon" and the Sabbath in the Old Testament, stand in juxtaposition in so many passages the Sabbath was originally the day of the "full moon," i. e., the fifteenth day of the month, need not concern us here.[14] Suffice it to say that besides the requirements for the king, specified in the calendar for the periods of seven days, including the 19th of the intercalary Second Elul, which are simply designated as "evil days," there are no data to show that the general activities of life in Babylonia were interrupted on what corresponds to the Hebrew Sabbath, not even on the fifteenth day of the month, which was designated as shapattu; that there is no etymological evidence to show that the root shabat, corresponding to the Hebrew, was in use in Babylonia; and that besides the occurence of the word shapattu in lists, or dictionaries of rare words, it is not found in the literature of the Babylonians except in the Amorite Enuma elish

---

[14] On this question see Jastrow, Amer. Jour. Sem. Lang. 30, 94 ff.

(V: 18). Moreover it is highly probable that *shapattu* is a reflection of the Hebrew *shabbath*.[15]

In view of all this, and also of the conclusion that the current of religious ideas flowed not in the direction of Syria and Palestine, as shown above in the second chapter, will scholars continue to promulgate the idea that the Hebrew Sabbath is of Babylonian origin? We have a right to expect more than this. Do not the scholars who have promulgated these ideas, if they have become convinced that their published views are wrong, have a responsibility to the Bible student in letting this fact become known?

[15] This is the view also of Professor Torrey, who says that the Babylonian *shabattu* was borrowed from the West-Semitic *shab'at* meaning "seven" (*AJSL* 33, 53.)

. VI

THE ANTEDILUVIAN PATRIARCHS

Many Assyriologists hold the view that the names of the antediluvian patriarchs of Genesis are translations of, or that they were otherwise made to be equivalents of, Babylonian names, in some instances of antediluvian kings, and in others, of kings from postdiluvian dynastic lists. It matters not whether those selected for the purpose belong to kings or sages. Some of the names used to show the origin of the early patriarchs are taken from Semitic, and others from Sumerian, lists, while several are deliberately changed to make them conform to those with which it is desired to identify them. The possibility that the ancestors of the Hebrews had their own traditional lists, is by them not even taken into consideration. It is in this way, we are informed, the Hebrew writers make up their fictitious lists of patriarchal ancestors.

A discussion of personal names is not ordinarily inviting to the average Bible student; nevertheless, I think even those not familiar with Semitic philology will not only be able to judge intelligently for themselves as to the merits of Babylonism, as it bears upon this subject, but will also find, I think, considerable interest in the display of effort made by scholars to prove the Babylonian origin of the Hebrew antediluvians, especially in studying the tabulated results on pages 125-7.

There are four sources of data used in trying to prove the Babylonian origin of these characters. The first of these is the Biblical. As is well known, there are two genealogical traditions or series of patriarchs in Genesis between the creation and the deluge, one having seven names, which is generally recognized as belonging to what is called the Jehovist version (J.), and the other having ten, as belonging to what is called the Priestly version (P.). There are also divergences as to the order and the form in which some of the names appear (see below).

The second source of the material used in identifying the Biblical patriarchs with the Babylonian is the list of antediluvian Chaldean kings which has been handed down by Berossus, as preserved in the writings of Eusebius and Syncellus, who had obtained their data from writings of Apollodorus, Abydenus, and Polyhistor.[1] As a result, the names said to have been copied by Berossus at Babylon, are handed down in variant forms (see below).

Professor Langdon of Oxford has recently published the third source, namely, a tablet of the Ashmolean Museum consisting of eighteen lines, some of which are unfortunately fragmentary.[2] This also gives ten kings who ruled before the flood, ending with the hero; but instead of the name Atra-khasis (Xisuthros), it gives the Sumerian form of the title he received after the deluge, namely Zi-û-sud-du (= Ûm-napishtim-rûqu) (see Chapter VII). Unfortunately only three of the names or titles are complete, and the reading of one of these is yet to be explained.

The fourth source of material used to show the origin of the Hebrew patriarchs is in the early dynastic list of kings who ruled in Babylonia subsequent to the deluge.[3] These have furnished additional material for certain scholars in their efforts to prove the Biblical patriarchs to be of Babylonian origin.

THE BIBLICAL LISTS

Jehovistic		*Priestly*		
1	Adam	1 Adam..........	130	930 years[4]
		2 Seth...........	105	912 "
2	Seth	3 Enosh..........	90	905 "

[1] See Cory, *Ancient Fragments*, from which the variants given below are taken.
[2] *Jour. Royal Asiatic Society*, Apr. 1923, 251.
[3] See Poebel, *Historical Texts* 73 ff., or Clay, *Jour. Am. Or. Soc.* 41, 241 ff.
[4] The first column gives the age at the birth of the son whose name follows, and the second column, all his years.

3		Enosh	4	Kenan.........	70	910 years
4	Cain		5	Mahalal-El......	65	895 "
5	Enoch		6	Yered..........	162	962 "
6	'Irad		7	Enoch..........	65	365 "
7	Mehuja-El		8	Methush°-Elakh.	187	969 "
8	Methusha-El		9	Lamech.........	182	777 "
9	Lamech		10	Noah...........	500	[950] "
10	Noah			Age at deluge...	100	"

1656

THE BEROSSUS LIST OF CHALDEAN KINGS

		Years		City
1	'Alōros................................	10 sars		Babylon
2	'Alaparos, Alapaurus......................	3	"	" (?)
3	'Amillaros, 'Amēlōn, Almelon...............	13	"	Pantibiblon
4	'Ammenōn...............................	12	"	"
5	Megalaros, Megalanos, Amegalarus...........	18	"	"
6	Daōnos, Daōs, Da(v)onus "shepherd"........	10	"	"
7	Euedōrakhos, Euedōreskhos, Edoranchus......	18	"	"
8	'Amempsinos, Amemphsinus.................	10	"	Larak
9	'Ardatās, 'Ōtiartās........................	8	"	"
10	Xisouthros, Sisouthros, Xisuthrus............	18	"	" (?)

	Years		
Total................................120	"	(432,00 years)	

THE ASHMOLEAN MUSEUM LIST

		Years	City
1	......x-alim.............................	67,200[5]	Khabur
2	.... lål-går.............................	72,000	"
3	..-ki-du-un-nu-sha-kin-kin.................	72,000	Larsa
4	.... x-x.................................	21,600	"
5	.. -zi-sib...............................	28,800	Dûr Tibiri
6	..-en-lù-an-na...........................	21,600	"
7	...... sib-zi an-na.......................	36,000	Larak
8	En-me-dur-an-na.........................	72,000	Sippar

[5] There is an additional sar at the end of the line unaccounted for. This may be the determinative kam which follows numbers.

9 *Su-kur-Lam dumu* ("son of") *Ubur-Tu-Tu* ... 28,800   Su-kur-Lam
10 *Zi-û-sud-du dumu Su-kur-Lam-Gi*........... 26,000   "

Total...............................460,400 years

Let us first discuss briefly the recently published Ashmolean inscription, concerning which Professor Langdon writes as follows: "The Weld-Blundell tablet proves that the legend of the ten prediluvian patriarchs preserved in Hebrew tradition and by the Greek historians of Babylonia was Sumerian." The post-exilic writer P., in Genesis X, he adds, "clearly borrowed the idea from the common Sumerian source."

Langdon reads the last sign of the first name *alim*, which he says "clearly represents the original of the Greek *'Alōros*." But even were this true, what is to be said about the three or more signs of the name which precede *alim*, one of which is partly preserved?

The second name he reads [A]-*làl-gár*, which he says "may conceivably afford an explanation of the name Alaparos given by Berossus. The Greeks corrupted Γ gamma to Π pe(pi)." I doubt whether scholars will accept the equation *Alalgar* = *'Alaparos*.

Langdon says that the sixth name of the Berossus list, "*Daōnus* is obviously a textual corruption for *Laōnus*, a transcription of *lù-an-na*." One thing can be said in favor of the identification, and that is both are the sixth in the lists. But what is to be done about the unpreserved first part of the name, which reads, ...*en-lù-an-na*?[6]

The next name, ...*sib-zi-an-na*, he says "was, somehow, corrupted into Amempsinos in the text preserved by Berossus, and occurs wrongly as the eighth king, not the seventh." In favor of this it is said that both ruled ten *sars* (36,000) of years; but there

---

[6] Since Anna reproduces El, as already shown, I would sooner think that this name would eventually prove to represent Mahalal-El.

are five of the ten rulers, three in the one list and two in the other, who are credited as having ruled ten *sars*. But see below.

Concerning the eighth ruler, called *En-me-dur-an-na*, he says "The variant readings" of Euedoranchos, etc., the seventh of the Berossus list, "prove that the Sumerian original was *En-me-dur-an-ki*." This identification with the name of the Sippar seer and king, made years ago by Zimmern, is very probably correct. In favor of the identification attention is called to the fact that one came from Pantibiblos and the other from Sippar, which are thought to refer to the same city (see further below). I cannot, however, follow Langdon in holding that it is originally a Sumerian name.

Langdon reads the signs *Su-kur-Lam* in the ninth name = *Arad* or *Aratti;* and the name *Arad-gin;* this he identifies with 'Ardatās. *Lam* might be a mistake for *ru*. However, even though his conjectural readings should prove correct, *Arad-gin* = 'Ardatās is not very convincing. The tenth name is, as stated above, the title that the hero received after the deluge.

This tablet, like the Biblical Priestly and the Berossus lists, gives ten antediluvians, the last of whom is the hero of the deluge story. This list gives also the name *Ubur-Tu-Tu* as the grandfather of the hero, which is nearly the same as *Ubar-Tu-Tu*, the *father* of the hero in the Gilgamesh story of the deluge. I presume since the proof that the Priestly Biblical writer borrowed his names from this Sumerian source is not found in the discussion, Langdon means that this statement is according to what he has previously presented (see below). I only desire to add here that the fact that the names are written in Sumerian does not imply or prove that the kings were Sumerians (see page 165). Moreover, it seems from what follows that the tradition goes back to a Semitic source.

In discussing the subject of the Hebrew borrowings, let us first consider a statement bearing upon the patriarchs as a whole. Professor Langdon says that the J. writer, in replacing the names in the Berossus list, reproduced the spirit of it as being connected with the arts, which was wholly misunderstood by the author of the P. list.   He also says that "the J. document with its seven patriarchs is obviously based upon the Sumero-Babylonian traditions of divine patrons of industries."[7]   It should, however, be stated that the text, on which the idea of these "patrons of industries" is based, is rather a myth concerning the birth of eight gods and goddesses to whom was given power over certain diseases of the cattle, the flocks, the mouth, the genital organs, etc.   Let us also look at this statement from another point of view.

As far as I can observe from all the sources used by Babylonists to show where the Hebrew writers secured their data, besides all the rulers being called "kings," it is added only that several were "shepherds," and in two instances, the names of seers or priests figure in these efforts.   Furthermore, besides the *sons* of Lamech, only one in both lists of the Old Testament patriarchs is said to be a so-called "patron of the arts," namely, Cain "the tiller" and "builder."[8]

Let us now proceed to examine the contentions concerning the connections of the Biblical list with that of Berossus.   The ten names which form the chief basis for this have been handed down as those of ten antediluvian kings of Babylon.   The variant forms given in parentheses are found, as stated, in the different Greek and Latin versions.

1. 'Alōros ('Aλωρος, *Alorus*).   This name Professor Hommel,[9] who is followed by Dr. Jeremias of Leipzig,[10] regards as having been

---

[7] *Sumerian Epic of Paradise* 52, 63, 81 f.

[8] Langdon makes the Biblical Mahalal-El to be "the patron of health," on the basis of his translation of the name: "God makes alive," or "God is my enlivener." Lamech he says is "a patron of psalmody," because he holds the name is a transcript of *lumkha*, a Sumerian title of the god Ea.   I cannot follow in this. (*Ibidem* p. 52).

[9] Hommel, *Proc. Soc. Bibl. Arch.* XV 243 f.

[10] Jeremias, *Das Alte Testament im Lichte des alten Orients* 118 ff.

corrupted from Aruru, which is one of the names of the mother goddess, who is said to be a "fashioner of mankind." In other words, they seem to think that this dynastic ruler of the land, who came from Babylon, was a creating goddess. Following another proposed identification of this name, Hommel more recently equated it with the Sumerian *Lal-ur*, a part of the name *Lal-ur-alim-ma*, said to be an early king of Nippur.[11] On Langdon's recent identification of . . . . . *alim* with this name, see above.

Before giving my own identification of this and of other names discussed below, let me refer again to the discovery that the name *Amur(ru)* was scratched on several tablets in the Aramaic characters *'wr* (= *Awur* = *Ûr*, see page 21). In other words, *Amur*, perhaps only found in *Amōrî*, meaning "the Amorite" in the Old Testament,[12] was here written, like many other words, with *w* instead of *m*; from which according to a well-established phonetic law, we have the formula *Amur* = *Awur* = *Ûr*.

Let me say for the benefit of those not versed in Semitic philology that the phonetic changes involved in this formula are well established. Let me add also that the doubling of the *r* in *Amurru*, probably marks the accented long vowel of *Amûr*; and also that the Babylonians used the same signs to represent the vowels *o* and *u*; in other words, the sign *Ur* can be read *Or*; *Amur* can be read *Amor*.

The nomenclature of early Babylonia is full of foreign names compounded with that of the god Uru.[13] After the time of the First dynasty of Babylon, this element is only occasionally found,

---

[11] In Nies, *Ur Dynasty Tablets* p. 206.

[12] Unless it is to be recognized in *Moriah*, 2 Chron. 3:1, for which the Septuagint and the Syriac give *Amoriah*.

[13] See Huber, *Die Personennamen in den Keilinschrifturkunden aus der Zeit der Könige von Ur and Nisin* pp. 170 and 189; Ranke, *Personal Names of the Hammurabi Dynasty* 208 f.; and the many editions of texts published since these works have appeared.

and then chiefly in family names, which is probably due to the fact that the city Mari, where apparently Uru was worshipped, was destroyed. As Babylon and Ashur later gave their names to the country, so Uru gave its name not only to its own land, but even to the upper part of Babylonia in the early period, which was called Uri.

In view of the prevalence of the god Uru in the early nomenclature, following the above mentioned discovery, I proposed that 'Alōros was El-Or; which probably means "El is Uru"; and I identified the name with El-Or ('l wr), in the list of gods found in the early Aramaic inscription of Zakir.[14] A little later in the same year, and independently, another scholar made the same identification; it has since been accepted by many scholars.[15]

In other words, instead of identifying 'Alōrus, the first king or emperor of the land, with the goddess Aruru, or with the Sumerian Lal-Ur, part of an early king's name of Nippur, or with . . . . . alim of the Ashmolean tablet, I maintain it is to be identified with El-Ur.

2. 'Alaparos ('Αλαπαρος, Alaporus, Alapaurus, Alaparus). Notwithstanding that the Greek and Latin forms of the second antediluvian Babylonian king are practically identical, this name is regarded by many scholars as incorrectly reproducing Adapa, the name of the sage of Eridu, already referred to, without any regard for the element oros or aros, which appears in all the forms at the

---

[14] *Amurru the Home of the Northern Semites* (1909) p. 64.

[15] See Schiffer, *Or. Lit. Zeit.* Nov. 1909, p. 478; Lidzbarski, *Zeit. für Ass.* 31 p. 196; Jensen, *Or. Lit. Zeit.* 1921, 269 f; etc. I note, however, that Professor Sayce, in commenting on this identification, writes: 'l wr, "it is needless to say, has nothing to do with Aloros of Berossos." He then identifies it with the god *Wir* or *Mir*. (*Proc. Soc. Bibl. Arch.* 1919, p. 208). I accept his identification, for it is the same as my own (see *Empire of the Amorites* p. 69); but the name of this god is also written *Wer, Mer, Mar, Mari;* and since *Mar* and *Amurru* (*Ūru*) are interchangeable (see *ibidem* p. 68), we have the same deity. Cf. the family name of the Cassite period *Pir'-ᵈAmurru* (*Kur-Gal; Martu*), written *pr wr* in Aramaic, at the time of Ashurbanipal (see Lidzbarski, *ibidem*).

end of the name. This change is made, so that Adapa can be regarded as "the first man," and the original of Adam. This conclusion, that 'Alaparos is Adapa, has been advanced by many Assyriologists: Sayce,[16] Hommel,[17] Zimmern,[18] Jeremias,[19] Ungnad,[20] Langdon,[21] and King:[22] as well as by many Old Testament scholars.

It is interesting to note that the changes proposed in the equation *'Alaparos = Adapa = Adam,* leave nothing of the original name except the first two vowels; reminding us of the definition once given by Voltaire for etymology, that it "is a science in which the vowels amount to nothing and the consonants very little." We have seen above that the identification of the sage Adapa (whose name is also written Adapa(d)) with Adam, is impossible. The same seems to be true of the more recent formula of Langdon, namely *Alalgar = 'Alaparos.* Moreover, since the element *oros* of this name, also written *aros,* is found in half of the names of the list, it ought to be needless to say, it cannot be ignored. My reading of the name 'Alaporos or *Alapaurus,* is *Alap-Uru.* It is Amorite, and probably means "Friend of the god Uru," or "Ox of Uru."[23]

3. 'Amillaros, 'Amēlōn ('Αμιλλαρος, 'Αμηλων, *Almelon*). Again, no account is taken by any of the Babylonists of the full forms of this name, which end in *aros,* and *ōn.* 'Amēlōn is alone considered and regarded to have been the Babylonian word *amēlu*

---

[16] Sayce, *Archaeology of the Cuneiform Inscriptions* 91.

[17] Hommel, *Ibidem.*

[18] Zimmern, *Keilinschriften und das Alte Testament*[3] p. 538.

[19] Jeremias, *Ibidem.*

[20] Ungnad, in Gressmann, *Altorientalische Texte und Bilder* p. 39.

[21] Langdon, *Ibidem.* In the light of his recent find, Langdon abandons this, but see above.

[22] King, *Schweich Lectures* 1916, p. 32 f.

[23] Cf. the Babylonian *Agal-Marduk* "Calf of Marduk;" *Immer-Ili* "Lamb of El," etc.

"man." This, they say, the Hebrew writers reproduced by Enosh "man." (Thus Hommel, Sayce, Zimmern, Jeremias, Ungnad, and King.) Barton reaches the same results in a different way. He proposes that the Sumerian *Enmenunna*, the fourteenth king of Kish, which he translates "Exalted man," if reproduced in Babylonian by one word, would become *amêlu* "man"; and this, if transferred into Hebrew, would give *Enosh*.[24] But *En-me-nunna*, if Sumerian, is a title meaning "the exalted lord of the oracle."

Assuming that the Hebrew scribes were intelligent men, we are prompted to inquire, why, if they desired to reproduce *amêlu* "man" in Hebrew, they did not use the element *mêth* "man" which is found in two of the Biblical names, or *îsh* "man," also found as a Hebrew name element, instead of making it Enosh, which really means "mankind," and which is only found in this name. It does not seem that the meaning "mankind" for this personal name, is correct, and especially in view of the common element *enshu* in Babylonian names. However, I feel that my own identification of the name Amillaros with Amêl-Uru, which accounts for both elements instead of only one, needs no comment; and that it is beyond cavil. And I propose that the variant name 'Amêlôn is *Amêl-Anu*. Attention has already been called to the fact that the name Anna or Anu is found in other names of Chaldeans mentioned in Berossus' story, namely Annadôtos, Anamentos, and 'Anôdaphos.[25] On the fact that we have these variant readings, etc., see below.

4. 'Ammenôn ('Αμμενων, *Ammenon*). This is generally regarded the same as the Babylonian word *ummanu*, "artisan," which it is declared was reproduced in Hebrew, and became Cain and Kenan "Smith." (Thus Hommel, Sayce, Zimmern, Jeremias, and Langdon.) Barton has proposed that the Hebrew Cain is from the

[24] Barton, *Archaeology and the Bible* p. 267.
[25] *Empire of the Amorites* p. 168.

Sumerian *Pilikam*, which is his reading of a postdiluvian name of the thirteenth king of the Kish dynasty, which he translates "with intelligence to build"; and this, he says, if rendered as one word in Babylonian, could become *ummanu* "artificer," which if reproduced in Hebrew, would become Cain.   King says the *n* in the Sumerian *En-me-nunna*, the king of Kish, above mentioned, was assimilated; and then he identifies it with 'Ammenōn.

In the more or less ten thousand Babylonian personal names now known, the supposed "Ummanu" is unknown.   And if *ummanu* "artisan" were the name in question, why did not the Hebrew scribes, if the Babylonists are right, use the corresponding Hebrew word *'ommān*, "artificer,"[26] or the very common *khārāsh* or *khoresh*, or even *'ammāl*, "artificer," to represent the word, instead of using Cain or Kenan, which is not found in Hebrew with that meaning; although to be sure there is an Aramaic word *kainaya*[27] and Arabic *kainu* meaning "smith."   And we should also ask, if the J. writer reproduced *ummanu* "artisan," by the name Cain, why did he frame the mother's expressed joy, at his birth, so as to explain etymologically the name of the child as if it was from the root *qanah* "to beget" (Genesis 4:1)?   Again, let us note that although there are men bearing the name "Smith" at the present time who are farmers and carpenters, we would hardly expect to find this same J. writer representing the first "Smith" who ever lived as a "tiller of the ground," and as a "builder" (see Genesis 4:2, 17).   It must be conceded that if the Babylonists are right, the J. writer has certainly produced a strange mixture of ideas in what he is supposed to have written about Cain.   I propose that *'Ammenōn* is *'Ammen-Anu* (probably Ammi-Anu).   It is to be noted that the Hebrew *Amīnōn* is somewhat similar.

[26] Torrey has suggested that *ummānu* and *'ommān* are borrowings from the Aramaic (*AJSL* 33, 53).

[27] It is used in this sense in the O. T. Targumim, see Kohut, ʻ*Arukh*, VII, 89a; see also Jastrow *Talmudic Dic.* p. 1363.

5. Megalaros (Μεγαλαρος, Μεγαλανος, *Amegalarus*). This is considered to be a corruption of a supposed *Amelalarus*, or *Megalalos*, which was reproduced in the Hebrew *Mahalal-el*[28] (thus Hommel and Sayce). Barton thinks that this name may go back to the Sumerian *Enmeirgan* or *Meskingashir*, who were also kings of Kish.

The first element of the name *megal* may mean "offshoot, branch;" compare the Hebrew *maqqēl*.[29] Elements with similar meanings are common. Megalaros is very probably Amorite, meaning "Offshot of Uru." Here also we have a variant name, Megalanos, which it seems to me is to be read *Megal-Anu*.

6. Daōnos, Daōs (Δαωνος, Δαως, *Da(v)onus*, "the shepherd"). Hommel, Sayce and Jeremias regard this as equivalent to the Biblical Jared. Langdon previously assumed a confusion of letters and made Daōs = Re'u. His later view, as given above, makes . . . . . *lù-an-na* = Laōnus = Daōnus. King transposed the initial vowel and offered the equation: Daōnos, "the shepherd" = Etana, "the shepherd." Etana was another king of the postdiluvian Kish dynasty. I do not think the above efforts need any comment.

It seems to me, in view of the above names with Anu, that Daōnos, and especially *Da(v)onus*, might well be *Dan-Anu*. *Dan* as an element in names is very common; compare *Dan-ili* (or *El*).

7. Euedōrakhos, Euedōreskhos (Ευεδωραχος, Ευεδωρεσκος, *Edoranchus*, *Edoreschus*). This name has been regarded as identical with the mythological sage, *En-me-dur-an-ki*, king of Sippar, by Zimmern, Hommel, Sayce, Jeremias, Ungnad, Langdon, and King. This king is generally regarded as the original of the Biblical Enoch (see *infra*). The identification with something like *En-me-dur-an-ki* seems reasonable, especially in view of the eighth name of

---

[28] It seems that Mahalal-El may be represented by Megalaros, and probably also . . . . . . -*en-lù-An-na*.

[29] I am indebted to Professor Torrey for this suggested comparison.

the Ashmolean tablet, *En-me-dur-an-na*. Zimmern, who originally made the identification, said that the name *Enmeduranki* was pronounced *Evvedoranki*.[30] *Evved*, or *Eved* of course, suggests the Hebrew *'Ebhed*, so commonly found in names. All the other names in the Berossus list are very probably Semitic, and it seems that this is the same. The Greek digamma having been lost at this time, I have, therefore, proposed that *Eued* represents the Hebrew *'Eved* "servant"; and that the name be tentatively read, *'Eved-Or akh* (see *infra*).

8. 'Amempsinos ('Αμεμψινος, *Amemphsinus*). This name has been generally regarded to be a corruption of *Amêl-Sin*. Hommel and Sayce translate it into *Mutu-sha-Arkhi*, "man of the moongod," or into *Metu-sa-el*, "man of the God."[31] The identification with *Amêl-Sin* seems possible; but not .... *sib-zi-an-na*, in the Ashmolean tablet.[32] It seems to me *sib* following the fifth name of the Ashmolean tablet, namely, ...-*zi-sib* is probably not to be read "shepherd," but is part of the name, and that in some way it may represent the name 'Amempsinos. Moreover, I cannot follow the efforts made to find it reproduced in the Biblical list of patriarchs.

9. 'Ardatās, 'Otiartās ('Αρδατης, 'Ωτιαρτης, *Otiartes*). Most of the scholars have proposed to change the name Otiartēs to Opartēs, in order to make it equivalent to *Ubar-Tu-Tu*, who is called the father of Atra-khasis in the Gilgamesh story of the deluge, and where he is said to be from the city Shuruppak. Since the reading of the ideogram *Tu-Tu*, in the above name, is not known, and for other reasons, I prefer to hold this identification in abeyance. Alexander Polyhistor, who has given us the best reproduction of the Berossus deluge story, hands the ninth name down as

[30] See *KAT*[3] p. 532.
[31] Sayce, *Proc. Soc. Bibl. Arch.* 1915 p. 10.
[32] See Langdon, *Jour. Royal As. Soc.*, 1923, 251.

'Ardatās. Langdon's recent identification of 'Ardatās with the conjectural reading *Arad-gin* (*Aradda* or *Araddagin*), I cannot follow. 'Ardatās reproduces perfectly the name of a city Ardata, situated along the coast of the Mediterranean. This name in the Amarna letters, is written *Ar-da-ta*, *Ar-da-at*, and once *El-da-ta*, showing that *Ar* very probably represents the name of a deity. Since the well-known name Arwad, in the Amarna letters, is written *Ur(Uru)-wada* (104:42), and also *Ar-wada* (101:13, etc.), as well as for other reasons, *Ar*, perhaps, originally *'wr*, seems to be a pronunciation of the deity's name, Ur. We need only recall here that the ancient Babylonian scribe has given us the reading *Ari* as an equivalent to *Amurri* (or *Uri*). Moreover, it seems reasonable to propose that the name 'Ardatēs in Berossus' list, is a personal name identical with the name of the city Ar-data. The element *data* in personal names of the early period, is also known.[32a] It is even found in the name of Annādōtos, mentioned by Berossus as living in the same era.

10. Xisuthros (Ξισουθρος, Σισουθρος, Σισιθρος, *Xisuthrus*). This name is generally regarded as transposing the elements of the name Atra-khasis, *i. e.*, Khasis-Atra, the deluge hero, which is also Amorite (see Chapter VI).

Other proposed identifications of the names of the Biblical antediluvian patriarchs are: 'Irad is surely a Sumerian or Babylonian word for some craft, which J. distorted into Yared "descent" (Langdon). Jared, meaning "descendant," may be from Dumuzi [Tammuz, a king of Erech], meaning "son of life" (Barton). In the name Lamech is seen "the Babylonian Ramku, 'the Priest'" (Sayce). The Sumerian *an-shu* "to heaven" may also be read *an-ku* which if mistaken for a proper name, would in Hebrew give Enoch (Barton). These identifications can speak for themselves.

[32a] Cf. *Dati-Enlil*, *Dati* (Dhorme, *Beiträge zur Assyriologie* VI 3 p. 78).

Following is a table of the identifications made by scholars of the names in the Berossus list:

1 'Alōros = *Aruru* (a goddess), *Lal-ur* (a part of *Lal-ur-alim-ma*), and ......-*alim*.
2 'Alaparos = *Adapa* (= Adam), and [*A*]*lalgar*.
3 'Amillaros, Amelōn = *Amêlu* (= Enosh), and *En-me-nun-na*.
4 'Ammenōn = *ummânu* (= Cain), *Pilikam*, and *En-me-nun-na*.
5 Megalaros, Megalanos = *Amêl-Aruru* and *Mahalal-el*.
6 Daōnos, Daōs = *Etana, Laōnus* from *lù-an-na* (of ..... *en-lù-an-na*).
7 Euedōrakhos = *En-me-dur-an-ki* (= Enoch).
8 'Amempsinos = *Amêl-Sin, Mutu-sha-Arakhi*, and ....-*sib-zi-an-na*.
9 'Otiartās = *Ubar-Tutu*. '*Ardatās = Arad-gin*.
10 Xisuthros = *Khasis-atra = Atra-khasis*.

My own identifications of these names follow:

1 'Alōros = *El-Ur*.
2 'Alaparos = *Alap-Ur*.
3 'Amillaros = *Amêl-Ur*. 'Amelōn = *Amêl-An*.
4 'Ammenōn = *Ammen-An* (or perhaps (*Ammi-An*).
5 Megalaros = *Megal-Ur*. Megalanos = *Megal-An*.
6 Daōnos, Da(v)onos = probably *Dan-An*.
7 Euedōrakhos = probably *Eved-Ur akh* "the brother."
8 'Amempsinos = (?).
9 'Ardatās = *Ar-data*. 'Otiartās = (?).
10 Xisuthros = *Khasis-Atra = Atra-khasis*.

On examination it will be observed that in the identifications proposed by others in every instance there is either the omission of the god's name, or one or all of the consonants have been changed; and that in my own identifications, all the elements are accounted for, and not a single consonant has been changed.

I am convinced that, in declining to follow the efforts of others to show that the Biblical names are borrowed from these lists, and in refusing to accept the conclusion that these identifications "make it clear that the Biblical list and the Babylonian are fundamentally identical," without appealing to the argument concerning the migrations of peoples and traditions, as discussed in Chapter II, I shall be in a large company; for it surely must be apparent to every unprejudiced student that it requires a very big stretch of the imagination to believe that Israel accepted as a list of its progenitors such a concoction made up from these as well as the other sources referred to. And further, it must be conceded as unfortunate that a statement like the following has gone broadcast everywhere: "The ten Babylonian kings who reigned before the flood have also been accepted in the Bible as the ten antediluvian patriarchs, and the agreement is perfect in all details."[33] Let us refer here also to an identification mentioned above, that has been made upon other grounds.

In the library of Ashurbanipal there was found a legend which had apparently been copied from a tablet that had come from Sippar, which relates how Shamash and Adad, the gods of divination, called a seer *En-me-dur-an-ki* to their assembly, and gave him the tablets of the gods whereby he could divine the mysteries of heaven and earth through the pouring of oil on water and with the cedar staff. This individual, as we have seen above, is regarded as the origin of the Biblical Enoch.

In the Old Testament the only light we have concerning Enoch, besides the fact that his father "built a city, and called the name of the city after the name of his own son, Enoch," is that he lived three hundred and sixty-five years and walked with God, and "he was not, for God took him."[34] From the apocryphal apocalyptic literature, however, of the later Jewish period, we get the impression that there was a wide circle of legends concerning Enoch. We are told that through visions he had gained much knowledge of what was going on in heaven and earth, whereby he was able to foretell the future. In the words of Jude, who apparently quoted

[33] Delitzsch, *Babel and Bible* p. 41.
[34] Genesis 4:17 and 5:23 f.

this literature, Enoch prophesied, "behold the Lord coming with ten thousand of his saints to execute judgment" (verses 14–16).

Zimmern, followed by nearly all Babylonists, would have us believe that the Old Testament character Enoch, as well as the legends which prevailed in the West, had their origin in this "mythological king of Sippar, *Enmeduranki*," who, they say, was "the father of Babylonian divination."[35]   Let us here inquire what proofs have been offered for this identification.

Assuming that Euedōrakhos in Berossus' list is the same as *Enmeduranki*, three arguments have been offered for the theory that he was Hebraized into Enoch:

1. Both Enoch and *Enmeduranki* were seers, who in the later period were recognized as having been in communion with their deities, and were able to reveal the mysteries of heaven and earth.

2. Euedōrakhos was the seventh in Berossus' list, while Enoch, although third or fifth in the J. list, was seventh in the P. list.

3. *Enmeduranki* being in the service of the sun-god Shamash, to Enoch were attributed three hundred and sixty-five as the years of his life, which is the number of days in the solar year.

If Enoch and Enmeduranki were the same, the second point, namely that both are the seventh in the list would naturally show an interesting coincidence, at least with one of the Biblical lists, but the corresponding name in the Ashmolean tablet is eighth in the list.

The third point, which has no support from the cuneiform text, for nothing is said concerning the number of years the seer lived, could just as well be said of any one of the myriads of devotees, not only of Shamash, but of all the many other sun-gods.   Moreover in both the Berossus and the Ashmolean lists, Euedōrakhos lived as long as the longest-lived of the kings.   A discussion of the remaining argument that both were seers, follows.

[35] See Zimmern, *Ibidem* pp. 540 f; Jeremias, *Ibidem* p. 119; Driver, *Ibidem* p. 78; etc.

In the Babylonian text we know of many of whom it is said they were sons of deity, to whom the secrets of the gods were revealed, and who interpreted the will of the deities. Thousands of seers, doubtless, in Babylonian history claimed to be able to divine the will of the gods. In the Old and New Testaments, as well as in the apocryphal literature, we also learn of seers, of whom it is said, that, through visions or otherwise, they knew the mysteries of heaven and earth and the will of God, whereby they were enabled to prophesy for the people.

There was, however, a great difference in the methods pursued, at least in Biblical times, through which the will of the deity was revealed. In Babylonia, the seers observed the markings of a liver of an animal, or the positions of the stars of the heavens, or the effect produced by the pouring of water upon oil, as well as many other methods whereby they ascertained the will of the gods. There are indications that their libraries were filled with omen tablets and texts containing magical formulae. While we know that the Hittites, Etruscans, and even the Greeks also practiced divination, it especially flourished in Babylonia. Ezekiel tells us that Nebuchadnezzar, "king of Babylon, stood at the parting of the way, at the head of the two ways, to use divination: he shook the arrows to and fro, he consulted the *teraphim*; he looked in the liver" (21:21). In the late period, the magician, enchanter, sorcerer, and Chaldean, as is well known, were important factors in the life of Babylonia.

In the wide range of history and custom, as represented by the literature of the Old Testament, we have considerable diversity of law, teaching, and practice. We find that the services of the diviner Balaam were used; that dreams were interpreted; that the *teraphim*, the rod, and the lot, were consulted; nevertheless, we know that the religion of Yahweh was fundamentally opposed to divination. This is summed up in Deuteronomy: "there shall not be found with thee anyone that maketh his son or his daughter to pass through the fire, one that useth divination, one that practiceth augury, or an enchanter, or a sorcerer, or a charmer, or a consulter with a familiar spirit, or a wizard, or a necromancer" (18:10 f). Situated as Israel was, the efforts to make the religion imageless and free from divination, were naturally never fully realized, in spite of the work of the prophets and the reformers. Nevertheless, the law and the prophets in spirit and in practice were against such.

In the light of what we know concerning Israel and divination, we are now asked to believe that the J. writer, and later the P. writer during the exile, having become acquainted with this *Enmeduranki*, king of Sippar, the supposed "mythological father of divination," whose name appeared as Euedōrakhos, the seventh antediluvian Chaldean king of Babylon, and that, in spite of the fact that divination by astrology, by hepatoscopy, by oil, etc., were so antagonistic to the Hebrew religion, these Jewish writers in the palmy days of Israel created the character Enoch, by Hebraizing this *Enmeduranki*; and the Jews accepted this fraud. This, in the light of research and our knowledge of Hebrew civilization, as well as what is written above, certainly is not plausible.

Sumerists say that *En-me-dur-an-ki* is Sumerian. If that were true, it should be translated "lord of the decree of the connecting-link of heaven and earth." This would not be a name, but a title. And if that were true, is it not strange that the gods of divination in whose service he was, should be the West Semitic Adad and Shamash? The identification with Euedōrakhos of Berossus seems reasonable, and especially in view of the eighth name of the Ashmolean tablet, written *En-me-dur-an-na*, the last sign of which, namely *na*, as Langdon has correctly said, should be *ki*, and especially since *na* and *ki* are quite similar in this period. As Zimmern, who originally made the identification, said, *Enmeduranki* was pronounced *Evvedoranki* or *Evedoranki;*[36] and since *Eved* represents perfectly the Hebrew '*Ebhed* or '*Eved*, so commonly found in names, and Eued of the Greek *Euedōrakhos*, in the absence of the digamma, also represents the same pronunciation, I have proposed, as already mentioned, that the name be read Eved-Urakh. This finds corroboration in the following.

In the P. list, the eighth name is written Methushelakh, which in the J. list is written Methusha'el or *Methu-sha-El* "Man of El." In other words, Elakh takes the place of El, and it parallels the Urakh of Euedōrakhos, instead of the usual Ur. If we separate the *akh* from both, we will have in the one case *Methu-sh‘-El akh*, which leaves the name the same as *Methu-sha-El;* and in the other *Eved-Ur akh*, which would be similar to five other names in the list, namely those compounded with Ur. A possible explanation of *akh* "brother" that is of the one who preceded, follows.

In the P. list, or the "book of the generations of Adam," the one thing in the entire chapter besides monotonous details of names and numbers, is the reference to Enoch having been taken by God. The years of his life are less than half of the shortest-lived of the other patriarchs. Probably in the original tradition, Methu-sha-El was not the son of Enoch, who was translated, but a "brother" who replaced him. In the Berossus list the only title added to any of the names is "shepherd," to Daōnos. Both Enoch and Daōnos immediately precede *Methu-sh‘-El akh* and *Eved-Ur akh*. What seems to substantiate this is found in the following.

The seventh of the Ashmolean list, which is unfortunately injured, appears thus: . . . .*sib-zi-an-na*. There is sufficient room for the name before these words, so that they probably are an epithet. They can be translated, "true shepherd of heaven," and also "true shepherd of Anu," or "El." But *zi* can also be translated "to lift up, to take up,"[37] and in view of the Biblical tradition which tells us that Enoch, the corresponding person in the list, was taken by God, it seems to me that this epithet can very properly be translated "the shepherd who was taken to heaven," or "who was taken by El (God)." As stated, both this king and Enoch stand seventh in the list, thus:

BIBLICAL

7 Enoch, "God took him"
8 Methu-sh^e-El, "brother"

ASHMOLEAN

7 ...., "the shepherd whom El took"
8 Eved-Ur *an-na* (or *an-ki* for *akh* "brother")

BEROSSUS

6 Da(v)onos, "shepherd"
7 Eved-Ur, "brother"

An-na, as already mentioned, is very probably a mistake for *an-ki* representing *akh* "brother." If this explanation of the epithet should prove correct, it will be the first connection that has been shown to exist between the so-called Chaldean lists and the Biblical, except that there are ten names ending with the hero of the deluge.

The fact that there are ten names, ending with the deluge-hero in the three lists, besides this probable explanation of the epithet, makes it reasonably certain that there is a common origin for the tradition, in spite of the fact that the Biblical lists give the "generations" of the first man created, and in the two Babylonian sources there is no thought of referring to primaevals or even aboriginals, but to ruling dynasties; in the case of Berossus to those of Babylon, Pantibiblos, and Larak; and in the other, which is written in

---

[37] See *sag-zi* = *rêsha nashû, shaqû sha rêshi*, etc., Delitzsch, *Sumerische Glossar* p. 224. In addition to *zi* meaning *nashû* "to lift up," it is thought to have the value also "to take," see Meissner *SAI* 1326. This is the same word used in the parallel passage in Genesis.

Sumerian, to Khabur, Larsa, Dur-Tibiri, Larak, Sippar, and Su-kur-ru(Lam). The lone city referred to in the Biblical lists was built by Cain, and called Enoch.

There is absolutely nothing in any of the lists to show that the Biblical were derived from the so-called Chaldean or Sumerian lists, in spite of all that has been written on the subject. And it must be admitted that the reverse is also true. It seems to me, however, in view of all that has been said in these lectures on migrations of peoples and their traditions, that we can only decide that the common source of the legend was in Amurru. As we have seen there are two versions in the Old Testament. In the list said to have been handed down by Berossus, there are marks also of two distinct versions, which show that one probably had received a local coloring at the Amorite city Mari, where Uru was worshipped; and that the other came from the Amorite Khana or 'Ana, where the god Anu was worshipped. In this way we can account for the names with variant deities, like Amêl-Ur and Amêl-Anu; Megal-Ur and Megal-Anu, as well as such variations as 'Ardatās and Otiartās, etc. The Ashmolean, it seems to me, is another version of this Amorite tradition, which was written in Southern Babylonia, where in the early period the Sumerian language was used in practically all the cities.

VII

THE DELUGE STORY

Ever since George Smith of the British Museum, in 1875, published the well-known story of the deluge, as found in the Gilgamesh epic, which had been discovered in the library of Ashurbanipal at Nineveh, most Assyriologists have held that this epic furnished Israel with its story. And following the discovery of a version, written close to 2000 B. C., Biblical scholars everywhere seem to have been convinced that "the Hebrew narrative must be derived from the Babylonian." Moreover, the clearest proof for the claim that Israel borrowed much of its religion and culture from Babylonia, it is asserted, is to be found in the deluge story or stories as handed down by the people of that land.

It is needless here to review the resemblances and the differences of the Biblical and the Gilgamesh stories of the deluge, for this has been done many times. Suffice it to say that there must be a common origin as shown by such details, as are found in both the Biblical and the Babylonian, as the divine decision to send the flood, the advice to construct an ark or ship, the use of asphalt to make it water-tight, the destruction of mankind, except the hero and those with him, the grounding of the ship on the mountain, the sending forth of birds, the smelling of the sweet savor; etc. These and other details of the two stories leave no doubt as to their being related. The version of the deluge in the Gilgamesh Epic, was written in the seventh century B. C.[1]

The early version, referred to above, is preserved, in the Pierpont Morgan Library Collection, in a fragment of a large tablet which

[1] For the translation and transliteration of all the deluge versions, see Appendix to Clay, *A Hebrew Deluge Story in Cuneiform.*

had been inscribed on the 28th day of Shebet, in the 11th year of Ammi-zaduga; which, according to our present understanding, was about 1966 B. C. This version, antedating Moses by several centuries, has given the Babylonists one of the two chief arguments advanced for the claim that the narrative was borrowed by Israel.

A recent study of this early version shows that it not only refers to the deluge, but to a dire famine which preceded; and what is very important, that it is an early version of a well-known inscription from Nineveh, written thirteen centuries later, known as the Ea and Atra-khasis legend. The latter, however, only referred to the famine. The early recension of the famine and deluge is of the greatest importance in this connection, in that many Amorite words of the original version are still to be recognized in it.

Besides these versions of the deluge story, others have been found. In the British Museum there is a fragment of one written also about the time of Ashurbanipal. It furnishes us with the conversation of the god Ea with the hero Atra-khasis concerning the construction of the ship, and with what it should be loaded. There is also a small fragment in the Museum of the University of Pennsylvania of thirteen partially preserved lines, written probably in the Cassite period, about 1400 B. C. To these must be added the version written in Greek, as handed down by Berossus, who lived about 250 B. C., in which the hero's name is given as Xisuthros, representing the transposition of the elements of the name, Atra-khasis.

A few years ago Professor Poebel, now of the University of Rostock, published a Sumerian version of the flood which had been found at Nippur. It is an epitomized story of the deluge, which Poebel holds was written some time between 2300 and 1300 B. C. This version has several points in common with the Gilgamesh story. The phrase, "when for seven days and seven nights the storm-flood overwhelmed the land," is paralleled in the Gilgamesh story by the phrase, "six days and nights the wind drives, the flood-tempest overwhelms the land; when the seventh day arrives the flood-tempest subsides in the onslaught." Both versions also refer to "the wall," when the hero was apprised of the impending deluge. The title which Atra-khasis received from the gods, namely, Um-napishtim-rûqu, meaning, "the day of life is extended," is reproduced in the Sumerian version, as Zi-û(d)-suddu, which means the same (see *infra*). These two versions have other details in common, as the opening of the hatch, the offering of a sacrifice, etc. It is perfectly clear, however, as others have pointed out, that the Sumerian story is only an epitomized narrative, for not a few details found in the other versions are wanting in it.

There are also striking differences between the Sumerian and the Gilgamesh versions, among which is the place where the hero lived after his apotheosis. In the Sumerian version he was caused to dwell in the land or mountain, which some scholars have called Dilmun; though the reading of the name is by no means certain. If it should prove correct that Dilmun is referred to, the version then very probably places the hero, after he received the gift of immortality, on an island to the south, outside of Babylonia.

In the Gilgamesh story, the hero was caused to dwell at the mouth of rivers; but in going there Gilgamesh traversed seas, and crossed over mountains to a place where a cedar tree was being felled, and where he was advised to cut a hundred and twenty trees in the forest to construct a boat. There can be little doubt from these and other facts mentioned in the story that the Gilgamesh Epic places "the waters of death" beyond the Mediterranean shore. This fact, it must be admitted, peculiarly identifies the legend with the West. If the mountain in the Sumerian version is Dilmun, and this, as is held, was on an island to the south of Babylonia, doubtless we have in this a coloring which is due to other influences.

The story of the Sumerian recension of the deluge is interrupted at the beginning of column six by an incantation formula, after which the story is continued. Whether other incantation formulae were found in the missing portions, of course, cannot be determined. This reminds us of the use to which the sorcerer put other myths and legends.

This is the only Sumerian version or story of the flood that is at present known. Professor Langdon has claimed to have another, which he published under the title "Sumerian Epic of Paradise, the Flood and the Fall of Man." As far as I can ascertain all scholars agree that it has nothing whatsoever to do with the deluge. In his original publication the crucial line bearing on the supposed deluge was not translated. In his French translation of the work,[2] he read it: "O Ninkharsag, I will destroy the fields with a deluge." Prince translated this: "The fields of Ninkharsag I will inundate"; but Witzel, followed by Mercer, translates: "Ninkharsag was made pregnant."[3] There can be no question but that the context fully bears out the last mentioned. In short, there can be no doubt, as stated above, that the poem has nothing to do with the deluge.

As is generally recognized, the Old Testament contains two different and originally independent accounts of the deluge which are combined into one, but which scholars feel, as in the case of the creation stories, can be definitely separated into what have been called the Jehovist and the Priestly versions. As already stated, most scholars hold that the former was written in the ninth or eighth century, and the latter in the fifth; others, however, hold that both stories are more ancient, which view, it seems to me, is very probably correct.

As has already been noted, the versions found in Babylonia have much in common with the Hebrew stories. This fact has given rise

---

[2] Langdon, *Poème Sumérien du Paradis, du Déluge et de la Chute de l'Homme.*
[3] See Mercer, *Jour. of the Soc. of Biblical Research* IV 51 ff.

to the conclusion, which has been many times restated, that either the Biblical stories are derived from the Babylonian, or the Babylonian is derived from the Biblical, or that they have a common origin.

Assyriologists, as far as I know, have generally dismissed as an impossibility the idea that there was a common Semitic tradition, which developed in Israel in one way, and in Babylonia in another. They have unreservedly declared that the Biblical stories have been borrowed from Babylonia, in which land they were indigenous. To me it has always seemed perfectly reasonable that both stories had a common origin among the Semites, some of whom entered Babylonia, while others carried their traditions into Palestine. The unanimous decision of Assyriologists, however, seemed difficult to cope with; nevertheless, this was attempted in *Amurru the Home of the Northern Semites*, with results which have already been mentioned. Now, after years of additional study, I feel that this can be done much more effectively.

In demonstrating that the views of the Babylonists are no longer tenable, let me present what I have to say under the four heads which have been outlined in the Chapter II.

The first of these four arguments has already been fully discussed, namely, that while no migrations from Babylonia into Amurru are known to have taken place, when such traditions would have been carried there, and that while there is no proof that Babylonian religious ideas were transplanted to Amurru, we have a mass of evidence to prove that in many periods Amorites not only poured into alluvial Babylonia, but carried with them their religion. This argument, which is fully discussed in Chapter II, the writer feels is most cogent in showing not only the futility of the Babylonist assertions, but that the origin of such legends, which both peoples had in common, was to be found in Amurru.

The second proof of my contention that these stories are not of Babylonian origin, but are Amorite, is based on a study of the forces of nature responsible for the deluge. As is well known, the more effective of the two chief arguments that have been advanced for the Babylonian origin of these stories,[4] is that they are either based upon nature myths, due to the climate, or upon recollections of an actual extraordinary inundation of Southern Babylonia, where the story was originated, and whence in time it was carried to Palestine. As the late Canon Driver, in quoting Professor Zimmern, puts it: "The very essence of the Biblical narrative presupposes a country liable, like Babylonia, to inundations; so that it cannot be doubted that the story was indigenous in Babylonia and transplanted to Palestine."[5] Or, as Sir William Frazer, in quoting the late Professor Jastrow says: the basis for the Biblical story "is the yearly phenomenon of the rain and stormy season which lasts in Babylonia several months and during which time whole districts in the Euphrates valley are submerged."[6]

The second quotation, which represents the view of many, we can peremptorily dismiss as a complete misunderstanding, as I have already shown, of the climatic conditions of Babylonia (see pp. 75 f.). A similar result awaits the first-mentioned quotation and argument.

Before discussing the force which caused the deluge as given in the narratives, let me refer again to the rains of Babylonia, and say a word with reference to the inundations as caused by the rise of the rivers.

The history of this land is the history of the two rivers. Without them, it would not have been inhabited by man. Permanent settlements were possible in this alluvial plain only after the two rivers were harnessed by the building of embankments and canals in order to direct the flood water into escapes, to be distributed later over

---

[4] The second argument, based on the antiquity of the Babylonian as against the Hebrew version, is discussed below.

[5] *The Book of Genesis* p. 107.

[6] *Folk-lore in the Old Testament* I p. 353.

areas to be irrigated.   In spite of heroic efforts and constant attention, the floods frequently played havoc.   The rise of the Tigris at
Baghdad is usually about sixteen feet, but occasionally an additional rise of about five feet causes trouble.   The danger of destructive inundations has always hung over the inhabitants of the plain.
The floods in Babylonia are mainly due to the rapid melting of
the snows in Armenia, and in the Kurdish mountains.   For further
information on the annual inundations, see Chapter III.   It must
be conceded that the people living in that land could appreciate
flood stories as well as any people known, because of the annual
rise of the rivers.   Of course this could be said nearly as well of
Egypt, which strange to say, among ancient peoples is a notable
exception in that it did not have a flood story.

We have already inquired into the rôle played by rains in Babylonia.   We have seen that while the rivers furnished the land with
its "life blood," rain had relatively little value.   We have seen that
the records kept by the German scientists show an average fall of
7 centimeters, or 2.80 inches, for the year, and those by the English,
4.98 inches.   We have further seen that the rains of Babylonia are
in character equivalent to New England summer showers, and that
the country, because of the scarcity of rain, could almost be classed
with desert lands.   While it would seem, as admitted, that Babylonia because of inundations was excellent soil for deluge stories,
certainly the force which caused the deluge could not have been
rain.   Let us now examine all the stories or versions that have been
preserved in Babylonia, and ascertain what force is mentioned in
them which brought about the deluge.

In the Gilgamesh story, Atra-khasis is told to say to the people,
in explanation as to why he was building the ship, beginning with
line 39:[7]

---

[7] See *A Hebrew Deluge Story* 74 f.

I know that Enlil hates me, and
I may not dwell in your city;
Nor on the soil of Enlil set my face.
I will go down to the ocean; with [Ea] my lord, I will dwell.
[Upon] you will he then rain abundance.

When the god ordered him to enter the ship, the hero was told:

The *muir kukki* at even will send a heavy rain.
Enter the ship and close the door.
That time arrived.
The *muir kukki* at even sent a heavy rain.

In his description of what happened, the hero informs us:

Of the storm, I observed its appearance,
To behold the storm, I dreaded.
I entered the ship and closed the door.
To the master of the ship, to Buzur-Amurru, the sailor,
I entrusted the great house, including its possessions.
On the appearance of the break of dawn,
There rises from the foundation of the heavens a black cloud.
Adad thunders in the midst of it.
Nebo and Sharru go before.
They go as messengers over mountain and land.
Urra-gal tears out the mast(?).
En-Urta proceeds; he advances the onset.
The Anunnaki raise the torches.
With their flashes they illuminate the land.

One day, the sto[rm . . . .
Quickly it overwhelms, and [covers] the mountains.

Six days and six nights
The wind tears and the flood-tempest overwhelms the land.
When the seventh day arrives, the flood-tempest subsides in its
    onslaught,
Which had fought like an army.

Does this sound like a description of an inundation caused by the
rise of the rivers of Babylonia?   And since we know that rain

played such an insignificant rôle in the Babylonian climate, is this flood story, caused by a mighty rain, due to Babylonian coloring? Surely, it must be admitted there is nothing found in this description of the force which caused the deluge to support the contentions of the Babylonists. And is it not strange that in this very level land the mountains should figure so prominently? And will the Babylonist and the Sumerist tell us whether this fact is also due to Babylonian coloring? Moreover, we have seen that the gods, Adad, Nebo, Sharru, Urra-gal, and En-Urta, who brought on the deluge, are all Amorite (see also below). But let us return to our study of the force which caused the deluge.

The small Babylonian and Assyrian fragments and the Berossus story, do not mention the cause of the deluge; but the ancient version found in the Pierpont Morgan Library Collection does. In the part referring to the deluge, which is unfortunately very fragmentary, the following passage occurs:[8]

> On the morrow let him cause it to rain a torrent.
> Let him in the night ....
> Let him cause it to rain a tempest.
> Let it come upon the field like a thief. Let ....

Where is any reference to the inundating rivers? Here again the cause of the deluge is clearly and definitely stated to be rain.

In the Sumerian version the flood was likewise caused by mighty storms. Beginning with Column V, it reads:[9]

> All the mighty windstorms together blew
> The storm-flood (amaru) .... raged,
> When for seven days, for seven nights,
> The storm-flood (amaru) overwhelmed the land.

Professor Poebel rightly considered that the Sumerian word amaru means "rainstorm, rain flood, cloud burst"; and that here

---

[8] See *A Hebrew Deluge Story* p. 60.
[9] See *ibidem* 70 f.

the two forces which caused the deluge are the same as those given in the Gilgamesh story, namely, *sharu* "wind," and *mekhû abûbu* "destructive rainstorm."[10]

The late Professor King, appreciating the difficulties involved by admitting this, argued that the Sumerian word *amaru* was equivalent to the Babylonian *abûbu* "deluge," more accurately "flood"; and that while "it is true that the tempests of the Sumerian version probably imply rain," he said, "in itself the term *abûbu* implies flood which could take place through a rise of the river unaccompanied by heavy local rain."[11]

True, a rise of the rivers could do this; but all the stories, including this Sumerian epitome, say that the deluge was caused by a storm. The view that *amaru* means "rainstorm, storm-flood, cyclone, whirlwind," is fully supported by many inscriptions, including those of Gudea, which belong to the classical Sumerian period.[12] Moreover, *abûbu*, the Semitic equivalent of *amaru*, means "whirlwind, tornado, cyclone";[13] even in the Gilgamesh story it also means "the storm" (see line 132). In the Code of Hammurabi, it means "hurricane." In other words, *abûbu* only in a special sense referred to "the deluge."

As a matter of fact, if this short Sumerian epitome had said the deluge was caused by the flooding of the rivers, it would only show that the scribe, who made it, had given the Amorite narrative a true Babylonian coloring; while later scribes either copied other versions just as they were, or they stupidly changed the cause of the deluge and gave the stories a coloring which belonged elsewhere. But, as already stated, the Sumerian version agrees with all the other versions in also making *rain* the force that caused the deluge.

---

[10] Poebel, *Historical Texts* p. 54.
[11] *Schweich Lectures* 1916, p. 70, note 2.
[12] See Delitzsch, *Sumerisches Glossar* p. 12.
[13] See Muss-Arnolt, *Assyrian Dictionary* p. 5.

The Babylonian word for the "river-flood," the "high tide of water," is *mêlu*. The word occurs in the famine story, but it is not found in any of the narratives of the deluge. Is it not remarkable, therefore, that in this so-called nature-myth which had its origin, it is declared, in the flooding of the rivers, the word for "river-flood" (*mêlu*) is not found?

Let us inquire also as to the cause given for the deluge in Berossus' story. It reads: "To him (Sisithrus) the deity Kronos foretold that on the fifteenth day of the month Desius there would be a deluge of rain."[14] Besides the hero's name, which is supplied from the preceding phrase, there are three nuts in this short passage for the Babylonists and Sumerists to crack, namely, the reference to the god Kronos who was Il or El, the name of the month, and the force that caused the deluge. Certainly they are not Babylonian.

Having ascertained that all the stories which have come from Babylonia which mention the force that caused the deluge, say it was rain, and that they make no kind of reference to the overflowing of the rivers, let us now inquire what the stories from Syria, or ancient Amurru, give as the forces. In the so-called Jehovist version we read:

> For after seven days I will cause it to rain on the earth forty days and forty nights. (Gen. 7:4).
> And the rain fell upon the earth forty days and forty nights. (Gen. 7:12).

In this version, the cause of the deluge is rain alone. In the so-called Priestly story, the forces are described as follows:

> On this self-same day were all the fountains of the great deep broken up, and the windows of heaven were opened. (Gen. 7:11).
> And the fountains of the deep and the windows of heaven were stopped. (Gen. 8:2).

[14] See Cory, *Ancient Fragments* p. 33.

In other words, the Priestly version, besides the rain which poured from the heavens, speaks of subterranean waters bursting forth. When, as we have seen, the average rainfall at Beirut is 35.87 inches, and in the mountains of Lebanon it is 50 inches, we can appreciate that this is truly an Amorite coloring. And when, for example, we see the water from three springs bursting forth from the earth at the foot of Mount Hermon and creating a river, we can appreciate that this reference to subterranean waters is also true to Amorite coloring. That this has been eliminated from the story handed down by the Babylonians, is perfectly intelligible, when we know that springs do not gush from the earth in the alluvial plain.

The story handed down by Lucian in *De dea Syri*, also gives rain as the force:

> The fountains of the deep were opened and the rain descended in torrents, when the rivers swelled and the sea spread far over the land, when there was nothing but water.

This coincides with the Priestly narrative. Moreover, we ought to credit Lucian, in his efforts to explain the deluge, with having presented what at least appeared to intelligent people as a reasonable cause. In short, the narratives from Amurru give, as the forces which caused the deluge, rain from the heavens; and also the breaking up of the fountains of the deep.

As long ago as 1883, Professor Suess of Vienna, appreciating the difficulty involved, and realizing that the cause as given in the Babylonian story was insufficient to account for a deluge in Babylonia, supplemented the fall of rain by a violent earthquake and the bursting of a typhoon, in the Persian Gulf.[15] Of course, Suess could find no proof for this in the Babylonian story; so he interpreted "the foundations of the deep" of Genesis, as referring to such seismic disturbances.

[15] See Suess, *The Face of the Earth* I 24 ff.

Professor Sayce, also apparently appreciating the difficulty involved, assumed that such a convulsion of nature took place; for he says, "the whole conception takes us back to the alluvial plain of Babylonia, liable at any time to be inundated by the waters of the Persian Gulf, and is wholly inapplicable to a mountainous country like Palestine where rain only could have produced a flood."[16]

The late Professor Delitzsch, in his famous lecture "Babel and Bible," also appreciating the difficulty presented by Suess, in order to be consistent in his views, without any regard for the cause as given by the stories, also says: that after the traditions "travelled to Canaan, owing to the totally different conformation of the land in this latter country, it was forgotten that the sea had played the principal rôle."[17]

It is needless to repeat here that this of course gives a different cause for the deluge than that clearly stated in all the stories that have come down to us. Moreover, there were myriads of intelligent residents of Syria and Palestine, including the Biblical writers and Lucian, who did believe in a deluge caused by "rain" and "the fountains of the deep."

The purpose of citing here what these scholars have said in their efforts to explain the deluge is to show how it had been appreciated by them that there is a real difficulty in believing that rain could have caused a deluge in Babylonia.

We have seen that the average fall of rain is 35.87 inches in Beirut, and 50 inches in the Lebanon mountains; and that most of it comes down in the three winter months. An average fall of 50 inches would mean a fall in some years of 80 inches, or even more. Suppose that at one time there had been a fall of 100 inches in the comparatively short period of "forty days and nights," what would

[16] *Early History of the Hebrews* p. 125.
[17] *Babel and Bible* p. 40.

have been the result in certain districts of that land?   Entire towns
and villages would have been wiped out.   I have no desire to
attempt to explain how the deluge might have taken place; nor
where it took place; nor even to attempt to prove that it did take
place.   I do desire, however, to show that under exceptional conditions, a great inundation could have occurred in certain parts
of Amurru with rain as the cause.   And furthmore, it is not at all
improbable that the seat of the deluge was in the great Central
Asian basin, north of "the mountains of Ararat," between the
Black and the Caspian seas.[18]

The study, therefore, of the versions of the deluge found in Babylonia, shows conclusively that although that land, which is liable
to floods, was good soil for deluge stories, the recensions found there
do not state that the force which caused the deluge was the flooding of the rivers; but they do say it was rain, the same as the
Amorite stories.   What becomes then of the much-vaunted Babylonian coloring which has been used hundreds of times to prove
that these stories originated in Babylonia?   And recalling that the
chief argument for the Babylonian origin of the story is based on
the annual inundations caused by the rise of the rivers, how are
Babylonists and Sumerists going to explain that this is not given
as the cause of the deluge in any of the stories?   –

Before dismissing this discussion I cannot help recalling and
emphasizing that Egypt in the Nile Valley, that great alluvium,
where life also depends solely on the flooding of the rivers, is a
notable exception among ancient nations in that it did not have a
deluge story.   True, the floods are not so large, and are better
controlled than in Babylonia; but whether this was always the
case is a question.   In thinking, therefore, of the widely heralded
idea that Babylonia was such good soil for deluge stories, one

[18] A theory advanced by Mr. Reginald A. Fessenden.

cannot help asking why Egypt should be such a notable exception in not having its story.

And now let us inquire what other arguments have been advanced for the Babylonian origin of the Hebrew stories.

One writer states that three passages in the "Jehovistic" narrative "seem to imply an acquaintance with the Babylonian poem." One of these is the statement that the Lord shut the door of the ark, which "differs from the Babylonian account, according to which Xisuthros closed it himself." The second passage is concerning the sending out of birds; for he says, "it is clear that the Babylonian version is older than the Hebrew record, and the position of the raven in Genesis seems less logical than in the Babylonian." The third passage refers to the smelling of a sweet savor, which is identical in both the Biblical and the Babylonian; and "it is impossible not to believe that the language of the latter was known to the Biblical writer."[19] It seems to me that there is but one point in these statements, which were made long ago, that need be discussed at the present time, and that is due to the Babylonian version being older than the accepted date of the Hebrew story. This is discussed in what follows.

The second of the two arguments for the Babylonian origin of the Biblical deluge story which have been effective above all others, is based upon the fact that the version, now in the Pierpont Morgan Library Collection, is dated above five hundred years prior to the time of Moses. The Sumerian epitome recently published, as we have seen, also may be earlier than the time of the lawgiver. It is, therefore, not a question as to whether the Jehovist writer could have borrowed these stories from Babylon to produce his narrative in the ninth or eighth century B. C., and the Priestly in the fifth century; nor even whether Moses produced these stories for the

[19] Sayce, *The Higher Criticism and the Monuments* 118 f.

first time. The discovery of the early dated tablet answers these questions. But the question is, did Syria, which was surrounded by the advanced cultures of Asia Minor, Crete, Babylonia, and Egypt, have a civilization of its own; and if it did, then did the predecessors of Moses and the patriarchs, or in other words, the Amorites, possess or know these stories?

The burden of my entire thesis is that the land of the Amorites had such a civilization. The answer to this part of the question is found in the sum and substance of these researches. Let me, however, refer in this connection to several points not previously discussed.

While certain critics have regarded it as impossible that these stories were as early as Moses, there are others who hold, because of their primitive simplicity, and also archaic character, that Genesis includes that which belonged to a great antiquity. The discovery of the Amarna letters has shown conclusively that an advanced civilization existed in Palestine in the time of Moses; and the recently discovered inscriptions in the Sinaitic peninsula at Serabit el-Khadim, prove that alphabetic writing was known to the Semites before the time of Moses.[20] There are also other recent discoveries including those made in connection with the culture of Byblos (see Chapter II), which put the whole matter now in a new light.

The Hebrews throughout their history used almost entirely a perishable writing material. This statement does not need any proof. Papyrus, skins, and potsherds were suitable materials for the Semitic alphabetic script; but plastic clay was not. A short rock inscription of a few lines, a few seals and ostraca, are nearly all the original indigenous evidence we have of the literary activity

---

[20] This is the view of Petrie, Gardiner, Cowley, Sayce, Sethe, Eisler, and Bauer. Schneider, however, takes issue with these scholars, and endeavors to show that the inscriptions belong to a later period. See *OLZ* 1921, 242 ff.

of the Hebrews. The Moabites, the Phoenicians, and the Aramaeans, also owing to climatic conditions, have likewise left us little evidence of their literary culture. While in Egypt considerable writings on papyrus have been found, in Palestine practically every trace of such has disappeared.

We know that the Hittites had their individual script, but they also used the Babylonian syllabary in writing their language, as did also the Mitanneans, the Vannic, and doubtless also many other peoples of Western Asia. There is no evidence that the Hebrews or other branches of the Western Semites used this syllabary for their language; for up to the present, not a single cuneiform tablet written in pure Hebrew or Aramaic has been found.[21] Knowing what a highly literary people the Hebrews were, had they used the Babylonian syllabary, we would unquestionably have found evidence of this use in Palestine, as well as in Babylonia, where in certain periods they lived in large numbers.

A very good explanation can be offered for this in the fact that a script requiring the mastery of twenty-two simple characters was somewhat easier to learn than a system involving hundreds of complicated cuneiform signs, nearly all of which having at the same time many values. This fact also makes it easy to understand how Aramaic in time supplanted the Babylonian as the inter-commercial language.

If the Egyptians wrote on papyrus as early as 3000 B. C., it would seem that a land whose civilization had provided Egypt with one of its prominent deities at that early date, and had sent its religion centuries before into Babylonia, also had its means of communication, as had its neighbors. What the exact character of their script was in that early period, is a question on which we have at present no light.[22]

[21] What I regard as Amorite literature in Babylonia has been Babylonized.
[22] On the script used in early Amurru, see also see *Empire of the Amorites* 61 ff.

There is another thought to which I desire to give expression in this connection. As has been said, we have not a scrap of evidence from any original source prior to the time of Christ to show that the Old Testament actually existed. Fortunately, however, we have the remains of a literature from Babylonia covering several millenniums, which illustrates for us what had taken place at the hands of redactors. We now have, for example, a portion of a version of the Gilgamesh Epic written 2000 B. C., or thirteen hundred years earlier than the redaction of it, which had been found in the Library of Ashurbanipal. The study of the two versions enables us to see what changes had taken place during these centuries. But we have another example that is even closer to the present subject.

A recent study of the Morgan Library deluge tablet, written in the eleventh year of Ammi-zaduga, about 1966 B. C., shows that it is an early version of what was written about thirteen hundred years later, namely, a redaction of a portion of it.[23] The study of the early and the late recensions, shows what has taken place during the intervening centuries. Moreover, the early dated version states that it is a copy of a still earlier document.

Naturally all this has been fully surmised by scholars, for it is exactly what should have been expected. Nevertheless, what has taken place in the handing down of literature in Babylonia, illustrates what certainly has taken place also in Syria and Palestine, where a more perishable writing material was used. And further, the illustration is helpful for those who, finding primitive thought and archaisms in Genesis, realize that in them they also have traces of very ancient documents.

In searching for other arguments for the Babylonian origin of the Biblical stories, I find the following: "The Babylonian home-

---

[23] *A Hebrew Deluge Story* 11 ff.

land of the story seems certainly to be indicated by the mention of two kinds of bitumen or pitch for caulking the vessel, Babylonia being the land of bitumen par excellence.[24]   Naturally in answer to this it need only be stated that the city Hit, whence the asphalt came, is in Amurru; and, moreover, vessels caulked with bitumen, of course, went westward from Hit on the Euphrates as well as eastward; and certainly, knowledge of its value for such purposes would have reached the sea-faring Phoenician.

It should also be stated that the late Professor King, since Professor Poebel published the Sumerian version of the deluge, maintained that the Hebrew story was directly influenced by the Sumerian.   One of his reasons was that both refer to the piety of the hero; which idea does not appear in the Gilgamesh story.[25] It seems to me that this simply shows the two stories have this thought in common.

Another and similar argument is that the Sumerian tablet contains, like the Old Testament, an account of the creation and deluge on the same tablet, while the Gilgamesh story divorces the deluge from the creation.[26]   This cannot be regarded as very weighty; for there were other "Outlines of History" written at that time, as there are at present.

Professor King also held, contrary to the position of many Babylonists that the story of the deluge is not a nature-myth, but a legend that had a basis of historical fact in Southern Babylonia. His idea is that the boat of the legend was nothing more than the *quffah*, the familiar coracle of Baghdad, which is formed of wickerwork, and coated with bitumen.   These crafts, he wrote, "are often large enough to carry five or six horses and a dozen men."

[24] Pinches, *The Old Testament in the light of the Historical Records of Babylonia and Assyria* p. 114.

[25] *Schweich Lectures*, 1916, 92 ff.

[26] *Ibidem* p. 93.

It is claimed that it was in one of these that the original hero saved himself and his property; and landed, after the waters had abated, not in a mountain, but in Southern Babylonia.[27] Naturally, this is simply a conjecture.

As further proof that the Sumerian story is the original, besides the argument already answered above, Professor King also quoted the use of the Sumerian term *mà-gur-gur* for the "great boat," which is found in the Babylonian fragment.[28] I cannot follow in this, since the script employed by the Semites in Babylonia was of Sumerian origin; and furthermore, Semitic Babylonian texts are full of such words. If this argument obtained, one could prove nearly every Semitic Babylonian inscription to be of Sumerian origin. Yet on the other hand, the use, for example, of the Babylonian *pukhru* "assembly," in the Sumerian version, instead of the Sumerian word *ukkin*, is a weighty argument against the Sumerian origin of the story. Yes, this interesting example of Semitic influence, together with other facts, speaks loudly against the view that this Sumerian epitome is indubitably the origin of the Semitic version.

The argument that a legend originated with the Sumerians because it is found in the Sumerian language, in my judgment is no more final than it would be to say that the work of Shakespeare was of German origin, because a copy of it, written in the German language, was found in Berlin. In certain cities, as for example Nippur, where the Sumerian epitome was found, practically everything in the Hammurabi period was written in Sumerian. Votive inscriptions written in Semitic, at an earlier period, were found at Nippur; but these were presented to the deity of that city by kings ruling in Semitic centres. The legends, chronological lists. hymns, prayers, contracts, letters—practically everything is written in

[27] *Ibidem* 80 ff.
[28] *Ibidem* 79 ff.

Sumerian in that period; and yet, if the nomenclature of this period is examined, it will be found that about two-thirds of the people bore names that prove to be Semitic.[29] And it is also to be noted that many of the names written in Sumerian, in these Sumerian documents, can also be read as Semitic; for example: *Lù-En-lil-la* can also be read *Amêl-Enlil;* and since the children of this individual bear Semitic names, it is probably correct to do so. This is true of many of the names written in Sumerian. There can be no other conclusion but that while the language of Nippur was Sumerian, the people were very largely Semitic. An examination of the thousands of tablets that have come from Drehem near Nippur, which were written in the III Ur dynasty (2475–2357 B. C.), also reveals an analogous situation, although every document is written in Sumerian. To maintain, therefore, that a legend is Sumerian because an inscription containing it, which was found at Nippur, was written in that language, would be equivalent to saying, if all other versions of the Talmud had been lost except an English translation preserved in the Bodleian Library, that it was of English origin.

I have in the above paragraphs given and answered all the arguments, with which I am acquainted, that have been advanced for the Babylonian origin of these narratives. Some presented years ago, doubtless, would not be offered to-day. My purpose in presenting even these, is that Biblical students may know upon what basis the theory has rested.

In 1909, when the writer, in his work called "Amurru the Home of the Northern Semites," in abandoning the prevailing theory concerning the origin of the deluge story, took the position that it had its origin in Amurru, he showed that besides many facts, proving that the Semites had carried the story into Babylonia, the

[29] See Poebel, *Babylonian Legal and Business Documents* (*BE*, VI 2).   125 ff., and Chiera, *Legal and Administrative Documents* (*UMBS*, VIII 1) 84 ff.

name of the pilot of the ship and the names of the gods were Amorite. This evidence based on the study of names was then regarded as most vital, as it is also at the present time.

In the first place, the hero of four of the fragmentary deluge versions, as preserved in Babylonia, is Atra-khasis, written also Atar-khasis, and in the Greek version, Xisuthros, or Khasis-Atra. In one of these four versions the hero's epithet is also given, namely, Ûm-napishtim-rûqu, meaning "the day of life is extended." This is reproduced in the Sumerian epitome, Zi-û(d)-suddu, which means the same. This is an appropriate title for the hero Atra-khasis, who was apotheosized.[30] Elsewhere I feel I have satisfactorily shown that the Gilgamesh story does not contain two different names of the hero.[31] Atra-khasis is unquestionably his personal name, while Ûm-napishtim-rûqu, which is frequently abbreviated Ûm-napishtim, is the epithet he received after his successful deluge experience. The reason scholars have failed in their efforts to explain it, is because they have regarded it as a personal name, for which there is no parallel.[32] Let us now inquire what is the origin of the name Atra-khasis.

Attempts have been made to show that Atra-khasis was composed of two words, and meant "most holy," "religious," "just and perfect man," "very intelligent," "open-minded," "very

[30] I previously translated the title Ûm-napishtim rûqu "Um-napishtim, the distant one;" see A Hebrew Deluge Story p. 72. Langdon has read it as a name, Ut-napishti-[arik] (JRAS 36, p. 190 and 1923, p. 259) which he says is a translation of the original Sumerian name Zi-ud-suddu, which he holds Lucian preserved in Sisythes. It seems this represents the form in Berossus, namely Sisouthros. Albright has also read it as a name, "Ut-napishti, the remote." (JAOS 38, p. 60). It would seem that in the late period, when the Gilgamesh Epic was written, the significance of the name was not understood.

[31] A Hebrew Deluge Story p. 23.

[32] The crude reproduction of the name U-ta-na-ish-tim (Meissner, Mitteilungen der Vorderasiatischen Gesellschaft 1902 p. 13, No. 1) is due to some scribe's misunderstanding.

wise," etc. There are no etymological grounds for any of these guesses, for in Assyrian the word *atru* means "abundant, surplus, excess," etc., and the verb *khasasu* means "to think, to remember, to reflect, to be mindful of." Atra-khasis, although used in these legends as an epithet, is a personal name.

There are two passages in the epics where the name is used as an epithet, apparently for "a wise man." Adapa, in the legend bearing his name, is called "the mighty one, the Atra-khasis of the Anunnaki." In the Etana legend, the wise young eagle is called "the young *admu*, the Atar-khasis." In both passages the name stands in apposition, and is not written grammatically as two words. There can be little doubt that the name was looked upon in these epics as synonymous with the idea of "clever one"; as if we would call a man "a Noah"; but it was, nevertheless, understood as a personal name. Moreover, the conclusive proof that it is a personal name is to be found in the fact that the determinative for man was placed before it in the early version of the deluge story. The name obviously means, "the god Atar is mindful (of the child)."

Names compounded with that of the god Atar and Attar, also written Atra, Atram, with and without the determinative for god, are numerous among the Amorite names found in Babylonian inscriptions. That they are Amorite is proved by the second elements of the names, as (Atra)-idri, -bi'di, -gabri, -sûri, -nûri, -khammu, -kamu, etc. The second element of Atra-khasis is found in the name Marduk-khasis, time of Samsu-iluna. In the late Assyrian period there is an Amorite named Atar-khasis, son of Au-shezib, from Kannu,[33] which city is mentioned in Ezekiel 27:23 between the names Haran and Eden. It is needless to add that Kannu is in Amurru.

---

[33] See Ungnad, *Vorderasiatische Schriftdenkmäler* I 88:15, and page X.

The name of the hero's father is given in the Gilgamesh story, Ubara-Tutu; but the reading is uncertain. He is said to have come from Shurippak. In the antediluvian kings' list of Berossus, the father of the hero hailed from Larak. In the Berossus story of the deluge, the hero seems to be identified with Sippar. These facts seem to point to there being a number of local variations of the tradition.

The only other personal name in the deluge legends is that of Buzur-Amurru, the name of the "governor" of the ship. Some years ago, as already mentioned, the writer discovered that the ideogram used for the second element of the name *Kur-Gal*, meaning the "great mountain," was to be read Amurru. This, of course, showed that the name of the pilot contained that of the Amorite deity. Although every translator of the text has since accepted this reading, two efforts have been made to show that it is incorrect. Both attempts endeavor to identify the sailor named Arad-Ea, of the time of Gilgamesh, with Buzur-Amurru,[34] the governor of the ship of the time of the deluge.

---

[34] The first effort in opposition to my explanation of the name was made by Professor Hilprecht. He says, "the very name of the boatman [*i. e.* Puzur-Amurru] which is Sumerian, demands a Sumerian original for the Akkadian versions thus far only known to us" (*BE* Sers. D. V. p. 41 note .5). Following is his proof for this, as well for his assertion that the governor and the boatman are identical. He interprets the name *PU-zu-ur-ᵈKUR-GAL*, as being another form of *Su-ur-Su-na-bu* or *Ur-shanabi*. Since *Pu = sir*, the first element, is either *Sirzur*, or the *zur* is a gloss for *PU*, standing also for *sur*, the name, therefore, should be written *PU-ᵈKUR-GAL*, and read *Z(S)u-ur-ᵈKUR-GAL*. And since the sign meaning 40 = ᵈ*Ea* = *sunabi* or *shanabi*, and a copyist wrote *Ea* by mistake with the number 50, which was interpreted as "Enlil" by another copyist, who now chose another ideogram for this god, namely *KUR-GAL*, when the name was rendered *Z(S)ur-Shanabi* (*Ibid.* p. 47 note 6). I will leave this opposition to my reading of the name and explanation to take care of itself.

The second effort was made by Professor Langdon, who said it is a Semitic translation of the name, Ur-Enlil, the sailor. He says "the reading *Puzur-ᵈⁱᵘAmurrū*, the name of the governor of the ark, is certainly false, for *kur-gal* became a title of the western Adad or ᵈⁱᵘ*Amurrū* only in the late period" (*Sumerian Epic of*

It scarcely seems reasonable even to try to prove that these two men of the sea are identical, and especially since the Gilgamesh Epic refers to the ferryman Arad-Ea as living in the hero's time, while in what immediately follows, the apotheosized deluge hero relates how in a previous era he had made Buzur-Amurru the governor of his great deluge-ship. Furthermore, we are not informed that others besides the hero and his wife became immortals. Moreover, it is hardly possible, even if we do not apply "the strictures of logic," for anyone to show, with the help of all the philological apparatus that is possible, that these two widely different names of the same text represent the same name.

As evidence for the Amorite origin of the tradition, these two Amorite personal names of the hero and the pilot are most significant. Supposing, for example, these two names were Agamemnon and Achilles, and there was no other definite distinctive coloring in the legend, what would be the conclusion of scholars concerning its origin? How are the Babylonists or the Sumerists going to explain that the two chief characters in the supposedly Babylonian, or Sumerian, stories bear Amorite names?

Let us now inquire what the study of the names of deities shows as regards the origin of the narrative. The gods mentioned in the

Paradise, p. 86). I am sure that Langdon will abandon this when he examines the Cassite documents published by Peiser, in which the deity of the chief contractor's name is written *MAR-TU*, *KUR-GAL* and *Amurru;* cf. *Urkunden aus der Zeit der dritten Babylonischen Dynastic* p. VII and X. And then let me suggest that the well-known family name Pir'-*d*Amurru (*KUR-GAL*, *MAR-TU*) (see Tallqvist, *Ass. Pers. Names* p. 181), of the Cassite period, written *pr wr* in an Aramaic letter, time of Ashurbanipal (see Lidzbarski *ZA* 31, 196), be compared.

The element *Buzur* is found in Buzur-Ashur, the name of a king of Assyria, who was a contemporary of Burna-Buriash, and is also found in several names from Nippur in the same era, compounded with Adad, Ishtar, and Marduk (see Clay, *Personal Names of the Cassite Period* p. 192). The element is apparently from the Amorite root meaning "to set apart"; and the name probably means something like "dedicated to the god Amurru."

lines quoted above from the Gilgamesh Epic, are all Amorite. No one to-day would question the Amorite origin of Adad. In Chapter II, I have shown that Nabû and En-Urta are Amorite. Elsewhere I have shown that Sharru, Urra-gal, and Ea, are also West Semitic.[35] The same is true of Anu in the legend, who was originally El.

Nisaba, in the part of the early tablet referring to the famine, is a goddess of fertility. Such a deity depicted on Babylonian seals, is also generally identified as this goddess, although officially she was regarded in Babylonia generally as the patroness of writing. In an inscription of Gudea she appears to the king in a dream, holding a reed-stylus and a tablet. She bestowed wisdom and the gift of prophecy upon rulers. She is also the one "who completes the fifty decrees."[36] In another inscription she is the great scribe of Anu.[36] Lugal-zaggisi king of Erech, about 2875 B. C., calls himself "Priest of Ana, the prophet of Nisaba, the son of Usham, the patesi of Umma, the prophet of Nisaba," showing that these rulers came from Umma, a city dedicated to Nisaba, and the Amorite god Shara.

In the syllabaries, Nisaba is connected with the deity Khani. Then we recall that the ancient laws found in the Yale Collection are the "decrees of Nisaba (the goddess who wrote decrees for Gudea) and Khani." Now Khani is unquestionably an Amorite deity. Since *kh* in cuneiform reproduces *'ayin*, Khani can be the same as Ani, Ana or Anu. Moreover, in the light of these and other facts that might be presented, there can be no doubt but that Nisaba is Amorite.

There is another god mentioned in the tablet to which Ungnad has called attention; namely, Shullat. Since the two gods of the Gilgamesh story, Nabû and Sharru, are equated with Shullat and Khanish respectively, Khanish is doubtless also to be supplied.

[35] *Empire of the Amorites* p. 184.
[36] See Thureau-Dangin *RA*, 7, 107 f, and also Clay, *BRM*, 4.

Like Nabû and Sharru, these seem to be storm-gods, and are West Semitic.

The Sumerian epitomized story, written at Nippur, has in it what I regard as being comparatively late. The principal deities in it are AN, Enlil, and Ea, besides the goddess Nin-Kharsag. This, in my judgment, is the triad and goddess which supplanted the early gods: El, Ea, Adad (*IM*), and Nisaba. I believe they are the same gods in a Sumerian dress. Several of the names were certainly epithets: En-Lil "lord of the storm," Nin-Kharsag "lady of the mountain," and Nin-Tu "lady of bearing." In brief, knowing that the text is an epitome of the fuller story, I can only conclude that the Sumerian translator, in using the names AN, Enlil, Ea, and Nin-kharsag, has given the corresponding deities from his language and adopted religion. Shamash and Ininna or Ishtar, also mentioned in this text, are also Amorite.

What is contained in the preceding paragraph reopens at least phases of a question which scholars have previously debated for many years. For this and other reasons, in order to avoid having the issue befogged, I prefer that it be not regarded as proof of my contentions.

Excluding then the consideration of the names of gods in the Sumerian epitome, let me assert that the study of names of gods and persons found in the Semitic Babylonian stories, shows that they are Amorite. The importance of the study of names in such legends has already been discussed briefly in Chapter II. In short, it seems to me the fact that the names of the hero, the "governor" of his ship, and the gods are not only Semitic but also Amorite, should in itself be sufficient proof to show that the story is Amorite.

If my contention is correct that the deluge legend, as handed down by the Babylonians, goes back to an Amorite original, we ought to find linguistic evidences of the dialect in which it was originally written, as well as traces of the coloring of the land whence it came; unless, as in the case of the creation story, it had been repeatedly edited. Naturally, in reproducing the legend century after century it was quite possible, and at the same time very easy, for the Babylonian scribe, if the root used was common to both dialects, to make a slight alteration in the form in order to make it conform grammatically to the Babylonian; also at the same time to replace foreign with Babylonian words; and even introduce a distinctive local coloring. Fortunately traces of this process are to be found in the versions; for not all of the distinctive marks of the Amorite origin of the story have been obliterated.

In presenting what I regard as linguistic and literary evidence of the original Amorite text, I fully expect to have certain scholars differ with me, because on the one hand, as already stated, our viewpoints are likely to be totally different; and on the other hand, it will be possible for them to point to the single occurrence of a foreign word in a cuneiform explanatory list of rare words, or even in a text under certain conditions, although the root is not in use in Babylonian, and it is commonly found in Hebrew.

Let us first direct our attention to the early version, as recently published under the title *A Hebrew Deluge Story in Cuneiform*; for as would be expected, it contains more traces of Amorite words than the late redaction of it, written thirteen hundred years later. The fragment is part of the "second tablet (of the series)," called *Inuma Ilu awîlu* "When El, man," being the first three words of the first tablet of the series. We shall probably later on find the full opening sentence. The first part of the fragment, *i. e.*, Column I, refers to the famine. After a break of about forty-seven lines, we find ourselves in the story of the deluge. As in the Old Testament, and also several texts found at Nippur, the series, doubtless, contained an outline history of the world. Following is a reproduction of the lines which contain the words we desire to consider in this connection.

I shall bring their clamor (?) ....?
The land had become extended; the people had multiplied.
The land like a bull had become satiated.
[In] their assemblage (*khu-bu-ur*) El (*I-lu*) was absent(*it-ta-akh-da-ar*).
5 .... heard their clamor.
He said to the great gods(?);
The clamor of men has become grievous.[36]
From their assemblage desolations (*shi-it-ta*) went forth (*u-ṣa-am-ma*).[37]
Let the fig tree (*te-i-na*) for the people be [cut off].
10 [In] their [bellies], let the plant become scarce (*li-'-zu*).[38]
..... the sheep (*shu*), let Adad destroy(*li-sha-qa-ṭi-il*).
...Injured .... let not flow([*li*]-*il-li-ka*).
[That the flood rise not at the sou]rce.
Let the wind blow.
15 Let it drive(*li-e-ir-ri*) mightily([*na*]-*ag-bi-ra*),[38a]
Let the clouds be held back(*li-im-ta-an-ni*); that
[Rain from the heav]ens pour not forth.
Let the field withhold its fertility.
[Let a change come over] the bosom of Nisaba."[38b]

(Forty-seven lines missing)

Let ....
Let ....

[36] The word *iq-ta-ab-ta* was incorrectly construed in my previous translation, as promptly observed by several friends.

[37] Thompson is right in reading *uṣamma*, but *shitta* "sleep" does not seem appropriate. I prefer the meaning "desolations" (cf. the Hebrew *she't*), if it refers to what follows, or the meaning "tumult", if it follows the thought of the preceding line. In Luckenbill's translation, "I (?) will proclaim a dispersion (?)," he might well have introduced more question marks.

[38] My previous conjecture for *li-'-zu* is also withdrawn. Professor Ungnad kindly called my attention to the occurrence of the form in an omen text which, although I had read, I had overlooked. It is, therefore, to be read the same as *li-me-ṣu* in the redaction (III:43 see *Ibidem* p. 66). Attention to palaeography would have kept Luckenbill from reading *li-ši*(?)-*ṣu* "let them carry off" the plants (see Addenda).

[38a] Luckenbill's question as to whether "Barth's law holds good for the Amorite," apparently shows that he does not know that similar *n* formations occur sporadically in Aramaic, including Biblical Aramaic, and according to the best authorities, even in Biblical Hebrew (see Ges.-Buhl s. v. *naftūlīm*).

[38b] I am unable to understand Luckenbill's improved (?) translation of [*li-ni-'ir-ta*] *sha Nisaba* "let Nisaba (——— vegetation) be restrained."

Let him destroy . . . .
70 On the morrow let him cause it to rain(*li-sha-az-ni-in*) a torrent(*ib-ba-ra*).
Let him give(*li-ish-ta-ar-ri-iq*) in the night . . . . . .
Let him cause it to rain a tempest(*na-ash-[ba]*)."[39]
Let it come upon the field like a thief; let . .
Which Adad had created in the city . . . .
75 They cried out and became furious . . . . .
They sent up a clamor . . . .
They feared not . . . .

A striking example of an Amorite word in this version, as well as
in the late redaction, which hitherto no scholar made any attempt
to translate except in one instance, is *khubur* "assemblage" in the
fourth line.

This interesting word has already been discussed in connection
with the title of Tiamat; namely, *Ummu-khubur*, see Chapter III.
This I regard as weighty proof for my contention that the legend
is Amorite.

The occurrence of the deity Ilu, the Amorite El, in this same
line, as well as in the name of the series to which the tablet belonged,
is really "unusual," as an unsympathetic reviewer has admitted;
it does not, however, "contain a problem"; it solves one. Yes,
it is so unusual and remarkable that at a single blow it makes the
contention impossible that the legend goes back to a Sumerian
original; and it is also weighty proof in showing that the legend is
Amorite. Furthermore, El, called Kronos, is the one deity mentioned in the Berossus version, who appeared to the hero in his
sleep and apprised him of the impending deluge.

The third word in this same line is *ittakhdar*, for which, in the
absence of anything known in Babylonian, my colleague, Professor
Torrey, has suggested that the root is the West Semitic *'adar*, which

---

[39] If *na-ash-[ba[* is correctly restored, it would also seem to be an Amorite word
from the root "to blow," although it is found in the Shurpu texts. See Muss-
Arnolt *Dic.* p. 738.

in the Nif'al, means "to be absent, lacking." How does this line appear in the late redaction?

It is apparent that some scribe who transmitted the legend did not understand the word, *ittakhdar*, for, in his paraphrase of the sentence, he used a Babylonian word which resembles it, and wrote "concerning their clamor he became troubled (*ittadir*, III:2)." In the eighth line *shitta* "desolation," falling together with the Hebrew *she't* appears to be an Amorite word.[40]

In the ninth line, the passage, "let the fig tree for the people be cut off," furnishes a most striking, and at the same time conclusive proof of the Amorite origin of the legend. Here the word for "fig tree," *te-i-na*, is the same as used in the Old Testament. In the late redaction, the form of the word has been changed and made to conform to the Babylonian word for "fig tree," namely *ti-ta*.

Scholars have heretofore divided the words differently, and read the line of the late text *lip-par-sa-ma a-na ni-she e-ti-ta*. In all the translations known to the writer, the last word has been left untranslated except in one instance, "la plante épineuse." "Thorny bush," however, would hardly fit the context.

When I found that the line in the early version reads *ni-shi te-i-na*, it became perfectly clear that the words in the late redaction had been wrongly divided, and that *e* belonged to *ni-she-e* and not to the following word *ti-ta*.

We are told that in the Garden of Eden Adam and Eve made aprons out of leaves from the fig tree. The people of Palestine, we know were prosperous "when every man dwelt under his vine and fig tree." Everywhere in the Old and New Testaments, plenitude of fruitful vines and fig trees was symbolical of prosperity. When Israel was to be punished, her vines and her fig trees were to be laid

---

[40] In the late paraphrase the word *nishitu* (III:8), replaces *shitta*. The passage in the redaction I now translate: "He said in their assemblage, the desolations are not effective" (literally, "have not taken hold").

waste or smitten.[41]   In short, "the fig tree," which flourished in Amurru, was used synonymously with the idea of prosperity in the literature of the land.

In ancient Babylonia, Herodotus tells us there was no fig tree (I, 193).   This slow-growing tree does not ordinarily grow in an alluvium.   While thousands of contract tablets refer to the fruit of the date palm, traffic in figs is little more than known.[42]   I know of no other literary use of the word in literature handed down by the Babylonians.

The point is so crucial, and its testimony so weighty, that it was not surprising to have a Babylonist come forward, and attempt to dispose of it.   The word *ti-ta* in the late text, Doctor R. C. Thompson, of Oxford, translates "food,"[43] creating a form not yet found in Babylonian; and then he raises the question, on the basis of the photograph, whether, instead of reading *te-i-na* in the early text, it is not to be read *"te-i-ta(?)."*   His translation of the phrase is "let food be cut off from men."   The following, however, will show the futility of his effort.

In the first place, if the word *ti-ta* or the supposed *te-i-ta*(?) meant "food," it would cover what is embraced in the two lines which follow, namely "the vegetable," and "the sheep."   In this well-written literary text the entire sustenance of the people is summed up in three consecutive lines, in which the subjects are the fig tree, the plant, and the sheep (or small cattle);[44] why, let me ask, should the writer have summed up these under the term "food," and then specify by giving details?

[41] Jer. 5:17; Hos. 2:12; Amos 4:9.

[42] Even this is on the supposition that Zimmern's restoration of *Gish-Ma* = *t*[*i-it-tu*] (see *SAI* 4837), is correct.

[43] See *The Times Literary Supplement* Oct. 12, 1922 p. 646.

[44] The text is unfortunately injured in line 11.   Justification, however, for reading *shu* "sheep," is found in the use of the word in the redaction (see III 49 and 59, *Ibidem* p. 67).

In the second place, while there is a word written *te-'u-u-tu*, and *ti-'u-u-tu* meaning "food," there is no word *te-i-ta* or *ti-ta* in Babylonian with that meaning. This in itself should be sufficient to prove the futility of the effort.

In the third place, even were the reading *te-i-ta*, the word, although in that case it would be Babylonian, would mean, according to our present knowledge, nothing else but "fig tree;" but the correct reading of the text is *te-i-na*, and not *te-i-ta*(?). I can appreciate the desire on the part of one who admits that he is "a little prejudiced against linguistic evidence for an Amorite origin," to discount this very crucial proof of it; but he will have to try again.[45]

Te-i-na in the early version is unquestionably the Hebrew *te'ēnā*. *Ti-ta*, which replaces it in the late redaction, is the Assyrian form of this word.[46] If no other example of an Amorite word were preserved in the text, the literary use of this one would speak volumes as regards the origin of the tradition; because as stated, "the fig tree" is not indigenous in alluvial Babylonia, and because it is a characteristic metaphor of Hebrew literature.

The word *lishaqṭil* "let destroy," in the eleventh line, was compared long ago by Père Scheil with the Hebrew root *qaṭâlu*; which is

---

[45] Luckenbill, who seems even more prejudiced, also reads *ta*, but strange to say, in his aggressiveness did not find a way out of acknowledging that it meant "fig tree." There are reasons why Père Scheil originally added a question mark after his reading *na*. In the first place the word *nishi* "people," was the lone word of the line that was understood, and the scribe had not given a perfectly written character, as he apparently had started to write the Babylonian form of the word, but after all he wrote *na* upon his erasure, thus reproducing the original from which he was copying. An examination of all the examples of *na* and *ta* in the text will leave no question in the minds of the unbiased as to the character being *na*. For this and other apparent purposes I have given the same but enlarged photographic reproduction of *na* in the Addenda, followed by other undisputed examples (see No. 4), and for comparison the sign *ta* (No. 5).

[46] *Te'ēnā*, which is feminine, in Assyrian would be written *te'ēntu = te'ēttu = tēttu* or *tittu = titu*. Both *tittu* and *titu* have been found. See Muss-Arnolt *Assyrian Dictionary* p. 1179.

not found in Babylonian. The causative in Hebrew, as is well known, is formed with *ha* not *sha*; although there are traces of the latter in Biblical Hebrew, but the Syriac which is also an Amorite language, forms it with *sha* as well as with *'a*. It is even found in the Zakar inscription, as Professor Torrey has shown. The *s* instead of *h* appears also in the Arabic and Ethiopic. I mention these facts, for I find one of my former students, after four years' instruction in Semitics, to my great chagrin, asking the question: "Did the Amorites have a shafel?"

The word *shu* of the same line, which occurs twice in the late version of the legend (III 49 and 59), is the Amorite word *seh*, meaning "sheep," or "small cattle,"[47] which also was not in current use in Babylonia. Here it is quite possible for my critics to say that *shu* is already in the Assyrian dictionaries as having been found in cuneiform. Let us briefly consider this anticipated criticism.

In Babylonian, the word *ṣênu*, the same as in the Hebrew, meaning "flock, sheep," occurs thousands of times in the early as well as the late period. The same is true of the word for a sheep, which in all periods is *immeru*. In the inscriptions of the Assyrian Sargon, however, the word *shu* "sheep" or "small cattle," the same as in Hebrew, is introduced. But when we recall that Sargon tells us in his reign he carried 27,290 of Samaria's inhabitants into captivity, without considering the fact that his predecessor Tiglathpileser had also taken many Israelite captives to Assyria, it is not difficult to understand how the Hebrew word *seh* for "small cattle" that were raised by the Hebrew slaves for the Assyrians, could come into use in that period in Assyria.

Besides the several occurrences of the word in the inscriptions of Sargon, and once in an Assyrian incantation text, where it is explained by *immeru*,[48] no other reference to the word is recorded

---

[47] See Muss-Arnolt *Assyrian Dictionary* p. 995.

[48] See Zimmern *Beiträge zur Kenntnis der Babylonischen Religion* p. 22.

in the dictionaries. In other Assyrian inscriptions, and in every Semitic Babylonian text known to the writer, the usual words *ṣênu* and *immeru*, are found, except in the early and late versions of the deluge story which I maintain is Amorite.

Here, it seems to me, the non-Assyriologist can also safely reach his own conclusion. Is this word so commonly used in Hebrew to be regarded as Babylonian; or is it a Hebrew loan-word? Does its occurrence in this legend, written 1966 B. C., twelve centuries before its first appearance in any other cuneiform text, as recorded in the available dictionaries, have any significance as linguistic evidence of the Amorite origin of the legend?

The twelfth line of the text contains the word *khibish*[49] meaning "injured," showing either that a previous scribe could not read the text from which he copied, or the tablet had actually been injured. At the end of the line he wrote [*li*]-*il-li-ka* "let not flow." Either he or some previous scribe had apparently changed the verb, which in the light of the redaction, it seems to me, should have been *lissakirû* "let be stopped." The late scribe very probably had before him a text that had come down from a source other than the early one which we now possess, for he wrote *lissakir*, which seems preferable to "let not flow." The word *lissakir* "let be stopped" in the late text, stands without a subject; and the scribe has not reproduced the word *khibish* in it, to show that anything is wanting. Instead he has reconstructed the line, but with rather poor results. If we turn to Genesis, we can supply the missing subject, not only for the early version, in the place which is occupied by the word *khibish*, "injured," but also in the line of the late redaction, where

[49] On this Luckenbill writes: "it is evident that the *khibish* of Professor Clay and others is a misreading of the remnants of *shaplish*. And so another argument for making this text a copy of one two thousand years old fades away into thin air." I think Luckenbill would have changed his characteristic style at this point had he examined the photograph published by Johns (*Cuneiform Inscriptions* p. 11) and the copy by Père Scheil (*RA*, XX p. 56) before the tablet was injured.

the subject is omitted. The words apparently are "springs of the deep," as found in Gen. 7:11 and 8:2. And the verb obviously was originally *lissakirû* in the cuneiform text, as is found in the late redaction, and also in Genesis. There are good reasons, if this is correct, why the Babylonian scribe had difficulty with the words "fountains of the deep," for springs gushing from the earth are unknown in the great alluvium. He knew that if a famine should ever occur in Babylonia it would be because the inundations failed to materialize. Unless he had been a traveller, he had never seen the clear water of a spring coming up out of the earth. Even the wells of the land, he knew almost entirely depended upon seepage from the rivers. Here, it seems to me, is another interesting detail in the text which points to a foreign origin of the legend. On the other hand, the man living in Amurru knew that a famine, to which this part of the legend refers, depended upon the failure of the springs, as well as of rain, and the flooding of the rivers.

In the fifteenth line, the word *li-e-ir-ri* "let it drive," is not Babylonian, but is from a very common Amorite or Hebrew root, meaning "to throw, hurl." In this line [*na*]-*ag-bi-ra*, if correctly restored, also seems to be an Amorite word.

The word *limtanni* (line 16) "be held back," is Amorite, from a root which has thus far not been recorded as occurring in the Babylonian language. In the Old Testament, *mana'* "to withhold, hold back," is a very common root; where it is also used of rain, Amos 4:7, and of showers, Jer. 3:3. It also occurs with the meaning "to withhold," in one of the Aramaic inscriptions found at Senjirli.[50]

The late scribe has omitted nearly all the Amorite words found in the early text. He replaced *khubur*, *ittakhdar*, and *teina* with the Babylonian words *pukhur*, *ittadir* and *tita*; and also *Ilu* appar-

---

[50] Professor Montgomery has kindly called my attention to this.

ently by another deity, which is unfortunately wanting, owing to the text having been injured. The seven lines containing the foreign words [n]agbira, lierri, limtanni, and lishaqṭil, he replaced by two lines containing only Babylonian words, which read:

> Above, let Adad make his rain scarce;
> Below, let [subject is wanting] be stopped; that the flood rise
>   not at the source.

Will anyone question the great significance of this fact?

Sir William Willcocks, in one of his recent papers, has said that "Joseph's famine would have been impossible in the Tigris-Euphrates delta." As far as I know Babylonian history does not record a famine as having taken place in the land. Certainly, for reasons already given, it is true that famines did not occur through want of rain. It seems to me, in view of these facts, that we need only recall from the Old Testament what a factor famines, due to the failure of the rain, have been in the life of the Semite in Syria, and also what an influence climate has had upon the literature of the people, to realize fully that we have in this element that which is characteristically Amorite, and not Babylonian.

There are other Amorite words in this fragmentary text besides those here given; but unfortunately the remaining lines are incomplete; and conjectural restoration would not be effective in this connection.

In these lines, as well as in what follow, there are words which show a peculiarity which is significant; namely, lishaqṭil, lishaznin, probably limtanni and lishtarreq, also liṣakhkhir in the Gilgamesh story (188). Although the precative with the Pa'el and Shafel is occasionally written like lishaznin instead of lushaznin, this seems to be due to Amorite influence. The precative is thus formed in Old Aramaic[51] and Arabic.

[51] See Montgomery, *Yale Review*, October, 1923.

The word *ib-ba-ra* I have heretofore translated "mightily" and proposed that it was apparently Amorite. My attention has since been called to an explanatory list of obsolete words in which *ib-ba-ra* is explained as being equivalent to the Babylonian *rihiṣti Adad*, "inundation (or cloudburst) of Adad."[52] The words *ibbara lishaznin* in the early version, therefore, mean "let him cause it to rain a torrent."

Here is another interesting confirmation of my contentions. This foreign word *ibbara*, which is Amorite, is found in an explanatory text, where its equivalent which is commonly found in cuneiform, is given. Naturally, some will very probably maintain that, since this obsolete word *ibbara* is explained in a Babylonian dictionary, it is Babylonian. It is also, at least, possible to assert that every loan word explained in our English dictionaries is English. In time, probably all such words from adopted legends may be found in dictionaries; but this fact will not make them Babylonian.

It seems to me that the only reasonable conclusion that the unbiased and unprejudiced can make, after considering these Amorite words, the grammatical peculiarities contained in the few lines of this fragment, the reconstructed and paraphrased sentences of the late version, as well as the literary evidence, above referred to, is that the legend had been brought from Amurru by the invading Semite. Since we know that before the scribe had copied the early text the Amorites had been ruling the country for several centuries,

---

[52] The line reads *ûm ib-ba-ra = ûm ri-khi-iṣ-ti ᵈAdad*, see Cuneiform Texts 18, 23:16. Professor Ungnad of Breslau kindly called my attention to the formula. The equation shows that the root is ʿ*abaru*, "to pass over, overflow, overwhelm." There is a common Hebrew word ʿ*ebra*, meaning "overflow, outburst." My colleague, Professor Torrey, calls my attention to the use of this root in Hebrew in connection with "water," Is. 8:8, etc., construed with ʿ*al*, Is. 54:9 (Noah's flood), etc., with rain, Hab. 3:10, etc. Luckenbill's knowledge of palaeography has · led him to read *dibbara* "pestilence" instead of *ibbara*. I think what is found in the Addenda will set him right on this.

and that the nomenclature of the era is full of Amorite personal names, it certainly does not require a stretch of the imagination to appreciate that this is the origin of the legend.

Five centuries later, when the Cassites ruled the land, these Amorite names had generally disappeared; and there is little evidence of the Amorite words that had been introduced in the previous era. It is not difficult to understand, therefore, how, in the dozen centuries which followed the age of Hammurabi, when there is no evidence that Amorite migrations took place, these legends suffered many changes at the hands of redactors, when foreign elements that had been previously retained, were eliminated; or by a slight change, the Amorite word was transformed into a good Babylonian word.

It must be conceded as remarkable, therefore, that in spite of the fact, as we have seen above, that scribes replaced Amorite words with Babylonian, there are traces of not a few Amorite words to be found in the redaction written thirteen hundred years later. We also find that a number of the foreign words which have been retained are glossed. In addition to *khubur*, already noted, which is glossed by *pukhru* in the late version, and also the word *shu*, let it suffice to call attention here to the following from the translation published in *A Hebrew Deluge Story*. In the late redaction these two lines occur (1:36 and 37):

> When the sixth year arrives, they prepare the daughter for a meal;
> For morsels(*ana patte*) they prepare the child.......

The words *ana patte* have been translated "aussitôt," "für Zehrung(?)," and "for food(?)." But these are only guesses, for there is no Babylonian word having such meanings. By considering it to be the Hebrew word *pat*, "morsel," and translating the passage as above, we have perfect sense. Moreover, since the text is not written in *parallelismus membrorum*, we can only conclude that the first line is a gloss to explain the second, containing the foreign word.

In line II:55, 56, we have the passage which has been usually translated:

> [He speaks] with his god,
> Ea, his lord, speaks not(*la-shu*) with him(*itti-shu*)

The parallel passage (III:19, 20) reads:

> He speaks with his god,
> Fa, his lord, speaks with him.

All scholars have read *la-shu* in the former passage as a negative particle, although such a particle is unknown. One scholar changed the text and made it read *la-a* "not." Two of the translators, appreciating the difficulty of such a translation, for the context does not require the negative, added a question mark. There can be little question but that *itti-shu* "with him" in the former passage, is a gloss explaining the meaning of *la-shu*, which is the Amorite inseparable preposition with the pronominal suffix, meaning "to him." In the parallel passage, *la-shu* is omitted. This is the third gloss referred to in the late redaction.

In I:43, *ma*, at the beginning of the line, is left by all translators wholly unaccounted for. Since the Babylonian *m* reproduced the Hebrew *w*, the explanation must be that *ma* is here the Hebrew waw conjunctive, meaning "and."

The words *shu-u ia i-'-ru* (III:49), have been translated "Korn nicht...ess!", "qu'elle ne germe pas!", "Getreide nicht kommen (?)!", and "lambs shall not fatten." There can be no question but that the words mean: "that sheep become not pregnant." The word *shu*, which we have discussed above, is the Hebrew *seh*, here used as in the Old Testament.

I have elsewhere called attention to a few other examples of words found in this text, which I hold are Amorite in spite of the fact that they occur once or twice in the cuneiform literature besides these legends.[52]   I shall omit them here, since Babylonists, whose viewpoint is totally different from mine, can point to these and refuse to acknowledge that they are foreign.

Let us now inquire whether any traces of the original Amorite version can be found in the Gilgamesh story of the deluge.

We have already called attention to such forms as *lişakhkhir* (188, etc.) instead of *luşakhkhir*, containing the Aramaic precative. *Qîru* (66) has been translated "Innerraum," "l'intérieur," "Schmelzofen (?)" and "outside (?)." There is no Babylonian word known to justify these guesses; but in Hebrew we have *qîr* "wall," which makes excellent sense for the passage.

In line 133, one text reads: *ta-ma-ta* "sea," but the variant text reads *û-mu*, which has been translated as usual, "day." The passage would then read: "I looked out upon the sea (variant "day"); the voice was silent." The contexts would seem to show that the meaning "sea" is preferable to "day." The common Babylonian word *ûmu* "day" represents the Hebrew *yôm* "day," but it here unquestionably represents the Hebrew *yām* "sea." This obviously is the correct meaning of the word; and it is Amorite, for *yām* "sea" is unknown in Babylonian. In other words both *tâmata* and *ûmu* mean "sea."

The word *pikhû* "governor" is another Amorite word. It is commonly used in the Old Testament, and in Biblical and old Aramaic. It is not found in current use in Babylonia. The Babylonian words for "governor" are *pakhâti* and *bêl pakhâti*. Besides our passage in the deluge story with *pikhû*, there is one occurrence known to the writer of this word in cuneiform; it is in a contract tablet.[53]   Now because in the five thousand, more or less, contract tablets which are now known, many of which refer to boats, there

[52] See *A Hebrew Deluge Story in Cuneiform.*
[53] Strassmaier, *Inschriften von Nabonidus* 180:1.

occurs in the record of a payment dated in the reign of Nabonidus, the passage: "one-half shekel of silver for the governor of the ship" (*bi-khi-e sha elippi*), and knowing that ships as now sometimes sailed from one land to another, and also that Nebuchadnezzar had previously filled the land with thousands of Jewish captives, shall we regard this *bikhû* or *pikhû* as a Babylonian, or as an Amorite word?[54]

The word *kha-aja-al-ti* (131), which is not Babylonian, has in previous years been compared with the Hebrew. The words *la-an* (60), *su-us-su-ul-lu* (68), *u-pa-az-zi-ru* (70), *na-a-shi* (142), I maintain are also Amorite, see *A Hebrew Deluge Story*.

There are other Amorite words in this text; but these suffice to show that in this legend from the West, even as late as the Assyrian period, linguistic evidence is still to be found to prove its origin.

In summarizing the results of our study of the versions of the deluge story, as handed down by the Babylonians, we find that the famine story is not Babylonian, but that it could have had its origin in Amurru; that the force in nature responsible for the deluge is not Babylonian, but it is true to Amorite coloring; that the reference to mountains and other literary details, as the fig tree, are not Babylonian, but are true to Amorite scenery; that the gods which brought on the deluge are not Babylonian, but are Amorite; that the names of the hero, and his pilot, are not Babylonian, but are Amorite; and that there is much Amorite linguistic evidence found in the different versions.

And having shown the overwhelming influence of Amurru, leaving out of consideration the Sumerian names of deities, as we do that of Yahweh in the Hebrew tradition, let us ask what are the dis-

---

[54] In view of these facts it appears somewhat surprising that scholars should have regarded the Hebrew *pekhah* as a loan word from Babylonia. See Brown, *Hebrew Lexicon* p. 808; Zimmern, *Akkadische Fremdwörter* p. 6, etc.

tinctive Babylonian features in the Babylonian versions? I know
of nothing that is distinctively Babylonian—nothing.

Now let us make a similar inquiry with reference to the versions
handed down by those living in Amurru, the Hebrews and the
Greeks. The famine story, the force in nature which caused the
deluge, the name of the hero, Noah, the mountains, the olive
branch—these are not Babylonian, but can be Amorite. The words
mabbul "flood," and *tebah* "ark" are not Babylonian. There is
also nothing in the Greek version that is Babylonian. How are
the Babylonists and the Sumerists going to explain these facts?
And let me finally ask, will they continue to publish the baseless
theory of the Babylonian origin of these versions for consumption
by the Biblical student and the student of general history?

VIII

THE TOWER OF BABEL

The Genesis story of the Tower of Babel, need not long detain us. Like the reference to Nimrod, an early emperor of Babylonia, it naturally deals with what is Babylonian. The light thrown upon the story of Babel by exploration and research, is well known; and need not be enlarged upon here. Suffice it to say, that one of the reasons why the Biblical writer made use of the story was to refer to the fact that people from his land journeyed eastward into the alluvium, for he tells us that they found a plain in the land of Shinar, and dwelt there.

These settlers, having come from Amurru, called the name of their city after their own god, Bab-El. Their temple they called Esagila "House (E) with a lofty (ila) head (sag)." Their tower they called E-temen-an-ki "house (E) of the foundation ($temen$) of heaven (an) and earth (ki)." As is well known, many other temple-names of Babylonia also refer to the heavens. Naturally, the names of these famous towers in Babylonia, and the idea expressed by them, namely, that they were intended to reach into the realm of heaven, an idea probably connected with all high places in the West, were, doubtless, known to intelligent people of the West. They probably even also knew of inscriptions referring to their reconstruction. If in Europe and America, museums now have not a few original inscriptions concerning the Tower of Babel, in which are found an expression almost identical with that of Genesis, namely, that they built up its head reaching into the heavens, it is quite probable that this conception was also well known at the time to the intelligent ancient of the Near East. Doubtless, also the fact that they had in mind making a name for themselves, which is also expressed in the inscriptions with which we ourselves are familiar, was also known to them. And naturally the fact that the Babylonians had to depend largely upon brick for this building material, instead of stone, and bitumen instead of mortar, was also very fully appreciated.

Having in mind the comparatively close connections between Babylonia and Canaan, there should be no occasion for any difference in views concerning the origin of the Biblical story of Babel. The story in Genesis is the story of a foreigner, not of a Babylonian. His interpretation of the facts which he uses, clearly indicates this. The story may even have been occasioned by the sight of the tower in a period when it had been allowed to fall into decay, for we have references in the inscriptions to this having occurred. Knowledge of such a condition, however, was not gained when the Hebrews lived in captivity; for at that time Babel was at its height.

The Biblical writer, doubtless, was also well acquainted with the fact that Babylon was a great metropolis of many tongues, especially in the period following its ascendency in the reign of Hammurabi. That it was the chief city of the land, following this period, was of course well known. Geographically, Babylon was built in a strategic position. There was always a great city or emporium in the vicinity—Kish, and Akkad before the days of Babylon; Seleucia, Ctesiphon, and Baghdad following its decay; which fact can easily be understood, for the trade routes between India, Persia, Assyria, and the West, owing to the position of the deserts, naturally passed through this part of the country. In short, the fact that so many languages were represented in Babylon, as is the case in Baghdad at present, was doubtless known to the Biblical writer, and was made use of in writing the story.

APPENDIX

A. THE AMORITE STORY OF CREATION (ENUMA ELISH)[1]

FIRST TABLET

When above the heavens were not named,
Below the earth was not called by name,
Apsu, the primeval, was their progenitor,
Mummu-Tiamat was the bearer of all of them,
5 Their waters had been gathered together (embraced each other),
Dry ground was not formed, grass was not seen,
When the gods, not one had been fashioned,
A name was not called, destinies were not fixed,
(Then) were created the gods in their midst.
10 Lakhmu and Lakhamu were fashioned, were called by name.
As they grew, they became lofty.
Anshar and Kishar were created; they surpassed them.
Long were the days, years were added.
Anu, their son, (became) a rival of his fathers.
15 Anshar made Anu, his firstborn, an equal.
Then Anu in his likeness brought forth Ea.
Ea, who became the ruler of his fathers,

---

[1] Parts of the text were published by Smith, *TSBA* 4, 364 ff, and Delitzsch, *Ass. Les.*³ 93 f; Bezold, *Catalogue* p. 716; Pinches, *Bab. and Or. Record* 1890; King *CT* 13; and *Seven Tablets of Creation;* Ebeling, *Keilschrifttexte aus Assur, Religiösen Inhalts.* Transliterations and translations appeared from the time of Smith by the above, including Sayce, *Higher Criticism* 63 ff; Jensen, *Kosmologie* 268 ff, 320 ff, and *KB* VI 1 2 ff; Zimmern in Gunkel, *Schöpfung und Chaos;* Delitzsch, *Das Babylonische Weltschöpfungsepos;* Bezold, *Die Schöpfungslegende;* Jeremias, *Das Alte Testament im Lichte des alten Orients;* Dhorme, *Choix de Textes Religieux Assyro-Babyloniens;* Jastrow, *The Religion of Babylonia and Assyria* 407 ff; see also the German edition, and Ancient Hebrew Traditions; Clay, *Light on the Old Testament from Babel;* Rogers, *The Religion of Babylonia and Assyria*, and *Cuneiform Parallels;* Budge, *The Babylonian Legends of the Creation;* Ungnad, *Altorientalische Texte und Bilder*, and *Die Religion der Babylonier und Assyrer;* Landsberger in Lehmann, *Textbuch zur Religionsgeschichte* 281 ff; Luckenbill, *AJSL* 38, 12 ff; Ebeling, *Das Babylonische Weltschöpfungslied*, etc.

FIRST TABLET (Continued)

Intelligent, thoughtful, mighty in strength,
Stronger by far than the begettor, his father, Anshar,
20 He had no equal among the gods his fathers.
(Thus) there came to exist the brotherhood of the gods.
They perturb Tiamat; they are satiated(?) with their ......
They disturb the soul of Tiamat
With horrible things in the heavenly dwelling.
25 Apsu could not quell their clamor;
And Tiamat was miserable because of their [conduct].
Their deeds were vexatious unto them;
Their conduct was not good; they made themselves masters(?).
Then Apsu, the begettor of the great gods,
30 Called Mummu, his messenger, saying to him:
"Mummu, my messenger, who rejoiceth my heart,
Come, to Tiamat let us go."
They went, and before Tiamat they reclined.
They discussed the matter concerning the gods their firstborn.
35 Apsu opened his mouth, addressing her;
To Tiamat, the glistening one, he said to her:
"Their conduct is [dis]tressing unto me;
By day, I cannot repose; by night I cannot rest.
I will destroy, I will ruin their course
40 That there be silence, and that we may rest."
When Tiamat heard this,
She was angry, and she cried out to her consort,
...... sorrowful; she alone was irritated.
She took the evil thing to her heart.
45 "[Wha]t, shall we destroy what we have created?
Their conduct truly is vexatious; yet we will act graciously."
Mummu having retorted, counselling Apsu,
Unfavorable [advice], was the advice of Mum[mu].
"Come let the troublesome conduct be overcome,
50 That by day thou may'st have repose, by night have rest."
When Apsu [heard] this, his countenance grew bright
[Because] of the evil-deed he planned against the gods, his children.
Mummu became faint in his head.
He sat down, his knees shaking violently.
55 Everything which they had planned in their assembly

FIRST TABLET (Continued)

Against the gods, their firstborn was repeated.
The gods hearkened; they became confused;
They were silent; they sat motionless.
The prodigious one, the prudent, the wise one,
60 Ea, who perceives everything, saw their plot.
He reproduced it; he determined the plan (picture) of the whole thing.
He devised cunningly his holy charm.
He recited it, and put it into water.
Sleep overcame him (Apsu); he slept soundly.
65 He caused Apsu to repose; sleep overcame (him).
Mummu, his minister, was woefully distressed.
He broke his restraint, he tore off his cr[own].
His majesty departed; he became delirious.
He bound him, namely Apsu, and slew him.
70 Mummu he tied; he used violence against him.
He established upon Apsu his dwelling.
Mummu he grasped, he held his adversary.
After he had bound, and executed his adversaries,
Ea established his triumph over his enemy.
75 In his chamber, he rested peacefully.
He named it *apsû*, he founded (appointed) shrines.
Around its place he established his dry ground.
Ea (Lakhmu), and Lakhamu, his spouse, in majesty sat
In the abode of fates, the dwelling of destinations.
80 The mighty one of the mighty, the leader of the gods, Anshar, he begat.
In the midst of the *apsû*, was Anshar created.
In the midst of the holy *apsû*, was Anshar created.
Lakhmu (Ea), his father, created him.
[Lakh]amu, his mother, conceived him.
85 The breast of the goddesses, suckled him.
The pregnant one who had conceived him, had implanted reverence.
Splendid was his st[atu]re, brilliant was the glance of his eye.
Noble was his going forth, a hero as of old.
Lakhmu (Ea), the begettor, his father, saw him;
90 He rejoiced, he beamed, his heart was filled with joy.
He exalted him; he endowed him with an equality of (god) El.
He was exceedingly tall; he overtopped them—all of them.
Indescribable was the comeliness of his appearance.

FIRST TABLET (Continued)

It was unimaginable; it was irksome visually.
95 Four were his eyes; four were his ears.
His lips, in emitting, breathed fire.
There grew four ears;
And eyes like that (number); they discerned everything.
Sublime among the gods was the preëminence of [his] features.
100 His members grew high; he was unusually tall.
             ?   ?   ?   ?   ?
He was clothed with the majesty of ten gods: he was exceedingly
     powerful.
Regard for their predicament overcame him.
. . . . begat Anu.
          (Twenty-two fragmentary lines follow.)
. . . . the word, the bright god;
. . . thou hast given; yes we will make a [fight].
125 . . . . the gods in the midst of [heaven].
. . . . the gods, the begettors.
[They are banded together], and they pr[oceed] at Tiamat's side.
They are an[gry]; they plan without resting, night and [day].
[They pre]pare for the conflict, fuming and ra[ging].
130 They formed a horde; they planned a re[volt].
Ummu-Khubur, who formed all th[ings],
Has [ad]ded weapons invincible; she bore monster serpents,
[Sharp of] tooth, and relentless in attack(?).
[With poison, instead] of blood, she filled their bodies.
135 Raging [monsters], she clothed with terror;
With [splendor] she endowed; [she made like] a god.
Those [behol]ding them, will be over[come with terror],
Their bodies will rear up; [their breasts] are not repulsed.
[She set] up serpents, dragons and Lakhamu,
140 Hurricanes, raging dogs, scorpion-[men],
Mighty storms, fishmen, and rams,
Bearing relentless weapons, without fear of bat[tle].
Powerful are her orders; they are irresistible.
In all, eleven like that [she made].
145 Among the gods her firstborn of the [assembly], she made him;
She exalted Kingu; among them she made him great.
Marching before the van of the army, leading the cr[owd],

FIRST TABLET (Continued)

Bearing the weapon of assault, the assembler of the hostility
Of the conflict, the chief conductor,
150 She intrusted in his ha[nd]s; she caused him to sit in the *karru*.
"I have cast thy formula in the assembly of the gods; I have made
thee great."
With the kingship of the gods, all of them, I have filled [thy] hand.
"Verily thou art exalted, my spouse, thou only one!
Let thy name be exalted above all of them—the Anunnaki!"
155 She gave him the tablets of fate, which on his breast she placed.
"Thy command shall not be altered; the [utterance of thy mouth]
shall be established."
When Kingu was exalted, he received [godship] (*anûti*).
Among the gods, his [so]ns, he [decreed] dest[inies].
"Open your mouth, the fire god [will be quenched].
160 In the conflict, let him be supreme; let his strength [increase]."

SECOND TABLET

When Tiamat made her work strong,
She colle[cted a force] against the gods her offspring;
[To avenge] Apsu, Tiamat planned evil.
As she had collected [her army], it was revealed to Ea.
5 Ea [gave attention to] this thing.
He was [grievously] affected; he sat in sorrow.
As the [days] passed by, his anger quieted down.
To the [place] of Anshar, his father, he set upon [his way].
[He went] before Anshar, the father who begat him.
10 [Everything] which Tiamat had planned, he repeated to him.
[Thus]: "Tiamat, the bearer of us, hates us.
She has called an assembly; she rages furiously.
The gods have turned to her, all of them;
[Including] those thou hast created, they go by her side.
15 They are [ban]ded together, and they proceed at Tiamat's side.
They are [an]gry; they plan without resting, night and day.
They [pre]pare for the conflict, fuming and raging.
They formed a horde; they planned a revolt.
Ummu-Khubur, who formed all things,
20 Has added weapons invincible; she bore monster serpents,

SECOND TABLET (Continued)

Sharp of tooth, and relentless in attack(?).
With poison, instead of blood, she filled their bodies.
Raging monsters, she clothed with terror;
With splendor she endowed; she made like a god.
25 Those beholding them, will be overcome with terror.
Their bodies will rear up; their breasts are not repulsed.
She set up serpents, dragons and Lakhamu,
Hurricanes, raging dogs, scorpion-men,
Mighty storms, fishmen, and rams,
30 Bearing relentless weapons, without fear of battle.
Powerful are her orders; they are irresistible.
In all, eleven like that she made.
Among the gods her firstborn of the assembly, she made him;
She exalted Kingu; among them she made him great.
35 Marching before the van of the army, leading the crowd,
Bearing the weapon of assault, the assembler of the hostility,
[Of the] conflict, the chief conductor,
[She intru]sted in his hands; she caused him to sit in the *karru*.
"[I have cast] thy formula in the assembly of the gods; I have made
     thee great."
40 [With the king]ship of the gods, all of them, I have filled [thy] hand.
[Verily] thou art exalted [my spouse], tho[u o]nly one!
[Let] thy name be exalted [above all] of them—the [Anu]nnaki!"
[She gave] him the tablets of fat[e, which on his breast] she [plac]ed.
"[Thy com]mand [shall not be altered]; the [utter]ance of thy mouth
     shall be established."
45 [When] Kin[gu was exalt]ed, he received godship (*anûti*).
[Among the gods, his sons], he decreed destinies.
"[Op]en [your] mouth, the fire god will be quenched.
In the con[flict], [let him be supreme]; let his strength increase."
     (Lines 49 to 71 are fragmentary.)
[Anshar, to] his son, spoke [the word].
. . . . . "this is my mighty hero.
[Lofty] is his strength, whose onslaught is invincible.
75 [Go], stand thou before Tiamat
That her spirit [may be appeased], her heart be merciful.
[If] she hearkens not to thy word,
Our [word] tell her, that she may be appeased."

SECOND TABLET (Continued)

When he [heard] the command of his father Anshar,
80 [He set out] on her road, he made his way upon her path.
Anu [drew nigh], he saw the design of Tiamat.
[He was impotent before her]; he turned back.
[He went to the father, his begettor], Anshar,
[Concerning Tiamat,] he said to him:
85 "...hand......against me."
Anshar was troubled; he looked at the ground.
He was oppressed(?); to Ea he lifted up [his] head.
They assembled at the place, all of the Anunnaki.
Their lips were covered; [they sat] in silence.
90 No god goes forth [to meet Tiamat].
From the presence of Tiamat, no one comes away [alive].
The lord Anshar, the father of the gods, was greatly [agitated].
His heart was stir[red]; and [to the Anunnaki] he spoke.
[He whose strength] is mighty, shall be the avenger for us.
95 ......battle, Marduk the hero.
................Ea, the place of his oracle,
[He came] and he told him, what was on his heart.
"Marduk, on a plan of advice, hear thy father!
Thou art a son, who has relieved his heart.
100 [Be]fore Anshar, proceed in the attack!
...............he shall observe thee, resting."
The lord rejoiced at the word of his father.
He approached, and he stood in the presence of Anshar.
Anshar saw him; his heart was filled with joy.
105 He kissed his lips, his fear departed.
"Before thine open lips be covered,
Let me go and satisfy all that is in thy heart.
Before thine open lips are covered,
Let me go and satisfy all that is in thy heart.
110 What man has brought against thee this battle?
....Tiamat, who is a woman, attacks thee with arms?
........creator, rejoice and be glad.
The neck of Tiamat, thou shall tread upon quickly.
.....creator, rejoice and be glad.
115 [The neck] of Tiamat, thou shall tread upon quickly."
"My son, knowing all wisdom,

SECOND TABLET (Continued)

Quiet [Tiamat] with thy holy incantation.

[The chariot] of the storm, speedily set out.

. . . . will not be cut off; return later!"

120 The lord rejoiced at the word of his father.

His heart [exulted]; to his father he spoke.

"Oh, lord of the gods, the destiny of the great gods,

If I, your avenger,

Enchain Tiamat, and give you life,

125 Proclaim an assembly, exalt my destiny;

In *upshukkinaki*, seat yourselves joyfully together!

Fix my status; let my fate like your own be fixed

That nothing shall be changed which I will do,

That the word of my lips is not altered, is not changed."

THIRD TABLET

Anshar opening his mouth

To Gaga, his minister, he spoke the word:

"O Gaga, minister, who rejoices my liver,

To Lakhmu and Lakhamu, I will send thee.

5 The [order] of my heart which thou hast obtained, thou shalt relate.

The gods, my fathers, bring before me,

Let the gods, all of them assemble.

Let a banquet be established; at the board let them sit.

Bread let them eat; let them prepare wine.

10 For Marduk, their avenger, let them decree the destiny.

Go, proceed Gaga, before them stand!

[Everything] I told thee, repeat to them.

Anshar, your son, has sent me.

[The command] of his heart he has caused me to comprehend.

15 [Thus: Ti]amat, the bearer of us, hates us.

She has cal[led an assembly]; she rages furiously.

The gods have [tu]rned to her, all of them;

Including those thou hast created, they go by her side.

They are banded together, and they proceed at Tiamat's side.

20 They are angry; they plan without resting, night and day.

They prepare for the conflict, fuming and raging.

They formed a horde; they planned a revolt.

THIRD TABLET (Continued)

Ummu-Khubur, who formed all things,
Has added weapons invincible; she bore monster serpents,
25 Sharp of tooth, and relentless in attack(?).
With poison, instead of blood, she filled their bodies.
Raging monsters, she [clo]thed with terror;
With splendor she endowed; she made like a god.
Those beholding them, will be over[come] with terror.
30 Their bodies will rear up; [th'eir breasts are not repulsed.
She set up serpents, dragons and Lakhamu,
Hurricanes, raging dogs, scorpion-men,
Mighty storms, fishmen, and ra[ms],
Bearing relentless weapons, without fear of battle.
35 Powerful are her orders; they are irresistible.
In all, eleven like that she made.
Among the gods her firstborn of the [assembly], she made him;
She exalted Kingu; among them she made [him gr]eat.
Marching before the van of the army, [leading the crowd,]
40 Bearing the weapon of assault, the as[sembler of the hostility]
Of the conflict, the chief conductor,
She intrusted in his hands; she caused him to sit [in the *karru*.]
I have cast thy formula in the assembly of the gods; [I have made
thee great]."
With the [ki]ngship of the gods, all [of them, I have filled thy] hand.
45 "[Verily], thou art exalted, my spouse, [thou] only one!
Let thy name be exalted above all of them—the [Anunnaki!"]
She gave him the tablets of fate, which on his breast she placed.
"Thy command shall not be altered; the utterance of thy mouth
shall be established."
When Kingu was exalted, he received godship (*anûti*).
50 Among the gods, his sons, he dec[reed] destinies.
"Open your mouth, the fire god will be quenched.
In the conflict, let him be supreme; let his strength increase.
I sent Anu; but he was impotent before her.
Nudimmud (Ea) feared, and turned back.
55 Then came Marduk, your son, the leader of the gods.
To set out against Tiamat, his heart moved (him).
He opened his mouth; he spoke to me,
If I, your avenger,

THIRD TABLET (Continued)

Enchain Tiamat, and give you life,
60 Proclaim an assembly, exalt my destiny;
In *upshukkinaki*, seat yourselves joyfully together!
Fix my status; let my fate like your own be fixed
That nothing shall be changed which I will do,
That the word of my lips is not altered, is not changed.
65 Hasten, and your destiny quickly determine
That he may go, and meet your strong enemy."
Gaga went, he set out on his way.
To Lakhmu and Lakhamu, the gods, his fathers,
He did homage, he kissed the ground under them.
70 He advanced, he stood, and spoke to them,
Anshar, your son has sent me,
The purpose of his heart, he has caused me to comprehend,
Thus: Tiamat who begat us, hates us.
She has called an assembly; she rages furiously.
75 The gods have turned to her, all of them.
Including those thou hast created, they go by her side.
They are banded together, and they proceed at Tiamat's side.
They are angry; they plan without resting, night and day.
They prepare for the conflict, fuming and raging.
80 They formed a horde; they planned a revolt.
Ummu-Khubur, who formed all things,
Has added weapons invincible; she bore monster serpents,
Sharp of tooth, and relentless in attack(?).
With poison, instead of blood, she filled their bodies.
85 Raging monsters, she clothed with terror;
With splendor she endowed; she made like a god.
Those beholding them, will be overcome with terror,
Their bodies will rear up; their breasts are not repulsed.
She set up serpents, dragons, and Lakhamu,
90 Hurricanes, raging dogs, scorpion-men,
Mighty storms, fishmen, and rams,
Bearing relentless weapons, without fear of battle.
Powerful are her orders; they are irresistible.
In all, eleven like that she made.
95 Among the gods her firstborn of the assembly, she made him;
She exalted Kingu; among them she made him great.

THIRD TABLET (Continued)

Marching before the van of the army, leading the crowd,
Bearer of the weapon of assault, the assembler of the hostility
Of the conflict, the chief conductor,
100 She intrusted in his hands; she caused him to sit in the *karru*.
"I have cast thy formula; in the assembly of the gods, I have made
thee great."
With the kingship of the gods, all of them, I have filled [thy] hand.
Verily thou art exalted, my spouse, thou only one!
Let thy name be exalted above all of them—the Anunnaki!"
105 She gave him the tablets of fate, which on his breast [she placed].
"Thy command shall not be alte[red; the utterance of thy mouth
shall be established."]
When Kingu was exalted, [he received godship (*anûti*)].
Among the gods, his sons, [he decreed destin]ies.
"Open your mouth, the fire god [will be quenched].
110 In the conflict, let him be supreme; let his stre[ngth increase]."
I sent Anu; but he was impo[tent before her].
Nudimmud (Ea) was afraid, and tu[rned back].
Then came Marduk, your son, the lea[der of the gods].
To set out against Tiamat, his he[art moved (him)].
115 He opened his mouth; [he spoke to me],
"If I, your aven[ger],
Enchain Tiamat, [and give you life],
Proclaim an assembly, [exalt my destiny];
In *upshukkinaki*, [seat yourselves joyfully together]!
120 Fix my status; [let my fate like your own be fixed]
That nothing shall be changed which [I] will do,
That the word of [my lips] is not altered, is not changed."
Hasten, and your [destiny] quickly determine
That he may go, and meet your strong enemy."
125 When Lakhmu and Lakhamu heard; they cried aloud.
The Igigi, all of them, howled bitterly.
"What is the enmity, unto their taking .. . ...
We do not know what Tiamat is thinking(?)."
They gathered together, they went.
130 The great gods, all of them, who determine [destiny],
Entered and before Anshar, they filled....
Brother was kissed by brother; in the assembly......

THIRD TABLET (Continued)

They held the feast; at the board [they sat].
Bread they ate; they prepared [the wine].
135 The sweet drink made them drunken(?)...
Becoming drunk in drinking to the fullness of [their] bodies,
They became very hilarious; their liver was exalted,
For Marduk, their avenger, they determined destiny.

FOURTH TABLET

They placed for him a princely seat.
Before his fathers, they endowed (him) for rulership.
"Thou art honored among the great gods.
Thy destiny is beyond compare; thy word is *Anu*.
5 Marduk, thou art honored among the great gods.
Thy destiny is beyond compare; thy word is *Anu*.
From this day thy command shall not be changed.
To exalt and abase, it truly is in thy hand.
The utterance of thy mouth truly is established; thy word is unchange-
able.
10 None among the gods shall trangresss thy prerogative.
Maintenance is desired at the shrine of the gods.
Where there is need, establish (it) for thy place.
Marduk, thou art our avenger.
We give thee sovereignty over the totality of everything.
15 Thou shalt sit in the assembly; thy word shall be exalted.
That thy weapon be unfailing, let it smash thy foes.
O lord, save the life of him, who trusts in thee.
But the god who has undertaken evil, pour out his life."
They placed in their midst a garment.
20 To Marduk, their firstborn, they spoke:
"Thy destiny, O lord, verily, is foremost of the gods.
To destroy and to create, speak; it will be accomplished.
Open thy mouth; the garment will be destroyed.
Command it return; the garment is whole.
25 He spoke with his mouth; the garment was destroyed.
He commanded it again; the garment was restored."
When the gods, his fathers, beheld the effect of his word
They rejoiced, they did homage: "Marduk is King!"

FOURTH TABLET (Continued)

30 They bestowed upon him sceptre, throne and *pala*.
They gave him an unrivalled weapon, the destroyer of enemies.
"Go, and cut off the life of Tiamat!
Let the wind carry her blood off to obscurity."
The gods, his fathers, decreed for the lord his destiny.
The path of peace and prosperity, they caused him to take the road.
35 He fashioned the bow; he appointed his weapon.
He seized the javelin; he fastened the rope to himself.
He raised the club; his right hand grasped (it).
The bow and quiver, he slung by his side.
He fixed the lightning in front of him.
40 With flaming fire, he filled his body.
He made a net in which to enclose Tiamat.
He caused the four winds to take hold, that nothing of her might escape:
The south wind, the north wind, the east wind, and the west.
By his side, he slung the net, the gift of his father Anu.
45 He created a bad wind, an evil wind, the tempest, the hurricane,
The four-fold wind, the seven-fold wind, the typhoon, the tornado.
He set forth the winds which he had created, the seven of them.
To trouble Tiamat's inward parts, they came on after him.
The lord lifted up the *abubu*, his mighty weapon.
50 He mounted the chariot, the unrivalled and terrible storm.
He harnessed the four-steed team which he yoked to it.
The destructive, the relentless, the overwhelming, the swift,
Their sharp teeth bearing poison.
They know [how to destroy], they had learned to overrun.
55 ....fearful in warfare.
Left and [right ....
..........., clothed with terror.
His overpowering majesty, was a covering for his head.
He took [his road]; he followed his pa[th].
60 To the place of the [rag]ing Tiamat, he set his face.
In his lips he held ....
A plant to destroy poison, he seized with his hand.
In his storm they gazed at him, the gods gazed at him.
The gods, his fathers, gazed at him, the gods gazed at him.
65 The lord drew near, he inspected Tiamat's battle array.

FOURTH TABLET (Continued)

He perceived the plan of Kingu, her spouse.
He gazes, and his way is confused.
His plan is destroyed, his action disturbed.
When the gods, his helpers, marching by his side,
70 Beheld their . . . . . . leader, their look was troubled.
Tiamat utt[ered a cry], she did not turn her neck.
With lips of boastfulness(?), she maintained the rebellion.
. . . . thy coming as lord of the gods.
They gathered at their places, they are in thy place.
75 The lord [raised] the *abubu*, his great weapon.
The challenge to Tiamat, who was raging, thus he sent it.
. . . . thou art raised above.
. . . . art prompted to slay.
. . . . their fathers . . . . :
  80 . . . . . thou hatest . . . .
. . . . Kingu, to be thy spouse.
. . . . to decree like Anu
. . . . thou hast pursued [ev]il. . . . .
[Against the gods] my fathers thou hast devised thine evil.
85 Let thy forces be joined; verily, they have girded on thy weapons.
Stand, I and thou, let us have the fight.
Tiamat, in her hearing these words,
Became like one possessed; her reason was distraught.
Tiamat cried out highly furiously.
90 Like roots, her legs to her foundations shook.
She recited an incantation, she pronounced her spell.
And the gods of the battle unsheathed their weapons.
Tiamat, and the leader of the gods, Marduk, stood before each other.
They approached each other for the fight; they drew nigh for the
  battle.
95 The lord spread out his net, and enclosed her.
The bad wind he had placed behind, he thrust into her face.
Tiamat opened her mouth to its full extent.
He drove in the bad wind that she could not close her lips.
The furious winds filled her belly.
100 The heart was shocked, and she opened her mouth.
He used the spear, he burst open her belly.
He cut into her inwards; he pierced the heart.

FOURTH TABLET (Continued)

He bound her, and destroyed her life.
He cast down her corpse, he stood upon it.
105 When he had slain Tiamat, the leader,
Her power was broken; her crowd was scattered.
And the gods her helpers, who went by her side
Trembled, feared and turned their backs.
They made an exit to save their lives.
110 They were surrounded by a cordon; they were not able to make an escape.
He caught them; their weapons he broke.
Into the net they were cast; in the snare they sat.
Put in an enclosed place, they were filled with wailing.
They bore his punishment; they were held in bondage.
115 And on the eleven creatures, who were loaded with fearfulness,
The troop of the devils going before her,
He thrust into fetters; their forces he .....
Together with their opposition, he trampled under him.
And Kingu, who had been magnified [above] them,
120 He bound him and with the god Dugga (god of death) he reckoned him.
He took from him the tablets of destiny which were not befitting him,
Sealed with a seal and placed on his breast.
After he bound and slew his enemies,
And the arrogant foe he treated like a bull(?)
125 The victory of Anshar over the enemy he completely accomplished.
The wish of Nudimmud he had attained, Marduk the warrior
Over the captive gods he had strengthened his hold.
To Tiamat whom he had bound, he turned back.
The lord trod upon Tiamat's foundation.
130 With his merciless club he smashed the skull.
He cut through the veins of her blood;
The north wind carried (it) to obscurity.
His fathers saw, they rejoiced, they were glad.
They brought greetings-gifts to him.
135 The lord rested, inspecting her corpse.
In parting the carcass, devising a cunning plan,
He split her like a *mashdê* fish, into two parts.
With her half he established and protected the heavens.
He drew the bolt; he stationed a guard.

FOURTH TABLET (Continued)

140 He ordered them not to let her waters escape.
He passed over the heavens; he encircled the regions.
He set before the *apsû* the dwelling of Nudimmud.
The lord measured for *apsû's* structures.
He founded the great house, Esharra, in its likeness;
145 The great house Esharra which he built in heaven.
Anu, Enlil, and Ea he caused to occupy their cities.

FIFTH TABLET

He formed the stations for the great gods.
The stars, their image he established *lumashu* constellations.
He ordained the year; he defined the divisions,
For twelve months he fixed three stars (each).
5 After he designa[ted] images for the days of the year.......
He founded the station Nibir, to determine their bounds.
That none might go wrong or err
The station of Enlil and Ea he fixed with him.
He opened the gates on both sides.
10 The bolt, he made strong on the left and right.
In its midst he established ....
The moon-god, he caused to shine, and entrusted the night.
He appointed him a being of the night, to determine the days,
Monthly without ceasing into a crown he formed,
15 In the beginning of the month, shining over the land,
Horns thou shalt show to determine six days.
On the seventh day, let the crown [be halved].
On *shapattu*, verily thou shall stand over against [the sun].
When the sun-god on the horizon of the heavens,
20 Divide the ..... look ......
[On the *bubbulu* day] the path of the sun-god approach,
[On the 28th day] thou shalt stand against the sun-god.
........to go her way.
........thou shalt approach, give justice
.............to destroy.
       (Many lines missing.)

SIXTH TABLET

When Marduk, on [hear]ing the words of the gods,
  his heart being stirred, and devising cunning plans,
Opened his mouth; to Ea he [spoke] concerning
  what he had planned in his heart, giving council.
"Blood I will gather, and bone I will fashion.
I will establish a *lù-gal-lu;* "man" shall be his name.
5 I will create a man—an *amelu.*
They shall do the work of the gods, that they may be reconciled.
I will change the ways of the gods; I will act cleverly.
Alike they shall be honored; into two (groups) they shall be divided."
Ea answered him, speaking the word to him;
10 For the reconciliation of the gods, he repeated to him the plan.
"Let one, their brother, be offered up;
  let him perish, and let people be fashioned.
Let the great gods assemble;
  let this one be offered up that they may exist."
Marduk assembled the great gods;
  presenting his plan; and giving the command,
He opened his mouth; commanding the gods;
  as king to the Anunnaki, he speaks the word:
15 "Let your former designations be established.
Trustworthy things, I swear the word with myself.
Who was he who created warfare?
Who incited Tiamat to revolt, and joined battle?
Let him be offered up who created warfare.
20 I will cause him to bear his sin; that you may dwell in peace."
The Igigi, the great gods, answered him;
To the king of the gods of heaven and earth, counsellor of the gods,
  their lord:
"Kingu was the one who created warfare.
'Twas he who incited Tiamat to revolt, who joined battle."
25 They bound him, and before Ea [brought] him;
  and the punishment they laid upon him; they extracted his blood.
With his blood he made mankind;
  he imposed [upon him the serv]ice of the gods; he released the gods.
When mankind was created, Ea [sav]ed (them);
  the work of the gods he placed upon him.
That work, which was not intelligently done,

SIXTH TABLET (Continued)

through the craftiness of Marduk. ......
Marduk, the king of the gods, divided the host of the Anunnaki;
.... above and below
30 He appointed for Anu to guard [the law];
[in] the midst [of heaven, he established] a watch.
He altered the ways of the earth, ... and earth .....
After Marduk had issued the oracles, ... the Anunnaki;
The Anunnaki [of the ....
35 To Marduk, their lord, they spoke:
"O Nannar, my lord, who had established our release,
What is our grace before thee!
Oh, let us make a shrine, whose name will be proclaimed,
An abode, truly our resting place, that we will have peace in it.
40 Come, let us found a shr[ine]; we will establish ....
In the day we have succeeded, we will rest therein."
Marduk, when he had heard this,
Like the day his countenance shone exceedingly.
"Like ... Babylon, whose work you have desired,
45 Let the city be build; let its bright(?) shrine be fashioned."
The [A]nunnaki carried the basket;
     the first year, [they made] their bricks.
As the second year approached, they reared the head of Esagil as
     against the apsû.
They built the ziggurrat in the upper apsû;
     for Marduk, Enlil, and Ea, in it they established a dwelling.
In majesty before them he sat;
     like a root [springs up], they watched its horns.
50 After they had constructed the work of E[sag]ila,
     the Anunnaki, [all] of them fashioned their shrines.
To Marduk, ki[ng of the great gods] on the border of the apsû, all of
     them assembled, they sat in the shrine, whose dwelling they had
     built.
The gods, his fathers, he caused to sit at his ......
     This is Babylon, the place of your dwelling.
They sacrificed to its place, [they made] a feast;
     the gods sat down.
They set up the drink[ing] vessel; out of the chalice they drank
     after the wine(?) was placed in their midst.

SIXTH TABLET (Continued)

55 In Esagil . . . .
Laws were established; plans were formulated.
The stations of heaven and earth were assigned to the gods, all of them,
The great gods sat down joyfully.
The gods, the destiny of their *Sibi*, for eternity he stationed.
60 Enlil raised [the weapon, he laid it be]fore them.
The net which he had made, the great gods saw.
They beheld the bow, how artful was its construction.
The work which he had done, his fathers praised.
Anu raised it, and speaks in the assembly of the gods.
65 He kissed the bow; it . . . .
Thus are the names of the bow he named:
     long-wood is the first; the second . . . .
The third of its name is bow-star in the heavens. .
He established the station . . . .
After the fates of . . . .
70 He laid the throne . . . .
Anu in heaven . . . .
They assembled . . . .
. . . . Marduk . . . .
     (Five lines missing.)
He made exceed . . . .
80 To their words . . . .
He opened his mouth . . . . . .
. . . .
Let Marduk be exalted . . . .
His lordship, verily, is magnified. . . . .
85 Let him do the shepherding of the Blackheaded . . .
That in later days, lest his deeds be forgotten . . .
Let him establish for his fathers the offerings . . . .
Their support let him [provide . . . .
Let him cause to smell the in[cense . . . . .
90 An image in heaven he made . . . . . .
Let him appoint . . . .
Not . . . .
. . . .
Let offerings be brought their god (and) their goddess.
95 Lest they be forgotten, let them support their god.

SIXTH TABLET (Continued)

Let them adorn their path; let them build their shrines.
. . . . the Blackheaded, our god.
For us whatever name we mention, he, verily, is our El.
[Yes], we will name his fifty names.
100 His triumph, truly, is magnificent; his deeds, verily, are the same.
Marduk, who on his going forth, his father Anu named him;
He establishes the storms against the enemies; he makes plentiful their violence;
Who with his weapon *abubu* bound the . . . . . .
The gods his fathers, he saved in distress.
105 Verily, his sonship of the gods, they proclaimed him.
In his shining light, they will walk continuously.
On the people, whom he created, creatures of life(?),
The work of the gods he imposed, that they were appeased.
. . . . the star . .
110 Verily their protection(?) . . . . . their glance, himself.
Marduk, verily his deity . . . .
Who gladdens the heart of the Anunnaki; who pacifies the . . . .
Marduk, verily the assistance of his land and his [people].
Him, let be honored, the people have . . . . .
115 Sharru, the decider, stood and the adversary is over[thrown].
Wide was his heart; warm his compassion.
Lugal-dimmer-an-ki, whose name, our assembly pronounced,
We will bring the word of his mouth unto the gods his fathers.
Truly, he is the lo[rd] of the gods of heaven and earth, all of them.
120 The king, whose consecration the gods . . . . .
Nari-lugal-dimmer-an-ki-a, whose name we have mentioned, a place for all the gods,
Who is heaven and earth, established our abode in distress.
To the Igigi and the Anunnaki, he divided the station(s).
At his name, let the gods tremble; let the shrines totter.
125 Silig-lu-dug is his name, which Anu his father pronounced.
He, verily, is the light of the gods; the mighty *gishtû*.
Who, like a cloth is spread out, is a protecting deity of god and land,
Who, in a mighty battle protected our dwelling in distress.
Silig-lu-dug, the god of life, again the gods named his name (?).
130 Who, like his creatures, strengthened the dejected gods.
The lord, who, with his holy incantation, resuscitated the dying gods.

SIXTH TABLET (Continued)

The destroyer of the .... the hater of .....
Verily, the shining god, whose name was named.
A pure god, who makes our path bright.
135 ... whom Anshar, Lakhmu and Lakhamu had na[med].
To the [gods their children], they spoke.
We(?) .... mentioned his name.
A true .... mentioned.
The gods rejoiced .... their name.
140 In Upshukinnaka, he caused them to lay aside(?) their fetters.
"Of the warrior son, our avenger.
We, who are patrons, will [exalt] his name."
They sat down in their assembly; they named his destiny.
In the ... of their totality, they proclaimed his name.

SEVENTH TABLET

Asari, the donor of fruitfulness, the founder [of agriculture],
The creator of grain and plants, who causes [the green herb to spring forth],
Asaru-alim, who in the house of counsel is hon[ored for surpassing counsel],
Whom the gods have rev[ered ....
5 Asaru-alim-nunna, the great, the light of [the father, his begettor],
Who directs the law of Anu, Enlil, [and Ea],
He is their patron, he ordained ....
Whose provision he supplies abundantly.
Tutu, the creator of their restoration is [he].
10 If he consecrates their sanctuaries, truly they are [pacified].
If he makes an incantation, the gods will [be appeased].
If they rise in anger, he will subdue [their breasts].
Truly, he is exalted, in the assembly of the gods. .....
No one among the gods is like him.
15 Tutu, the Zi-ukkinna, the life of the host ....
Who established for the gods the holy heavens .....
Who set their way, and ordained .....
Lest there be forgotten among men the deeds .....
Tutu, the Zi-azag, as the third they named, who effects purification;
20 The god of the good wind, the lord of the obedient and benevolent.

SEVENTH TABLET (Continued)

The creator of fullness and plenty, who establishes abundance.
Whatever is lacking, he turns to plenty.
In sore distress, we caught his good wind.
Let them proclaim, let them exalt, let them render his service.
25 Tutu, the Aga-azag, as the fourth, mankind will magnify.
The lord of the holy incantation, who brings the dead to life.
Who granted mercy to the captive gods.
He removed the yoke which he had imposed upon the gods, his enemies.
For their deliverance, he created humanity.
30 The merciful one, with whom there is power to give life.
Let them be established, lest his word be forgotten
In the mouth of the Black-headed, whom his hands have created.
Tuti, the Tu-azag, as the fifth, his holy incantation, he will pronounce
     pashina
Who, through his holy incantation, destroys all the wicked.
35 Shazu, who knows the heart of the gods, who sees the innermost parts,
The doer of evil he taketh not out with him;
The founder of the assembly of the gods, [who appeases] their hearts;
The subduer of the disobedient . . . .
The director of righteousness, who guards . . . . . .
40 Who, the rebellion and . . . .
Tutu, the Zisi, the . . . . . .
Who banishes the fury . . . . . .
Tutu, the Sukh-kur, as the third, who destroys . . . . .
Who confuses their plan . . . . . .
45 Who destroys all the wicked . . . .
          (About sixty lines missing.)
Verily, he takes . . . . their . . . truly they look upon him.
Thus: who passed through the midst of Tiamat . . . .
His name truly is Nibiru, who seizes its midst.
110 He will uphold the ways of the stars of heaven.
He will pasture the gods like a flock, all of them.
He will bind Tiamat, he will trouble and oppress her soul.
In the future of men, in the oldness of days,
He will bear up without ceasing; he will rule for eternity.
115 Since he built the places (heaven), fashioned the fastnesses (earth),
"The lord of lands," Enlil the father, has pronounced his name.
The Igigi named the names, all of them.

SEVENTH TABLET (Continued)

Ea heard, and his liver rejoiced.
Thus: "He whose names his fathers have magnified,
120 He, like me, Ea, truly is his name.
The sum-total of my commands, all of them he will observe.
All my oracles he shall observe."
By the fifty names, the great gods;
His fifty names they named, they made his path excel.
125 Let them be held fast, let the foremost reveal (them).
Let the wise and the understanding consider them together.
Let the father repeat (them), and teach the son.
Let the shepherd and the herdsman open their ears.
Let them rejoice, for the Enlil of the gods, Marduk,
130 Will make his land prosperous; it verily will succeed.
His word is established; his command is unchangeable.
The utterance of his mouth, no god shall revoke.
When he looks about, he turns not his neck.
In his anger (and) his wrath, no god can face him.
135 Extended is his heart; wide is his compassion;
The sinner and evil-doer, before him . . . .
They received instruction, they spoke in his presence
. . . .
. . . . Marduk, verily the gods . . . .
. . . . they drank . . . .

B. BILINGUAL BABYLONIAN STORY OF CREATION[2]

The holy house, the house of the gods, in the holy place, was not made.
The reed had not come up; the tree was not created.
A brick was not made; the mould was not fashioned.
A house was not made; the city was not built.
5 A city was not made; a creature was not constituted.

---

[2] For the text see *CT* 13, 35 ff. It was first translated by Pinches, *JRAS* 23, 393 ff. See also Sayce, *Higher Criticism and the Monuments* p. 39; Zimmern in Gunkel, *Schöpfung und Chaos* 419 f; Jensen, *KB* 6, 38 f; King, *Seven Tablets of Creation* 130 ff; Dhorme, *Choix de Textes Religieux Assyro-Babyloniens* 83 ff; Rogers, *Cuneiform Parallels* 47 ff; Jeremias, *Altorientalischen Geisteskultur* p. 24; Jastrow, *JAOS* 36, 280 ff; Budge, *The Babylonian Legends of Creation* 5 ff; Ungnad, *Die Religion der Babylonier und Assyrer* 52 ff, etc.

Nippur was not made; Ekur was not built.

Erech was not made; E-anna was not built.

The *apsû* was not made; Eridu was not built.

The holy house, the house of the gods, his habitation, was not made.

10 All lands were sea.

Then, what was in the midst of the sea was squeezed out.

At that time, Eridu was made, Esagila was built,

The temple .... where in the *apsû* Lugal-du-azag had dwelt,

Babylon was made; Esagila was finished.

15 The gods, the Anunnaki, altogether, he made.

The holy city, the dwelling of their hearts' desire, they proclaimed supreme,

Marduk laid a reed work upon the face of the waters.

He created dirt, and poured (it) with the reed-work.

To have the gods dwell in a desired habitation,

20 He created mankind.

The goddess Aruru with him created the seed of mankind.

The beast of the field, the living things in the field, he created,

The Tigris and Euphrates, he created and fixed (their) course;

Their names he appropriately announced.

25 The grass, the rush of the marsh, the reed, and the forest, he created.

The green herb of the field, he created.

The lands, the marsh, the swamp,

The cow, her offspring, the young, the ewe, her kid, the sheep of the fold,

Groves and forests,

30 The he-goat, the mountain-goat, he brought into existence.

The lord Marduk filled in an embankment at the edge of the sea.

.... a secure place he established.

.... he caused to exist.

.... wood he created.

35 .... in the place he created.

.... (the mould) he created.

....

.... [he established.

.... E-kur, he created.

.... he created.

C. THE PHOENICIAN COSMOGONY ASCRIBED TO SANCHUNIATHON BY PHILO OF BYBLUS[3]

As the first principle of the universe he posits murky, windy air, or a breath of murky air, and turbid chaos, dark as Erebos; these were infinite and throughout a long lapse of time limitless. "But," says he, "when the windy breath became enamoured of its own first principles and an intermingling took place, that union was called Desire. This was the beginning of the creation of all things; but it was not aware of its own creation. From the self-embrace of the windy breath was engendered Mot; this some say was mud, others the corruption of a watery mixture. From this was engendered all seed of creation, and the origin of the universe. There were certain beings devoid of sense-perception, out of which were engendered sentient beings; and they were called Zophasemin, that is, beholders of Heaven, and were fashioned like the shape of an egg. And Mot was illumined[4] by the sun and moon, and by the stars and the great stellar bodies."[5]

Such is their cosmogony, which brings in downright atheism. But let us next see how he says the origin of life came about. He says, then:

"And after the air had become glowing, through the burning of the sea and the earth were engendered winds and clouds, and very great downfalls and outpourings of heavenly waters. When these had become disjoined from each other and disparted from their own place through the burning heat of the sun, and when they all encountered again in the air, one with another, and collided, claps of thunder and bolts of lightning were created. At the noise of the thunder-claps, the previously mentioned sentient beings awoke, and started at the sound, and moved upon the earth and in the sea, male and female."

Such is their view of the origin of life. Directly after this the same writer adds the remark:

"All this was found written in the cosmogony of Taautos and his commentaries; by means of indications and proofs which his intelligence had discerned, he discovered it and enlightened us."

---

[3] These quotations, from the first book of the *Phoenician History* of Philo of Byblus, are given by Eusebius, *Praeparatio Evangelica*, i, 10. The translation, which has been made by my colleague, Professor A. M. Harmon, follows the text of Müller, *Fragmenta Historicorum Graecorum*, iii, p. 565. The interspersed comments are those of Eusebius.

[4] Or, "set aflame."

[5] The five planets.

D. STORY OF CREATION ASCRIBED TO OANNES BY BEROSSUS[6]

"There was," he says, "a time when everything was darkness and water, and in these were bred portentous creatures with peculiar appearances; for men with two wings were born, and some, too, with four wings and two faces; they had only one body, but two heads, a man's and a woman's also, and double privates, male and female. And there were other men, some of whom had goat's legs and horns, some had horse's hooves, and some had the hinder parts of horses and the fore parts of men, so as to look like hippocentaurs. Bulls with human heads were bred, too, and four-bodied dogs, with fish-tails attached to their hind quarters, and horses and men with the heads of dogs, and other creatures that had the heads and bodies of horses but the tails of fish, and still other creatures with the shapes of all manner of beasts. In addition to these, there were fish and creeping things and serpents and many other marvellous creatures that had appearances derived from one another. Images of all these are set up as offerings in the temple of Bel. The ruler of them all was a woman whose name was Omorka, which in Chaldean is interpreted Thalatth, and in Greek Thalassa (sea); but by numerical equivalence (it is) Selene (the moon).[7]

"After the universe had thus come into being, Belos made his appearance and clove the woman in two; he made half of her Earth and the other half Heaven, and did away with the creatures in her. This, he says, is a physical truth allegorically set forth; for when the universe was liquid and only animals had come into being in it, [this god removed his own head, and the other gods mixed with earth the blood that flowed and moulded men; hence they are intelligent and partake of divine wisdom][8]

[6] For the text see Schoene, *Eusebi Chronicorum Liber Prior* pp. 14–18. It may also be found in Müller, *Fragm. Hist. Graec.* ii. pp. 497–498. The translation and notes are by Professor A. M. Harmon, of Yale University.

[7] The two words Omorka and Selene not only have the same number of letters, but if the letters are given their numerical value, according to the Greek system, the sum of the letters in Omorka (301) is the same as the sum of the letters in Selene.

[8] I have bracketed these words following Gudschmid, and on my own responsibility have indicated a lacuna between what precedes them and what follows. The bracketed passage interrupts the rationalistic explanation of the myth, and is evidently a double of the continuation of the myth itself. Out of the interpretation of the myth we have lost at least the explanation that Belos is light (A. M. H.).

.... but Belos, whom they interpret to be Zeus, sundered the darkness in twain, disparted Heaven and earth from each other, and established the world-order; and the animals, not being able to endure the strength of the light, perished. When he saw land unoccupied and fruitful, Belos ordered one of the gods to take off his head, to mix earth with the blood that flowed from it, and to mould men and beasts that could endure the air.* Belos created also the stars and the sun and moon and the five planets." All this, says Alexander Polyhistor, Berossus asserts in his first book.

E. DAMASCIUS ON THE THEOGONY OF THE BABYLONIANS[10]

"Among the Barbarians, it would appear that as far as the Babylonians are concerned they have passed over in silence one of the three first principles of the universe[11] and have made two, Tauthe and Apason, making Apason the husband of Tauthe, and naming her the mother of the gods. Of these a single son was born, Moymis—the visible world itself, I take it, derived from their two first principles.[12] But other issue came from the same parents, Daches and Dachos, and then again a third, Kissare and Assoros. Of these two were born three children, Anos, Illinos, and Aos; and the son of Aos and Dauke was Belos, who they say is the Creator."

* I. e., the light of day.
[10] Damascius, Ed. Kopp, p. 384. It is supposed to have been handed down by Eudemus of Rhodes. The translation and notes are also by Professor Harmon.
[11] Damascius is an ardent Neo-Platonist; he finds triads if he can.
[12] This may be pure conjecture on the part of Damascius.

ADDENDA

The signs from the text published in *A Hebrew Deluge Story*, which Luckenbill, one of my former pupils, has declared were misread (see *AJSL* 39, 153), are placed at the top of each column, beneath which are given other examples of the same sign (if they occur), on which there is no question as to the reading. Although all experts know that the eye can see and the camera will reproduce wedges, when the light is thrown from a different angle, which in some instances are not clearly visible in a single photograph, nevertheless I have used the *same* photograph, but enlarged, which was previously published, so that, without a glass, anyone, including even

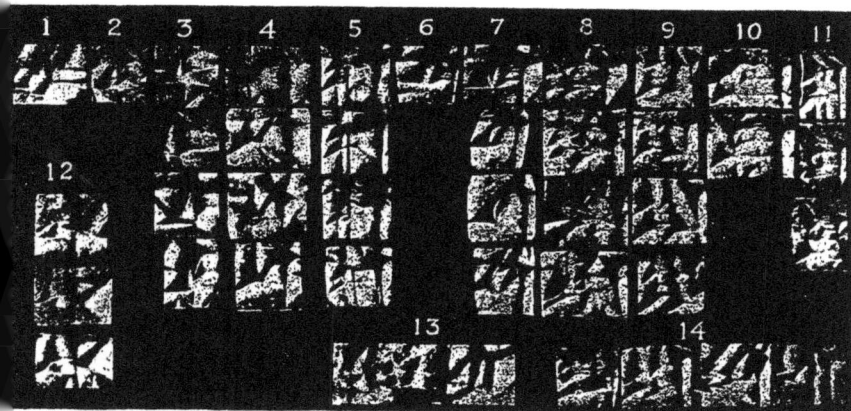

those who have not studied cuneiform palæography, may judge for himself whether my readings are "misreadings," and whether they "fade into thin air."

No. 1 is *akh* from *it-ta-akh-da-ar*, line 4, which Luckenbill declares is ', see No. 2.

No. 2 is ' from *li-'-zu*, line 10; but all the wedges are not visible in the photograph. This he has read *shi*, i. e., No. 3. Note the oblique instead of horizontal wedge.

No. 3 is *shi* for comparison with ', i. e., No. 2.

No. 4 is *na* of *te-i-na*, line 9, which he has read *ta*, for which see No. 5.

No. 5 is *ta* for comparison with *na*, i. e., No. 4.

No. 6 is *ṭi* from *li-sha-aq-ṭi-il*, line 11, which he has read *qi;* see No. 7

No. 7 is *qi* for comparison with *ṭi*, i. e., No. 6.

No. 8 is *il* from *li-sha-aq-ṭi-il*, line 11, which he has read *ra;* see No. 9

No. 9 is *ra* for comparison with *il*, i. e., No. 8.

No. 10 is *ib* from *ib-ba-ra*, line 70, which he has read *dib;* see No. 11.

No. 11 is *dib (lu)*, for comparison with *ib.*, i. e., No. 10.

No. 12 is *ti* from . . . *-ti*, line 10, which he says may "have the rem nants of *shi*"; but for which see No. 3.

No. 13 is *khi-bi-ish*, line 12, which is from the photograph publishe by Johns, *Cuneiform Inscriptions*, p. 11, because through an injury to th tablet the word is no longer preserved. In spite not only of this photograp but Scheil's clear copy (*RT* 20, 56), Luckenbill says, "it is evident th *khibish* of Professor Clay and others is a misreading of the remnants o *shaplish*"; but see No. 14.

No. 14 is *sha-ap-li-ish* made up from other lines for comparison wit *khi-bi-ish*, i. e., No. 13.

The answer to his other strictures of my work will be found on pag 96[55], 174[37, 38, 38a,38b], 178[45], 179, 180[49], and 183[52]. An examination of all the facts, it is believed, is sufficient to convince anyone competent to weig the evidence that his criticisms, presented in such an aggressive tone, wit the exception of one or two things previously noted by others, are withou foundation.